17/22

When a Baby Dies of SIDS

The Parents' Grief and Search for Reason

by

Karen Martin

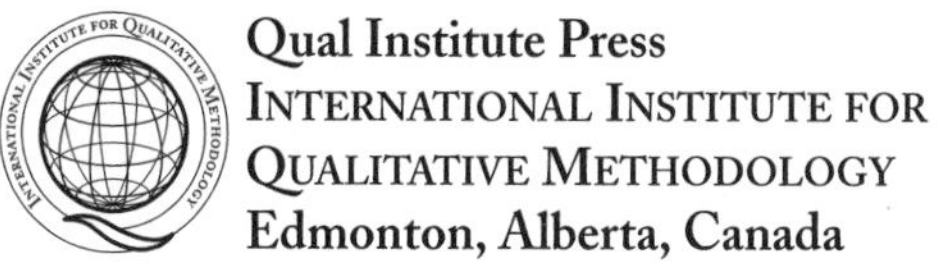

Qual Institute Press
INTERNATIONAL INSTITUTE FOR
QUALITATIVE METHODOLOGY
Edmonton, Alberta, Canada

Copyright © 1998 Qual Institute Press

All rights reserved. No part of this book may be reproduced or used in any form or by any means, electronic or mechanical, including photocopying, recording, or by any information storage and retrieval system, without permission in writing from the publisher.

For information:

Qual Institute Press
INTERNATIONAL INSTITUTE FOR
QUALITATIVE METHODOLOGY
Sixth Floor
University Extension Centre
8303–112th Street
University of Alberta
Edmonton, Alberta, Canada T6G 2T4
Phone: 1-403-492-9041
Fax: 1-403-492-9040
Email: qualitative.institute@ualberta.ca
Or order books from our website: http://www.ualberta.ca/~iiqm/

Printed in Canada

Canadian Cataloging-in-Publication Data

Martin, Karen
When a baby dies of SIDS: the parents' grief and search for reason
Includes bibliographical references and indexes.
ISBN 0-9683044-3-5
1. Sudden infant death syndrome—Psychological aspects.
2. Bereavement—Psychological aspects. I. Title.
RJ320.S93M37 1998 155.9'37'085 C98-900173-3

Editor:	Janice M. Morse
Managing Editor:	Don Wells
Graphic Design:	Murray Pearson
Front Cover Artwork:	Jill Watananiuk
Back Cover Photo:	Jill Watananiuk

CONTENTS

DEDICATION

To all the babies stolen by SIDS and
to all their parents and brothers and sisters and grandparents

and

To Sarah who keeps teaching me about the depth of parental love.

Acknowledgments

There are so many people to thank. I could not have done this study without their generosity, support, and love. Thank you first to the parents who participated in the study. By sharing your experiences with me, you taught me how to endure pain with dignity. You also taught me about the strength of the human spirit. I will never forget you. Thank you to the Executive of the Edmonton chapter of the Canadian Foundation for the Study of Infant Deaths (CFSID). Your support and interest in this project kept me going when the enormity of it all overwhelmed me. I feel privileged to know you and to call you friends. Thank you, too, to the members of the Board of Consultants of the CFSID for agreeing to fund this study. I know my study was unusual. Thank you for seeing its merit and going out on a limb to fund it.

Thank you to the original members of my committee: Dr. Larson, Dr. Kent, and Dr. Morse. You each gave me something special. Thank you, Dr. Larson, for your ongoing support and respect for my work; thank you, Dr. Kent, for your inspiring enthusiasm and excitement about my findings; and thank you, Dr. Morse, for your intellectual challenges, for sharing your knowledge about qualitative research, and for your continued interest in my work. Thank you also to Dr. Peggy Anne Field who took Dr. Morse's place when she moved to another university. I appreciate your input and your willingness to be involved so late in the process. Thank you also to Dr. Judith Golec, my current supervisor, for believing in me and the merits of this research.

A special thank you to my family, particularly my husband who held me while I cried my way through this study, talked with me about what I was learning, and believed in me enough to encourage me to attend university in the first place. Thank you also to all the members of my family and my friends for understanding my obsession with this project and for doing what you could to help me survive it.

Preface

Ever since I began my training as a psychiatric nurse in the late 60s, I have been trying to understand why traumatic events such as deaths, major illnesses, and relationship difficulties seem to devastate some people and strengthen other people. This question has followed me over the years as I worked in mental hospitals, general hospitals, nursing homes, group homes, community treatment centers, and mental health clinics and as I worked with the mentally ill, mentally challenged young adults, emotionally troubled youths, physically ill women, adults seeking a divorce or dealing with depression, and, finally, with people who were grieving. I began working with the bereaved while serving as the Family Development Coordinator for the Family Service Association of Edmonton (now called the Family Centre) in the late 70s. In response to requests from people who were grieving and had nowhere to turn for support, I established a bereavement support program at the agency. Little did I know what effect it would have on my life.

Some of the people who came to the grief support groups were parents. Being a parent myself, my heart went out to these parents who had lost a child to stillbirth, a neonatal condition, accidents, illnesses, and suicide. Each loss was unique and devastating in its own way, and yet somehow these parents managed to get up every morning and, most days, to find a reason to go on with their lives. I could not understand how they managed to do this. To answer this question, I began to read all I could about grieving. In the course of my reading, I discovered an article by Cornwell, Nurcombe, and Stevens (1977), who described the grief experiences of Australian parents who had lost babies to Sudden Infant Death Syndrome (SIDS), something with which I was not familiar. On top of dealing with their grief, these parents were dealing with the fact that no one knew why their babies had died of SIDS. I wondered how these parents managed to survive this tragedy and whether any parents were strengthened by such a devastating loss. This question accompanied me to university, where I took every opportunity to explore it in the research papers I wrote as an undergraduate student in home economics. Even before I began my course work in the Master's program in sociology, I knew what my thesis topic would be. I just had to understand how parents who lost a baby to SIDS survive. I knew that the only way I could do that would be to talk with those who had lived this experience. I am pleased to finally have the opportunity to share what I learned.

Before getting into the study itself, I would like to describe what it was like for me to do this research. Although it took me a while to realize this, I eventually discovered that my research experience paralleled, to some degree, the parents' grief experience. Like the parents who tried to rush their grief, I tried to rush the research process. Like the parents who had to learn that grief takes its own time, I had to learn that this kind of research cannot be rushed. Eventually, I learned to let my understanding unfold naturally rather than trying to force it.

The parents' journey into grief began when they conceived, delivered, and loved their new baby for without love and attachment there can be no grief. My journey began when I decided to do the study; I felt enthusiastic about what lay ahead. Like the parents who discovered that their baby required constant attention, I soon found that the study crowded into my personal life. I walked, talked, and slept with the study. In short, I became so obsessed with it that I set aside positive and distracting interests and relationships. Soon I felt overwhelmed. At first I thought it was because I had so much information to analyze. While it was true that it took some time to learn how to manage the interview data effectively, this was not the real problem. My problem was the emotional content of the interviews. The pain behind the words on the tapes and pages of transcripts soon began to overwhelm me.

As I listened to the parents' stories, first in person and then on tape, I began to feel devastated by the parents' stories of finding their baby dead, of considering suicide, of struggling to survive. I had entered the parents' nightmare, and for a time, I could not find my way out. I wondered whether I could ever function as a detached researcher. But, like the parents, I had good days and bad days. On the good days, I tried to carry on with the research, dutifully coding and writing about what I saw in the data and in myself. On the bad days, I struggled for control of the research process and my emotions. When I tried to force an objective stance so I could be productive, I usually had to give up and just let myself feel. The pain of what these parents had been through made me fall apart. Ashamed of what was going on, I kept this "yo yo[ing]" a secret from everyone but my family. Like the parents, I kept trying to understand the cause of the problem. Initially, I blamed myself and decided that I was not cut out to do this kind of research. Gradually, I learned to be kinder to myself. I decided that living inside the parents' experience was teaching me more than I could have learned any other way. Like the parents, I kept trying to make sense of everything that was happening to me.

Once I understood the logic behind my apparent inability to function, I began to feel better. Gradually, I learned to let go. When I gave myself permission to stop fighting to control my emotions, their intensity seemed to subside. Soon I could work at the theoretical level. This proved to be easier than letting go of my need to understand everything about this experience. In addition to feeling the parents' pain, my obsessive curiosity slowed me down as well. My curiosity also drove me to continue to analyze and understand more and more of the parents' experience.

I did not let go of everything though. Like the parents who chose to maintain a strong connection to their baby through "do[ing] for," I still feel a strong need to care for parents who are still struggling with their grief. When I had almost completed the data analysis, I agreed to act as the advisor for the local parent support group, something I am still doing to this day. Like the parents who were changed by the death of their baby, this research project changed me, too. Despite the pain I had to endure along the way, the journey was worth it.

One reason many of these parents agreed to participate in this study was to help newly bereaved parents and helping professionals understand what this experience was like. I am happy to have been a part of bringing these stories to light.

Chapter 1
Understanding SIDS and Its Impact

UNDERSTANDING SIDS

Every year hundreds of Canadian families (Statistics Canada, 1994) and thousands of American families (Valdes-Dapena, 1991) experience an "unpredictable, unpreventable, and unexplainable tragedy" (Valdes-Dapena, 1991, p. 11): Their apparently healthy baby dies of Sudden Infant Death Syndrome or SIDS as it is commonly known. The most common cause of death for children between the ages of 1 week and 1 year, SIDS is defined as

> the sudden and unexpected death of an infant who has seemed well, or almost well, and whose death remains unexplained after the performance of an adequate postmortem investigation including an autopsy, examination of the death scene, and review of the case history. (Valdes-Dapena, 1991, p. 3)

As this definition indicates, the diagnosis of SIDS requires the involvement of both police and medical experts. The police must be involved because they investigate all sudden and unexplained deaths. They begin their investigation by first noting the circumstances of the death. Then they examine the baby and scene of death for evidence of "accidents and child battering" (Valeriote & Fine, 1987, p. 202). They also question the parents.

Once the police rule out physical harm as the possible cause of death, they turn the investigation over to a pathologist. Using an autopsy as the primary investigative tool, the pathologist examines the body for signs of undetected abuse, congenital problems, and illness. If there is no indication of a problem "sufficient to cause death" (Hillman, 1991, p. 23), then the pathologist certifies that the baby died of SIDS. This diagnosis merely excludes all other reasonable explanations (Zielke et al., 1989); it does not explain how or why the baby died. It just gives the mysterious killer a name.

Nevertheless, legal and medical authorities, family doctors, ministers, and others often assume that this diagnosis settles the question of why the baby died. People expect parents to accept the diagnosis, quickly grieve the loss of their baby, and get on with their lives. The problem is that many parents refuse to believe that an apparently healthy baby can die for no reason at all. For their own peace of mind, parents need to understand the reason for their baby's death. As long as the actual cause of SIDS remains unknown, parents will continue their own secret inquiry into their baby's death (Fetus and Newborn Committee, 1983). This inquiry may affect the nature of the parental grief process.

Defining the Research Problem

For many years researchers paid little attention to the impact that a SIDS death has on the individual survivors: the parents, siblings, and grandparents of these babies. Instead, researchers focused their energies on the search for the cause of SIDS. Then, in 1969, Bergman, Pomeroy, and Beckwith published one of the first articles about the problems of families who had lost a baby to SIDS. Entitled "The Psychiatric Toll of the Sudden Infant Death Syndrome," the article reports on the authors' observations and interviews with 225 families. Since the publication of this article, many other researchers have explored various facets of this unique and devastating grief experience.

Unfortunately, instead of trying to understand the nature of this experience over time, many researchers have tried to quantify and compare the parents' pain. As a result, much of the information about what it is like to lose a baby to SIDS is fragmented, disconnected, time bound, gender biased, and emotionally detached from the parents' pain. Studies that do give families a voice often focus on a small period of time after the baby's death. These results do not provide us with any information about how families deal with this tragic loss over the years. Generally, we still have much to learn about what it is like to lose a baby to SIDS. We know even less about how parents conduct their inquiry into the reason for their baby's death and how these personal investigations might affect the parental grief process.

Defining the Study's Purpose and Rationale

While parents attempt to deal with their grief, they meet a variety of professionals and nonprofessionals whose attitudes, comments, and behavior can greatly affect the parents' ability to deal with their loss. For a variety of reasons, these professionals and nonprofessionals could benefit from knowing more about the unique issues and needs of parents who lose a baby to SIDS.

First, parents have no choice but to deal with a variety of professionals. These include first responders (paramedics, firefighters, police, medical examiner's investigators, emergency room doctors, and nurses) then ministers, funeral directors, family doctors, public health nurses, and, sometimes, counselors of various kinds. Because parents encounter professionals at the beginning of this painful experience, it is crucial that these professionals understand how their behavior affects the parents and what the parents need from them.

Second, nonprofessionals who provide both formal and informal support to these parents could also benefit from understanding the complex issues underlying this experience. This group of helpers includes the board, staff, and volunteers of the Canadian Foundation for the Study of Infant Deaths (CFSID), volunteers for The Compassionate Friends (TCF), and the relatives, friends, and coworkers of the bereaved parents.

Third, parents who lose a baby to SIDS can benefit directly from this study. The results can be shared in parent support meetings, information sessions, and through CFSID newsletters and conferences.

With all these needs and people in mind, I designed a research study that

- provides an opportunity for individual fathers and mothers to share their perspective on what it was like to lose their baby to SIDS;
- uses the collective experiences of a number of parents to identify the unique but common issues that parents who lose a baby to SIDS must confront; and
- builds on these collective experiences to develop a theoretical understanding of the grief process and the factors that affect the parents' ability to cope with it effectively.

Critiquing Our Current Understanding of the Impact of SIDS

Review of the literature

When a loved one dies, people experience varying degrees of emotional, physical, intellectual, spiritual, and interpersonal pain. We call this pain grief (Dershimer, 1990; Simos, 1979; Walsh & McGoldrick, 1991; Worden, 1982). Dealing with one's grief means going through a process of gradually learning to live with a loss, integrating it into one's life, and deriving some kind of meaning from it (Arnold & Gemma, 1991). Learning to deal with grief is hard work, but the grief that comes from the death of a child seems particularly difficult to bear.

Of all the "threads of human connectedness" that bind people to one another (Lofland, 1982, p. 222), the most unique, intense, and timeless bond is the one that connects parents to their children (Klass, 1988; Knapp, 1986; Rando, 1986a; Rosof, 1994). Consequently, when a child dies, parental grief is difficult and painful no matter what causes the child's death and no matter how old the child is at the time of death (Arnold & Gemma, 1991; Bolton, 1986; Day & Hooks, 1987; DeFrain, Taylor, & Ernst, 1982; Feeley & Gottlieb, 1988; Hutchins, 1986; Klass, 1988; Klass & Marwit, 1988; Knapp, 1986; Kupst, 1986; Lietar, 1986; Nichols, 1986; Rando, 1986a, 1986c; Riches & Dawson, 1996; Rubin, 1996; Sanders, 1986; Schmidt, 1986; Simos, 1979; Smith & Borgers, 1988; Sprang & McNeil, 1995; Worden, 1982). Research shows that the death of a child causes a "more intense grief reaction" than the death of either a spouse or a parent (Sanders, 1980, p. 309).

Because "the sense of selfhood involved in parenting is a central part of [people's] being" (Klass, 1988, p. 4) and because a child "is at once from the parent, part of the parent, and a separate self" (Arnold & Gemma, 1991, p. 47), the death of a child makes parents feel like they have lost a part of themselves (Klass, 1996). Rando (1986b) suggests that parents think of their children as "an extension of [them]selves" and "invest [their children] with a myriad of meanings, along with parental hopes, dreams, needs, and wishes for immortality" (p. 49). In fact, for many people, children symbolize a commitment to life itself. As George Bernard Shaw once wrote, "Life is a flame that is always burning itself out, but it catches fire again every time a child is born" (Wallis, 1965, p. 53).

When an infant dies within the first year of life, the grief is especially difficult to bear. The death of an infant to SIDS, however, triggers one of the most severe parental grief reactions (Dyregrov, 1990). Parents experience significantly more intense early grief and more anxiety, anger, self-reproach, restlessness, sleep disturbances, and intrusive thoughts than parents who lose infants to either stillbirth or neonatal death (Dyregrov & Matthiesen, 1987b). Losing a baby to SIDS triggers the "most severe crisis [parents] have experienced in their lifetime" (DeFrain & Ernst, 1978, p. 987). Parents must find a way to endure grief that may last for the rest of their lives (Arnold & Gemma, 1991; DeFrain, Ernst, Jakub, & Taylor, 1991; Rubin, 1985). Some never recover (DeFrain et al., 1991).

Unique circumstances of a SIDS death

Markusen, Owen, Fulton, and Bendiksen (1978) suggest that family members left behind after a baby dies of SIDS are the living "victims" of the syndrome (p. 277). These victims often suffer a traumatic and problematic "aftermath" (p. 277). To understand what contributes to the production of this difficult aftermath, Markusen et al. reviewed studies published between 1944 and 1975. Using their review as my foundation, I looked at more recent studies and reexamined some of the studies they reviewed. Like Markusen et al., I found support for four unique circumstances of the death that may contribute to intense parental grief reactions:

- SIDS takes the lives of infants;
- SIDS strikes suddenly and without warning;
- sudden and unexpected deaths must be investigated; and
- the cause of SIDS is not known.

SIDS takes the lives of infants

"The complex grief parents experience after the death of a child is in a sense a continuation of the complex dynamics by which attachment of the child was created and developed" (Klass & Marwit, 1988, p. 31). Therefore, I explore the "complex dynamics" of the parent-infant relationship before discussing why the death of an infant creates such intense grief. The more central the attachment, the more intense the grief reaction (Bugen, 1983; Worden, 1982). I track the history of this attachment from before the baby is even conceived to the early months of life.

The prebirth relationship

With the arrival of effective family planning methods, most women can decide if and when they want to have a child. Consequently, a woman may begin a "pre birth relationship" (Stainton, 1985, p. 325) with her baby either when she first "conceives of" the idea of becoming pregnant (Winnicott, 1987a, p. 51) or when she begins to plan a specific pregnancy (Peppers, 1987). With confirmation of a wanted pregnancy, a "mysterious union" between mother and baby begins and intensifies over time (Bergum, 1986, p. 96). As the months pass and the baby makes its presence felt, "child and woman are truly one body," creating a setting for an "intimate relationship that no one else [can] share" (Bergum, 1989, p. 58).

First pregnancies change women's identities, transforming them from women into mothers (Bergum, 1989). The "social process of identity construction" (Lovell, 1983, p. 760) occurs through the interaction of physical and emotional changes, the way others treat women when they are pregnant, and the experience of giving birth (Bergum, 1989; Lovell, 1983). Writing about her own experiences during pregnancy, Jackson (1992) says that for women

> pregnancy ends the illusion of autonomy. You are housing somebody else, a living presence. It's a third party to the relationship long before the father suspects. He may sing to the baby and converse with your belly, but it's just an idea, until the baby is born. For a woman, it's already the root, the core around which she walks and dreams. (p. 35)

Research confirms that, as Jackson (1992) suggests, men's relationships with their unborn children are more distant. Most men do not "define [themselves] as a father and the world around [them] in terms of [their] future fatherhood" (May, 1982, p. 341) until about the twenty-sixth week of an actual pregnancy. This redefinition of self during the last trimester of the pregnancy occurs as expectant fathers begin to feel intellectually connected to their baby (May, 1979, 1982; Peppers & Knapp, 1980; Smith, 1983). Peppers and Knapp (1980) contend that unlike mothers fathers may not bond with their baby until it is born. On a practical note, perhaps many first-time fathers have difficulty connecting to or even imagining their baby any earlier because they have little experience caring for babies (Lewis, 1982; Soule, Standley, & Copans, 1979).

Before the baby's birth, expectant fathers can choose the degree to which they will be involved (Brazelton & Cramer, 1990). Even after making a commitment to their unborn baby and beginning to think of themselves as fathers, some men do not show their "sense of fatherliness" (Soule, Standley, & Copans, 1979, p. 261) by becoming emotionally involved with the pregnancy. Instead, they increase their commitment to their jobs or careers during the latter months of the pregnancy (Brown, 1987). May (1980) found three distinct styles of father involvement during pregnancy. "Observer" expectant fathers act like "bystanders" (p. 449), investing little emotional energy in the pregnancy or their unborn child. In contrast, men who adopt an "expressive style" become emotionally involved with the pregnancy; they consider themselves "full partner[s]" in the experience. Men who assume the "instrumental" style act like a "caretaker or manager of the pregnancy." Although interested in making sure the pregnancy goes well, these men do not connect to the baby on an emotional level.

The parent-infant relationship

Both before and after a baby is born, family members begin "making [a] place" (Bright, 1992, p. 86) for the baby, both physically and socially. Bright calls the preparation of the baby's spot in the house "nesting" (p. 86). Social space making includes: naming the baby, attributing the baby's characteristics to others in the family, and welcoming the baby by giving gifts, speaking to or about the baby, and interacting with the baby. While Bright studied how parents and grandparents make a place for a first-born child, this concept seems equally applicable to families welcoming their next child as well. The point is that the arrival of a baby changes the dynamics of the family as everyone learns to make room.

Parents are also forced to make time for their baby. Babies require constant and continuous care and attention: "What makes the transition to parenthood so unique, and for some parents especially frustrating, is the amount of attention that infants require" (LaRossa, 1986, p. 88). Because the need for attention is continuous, parental involvement must also be continuous. According to Lamb (1987, cited in LaRossa, 1988), parental involvement can be divided into three components: engagement ("time spent in one-to-one interaction with a child"); accessibility (time spent being in "a less intense degree of interaction" in which the parent may be available to the child but is not focused specifically on the child); and responsibility (time spent physically and mentally being "accountable for the child's welfare and care") (p. 452). Someone must always be "on duty," particularly during the early years of a child's life (LaRossa, 1986, p. 90).

It has been estimated that mothers assume about 90 percent of this responsibility (LaRossa, 1988), so they have many opportunities to interact with the baby. The seemingly endless and intimate tasks involved in feeding and caring for a baby can intensify the mother-infant relationship significantly, creating the potential for both increased satisfaction and increased stress in the maternal role. Many new mothers struggle to maintain their identity in the midst of the demands of motherhood (Jackson, 1992).

In contrast, many fathers struggle to find a way to stay involved with their new baby. Although some fathers become interested, intensely preoccupied, and absorbed with their newborn baby, this intensity may wane over time (Greenberg & Morris, 1974). Within a few months, the level of involvement approaches a traditionally detached stance (LaRossa, 1988). Today's fathers are more involved with their children than their own fathers were with them. Nonetheless, on average, fathers typically devote "only a fraction of the mothers' [total time]" (LaRossa, 1988, p. 454) to direct and indirect child care.

LaRossa (1988) suggests that when fathers are with their children, they are often "technically present but functionally absent" (p. 454). While caring for or playing with their children, fathers are often simultaneously involved in another activity, either mentally or physically. Detached caretaking reduces the potential for the intensification of the father-child relationship. Although modern fathers may want to be more involved with their children, many are not. The discrepancy causes men to feel "ambivalent and guilty about their performance as fathers" (LaRossa, 1988, p. 456). Those fathers who are intensely involved with their children may hide their involvement, fearing others might think their behavior is "unmanly" (Greenberg & Morris, 1974, p. 527).

The way in which each new parent responds to a baby's "invitation to love" (Rosof, 1994, p. 6) and is involved with caretaking differs in terms of timing, intensity, and activities. It follows then that mothers and fathers might also derive satisfaction from different aspects of their parental role. Scott and Alwin (1989) found that when parents speak about their positive parenting experiences mothers focus more on the immediate and intimate aspects of relating to and caring for their children. Fathers tend to celebrate their children's achievements. In addition, motherhood can offer a feeling of personal fulfillment to women, while fatherhood offers men a feeling of accomplishment (Knapp, 1986).

Despite the potential for rewards, in our society we have impossible expectations for both mothers and fathers. As Rando (1986a) says, "Parents are to be all-loving, all-good, all-concerned, totally selfless, and motivated only by the child and his welfare" (p. 9). Klass (1988) adds that we also expect competent parents to be able to protect their children from all harm. These expectations make it difficult for parents to admit to themselves and to others that sometimes they make mistakes and that sometimes they feel angry, frustrated, and ambivalent about their parental role and their own children.

When parents commit themselves to caring for a new baby, they begin a new chapter in their lives. Some are ill-prepared to handle all the demands.

Parenthood involves a commitment to helping children move away from "absolute dependence" to "lessening degrees of dependence, and [helping them] grope towards independence" (Winnicott, 1987b, p. 83). Each stage of a child's development stimulates new and different parent-child issues. Rando (1986a) says there is a connection between these issues and the nature of parental grief.

During the first year of life, children are completely dependent upon their parents to meet their every need (Rosof, 1994). Thus, two issues may arise for parents during this time: the feeling of immense and overwhelming responsibility for the baby's well-being and the struggle to find time for oneself occasionally (Jackson, 1992; LaRossa, 1986). It may take parents several months to balance their needs and their children's needs. With the complex meanings assigned to children, the high expectations of parenthood, the development of parental identities and roles, the unique and intense histories of the mother-infant and father-infant relationships, and the dependency related issues that occur for the parents during the first year of a child's life, it is no wonder that the sudden death of an infant triggers an intense grief reaction.

The literature offers further suggestions about why losing an infant may trigger such intense grief. First, babies are completely dependent upon their parents, making parents feel responsible for anything that happens to them. Therefore, when a baby dies, parents feel like they have "failed totally and completely" at their job (Klass, 1988, p. 15). Second, the death of an infant occurs at a time when physical and "psychological boundaries [between the parent and the child] overlap significantly" (Rubin, 1985, p. 347). This makes the death a physically and emotionally wrenching experience. Third, although parents in all cultures and times have experienced the death of their children (Smart, 1993–1994), people in modern Western societies no longer react to child death with what Bluglass (1993) calls "philosophical acceptance" (p. 59). In this time and society, "children's deaths make no sense, have no precedents, are part of no pattern [and they seem] unnatural and wrong" (Finkbeiner, 1996, p. xiii). And when a baby dies, people believe that "the natural order of things [has been] disrupted" (DeFrain et al., 1991, p. 86). They use words like "untimely" (Dyregrov, 1990, p. 274) and out of the natural order (DeVries, Lana, & Falck, 1994) to describe such deaths. Finally, instead of receiving support for their grief, grieving parents may be socially isolated (Ford, 1993) and marginalized (Farnsworth & Allen, 1996). Instead of understanding the depth of their love for the baby, others may say that the parents "are lucky they did not have a longer time to become attached to [the baby] or…that they can have other children" (Rando, 1986a, p. 6) or "at least you've got your other children" (Zagdanski, 1995, p. 301).

Since these issues are present whenever an infant dies (Nichols, 1986; Stinson & Stinson, 1979), they are not enough to explain the intensity of the parental grief reaction after a baby dies of SIDS. Exploring the unique circumstances of the death itself provides a better explanation.

SIDS occurs suddenly and without warning

SIDS strikes without warning, often during the night or while the infant naps during the day. Consequently, a SIDS death hurtles parents into grief; they have no time to prepare themselves psychologically (Arnold & Gemma, 1991; Bergman, Pomeroy, & Beckwith, 1969; Cornwell, Nurcombe, & Stevens, 1977; DeFrain et al., 1991; Dyregrov & Matthiesen, 1987b; Halpern, 1972; l'Hoir & Wolters, 1993; Markusen et al., 1978; Valdes-Dapena, 1991). At least parents who know their child is ill and likely to die can brace themselves for the emotional pain that lies ahead (Knapp, 1986; Kupst, 1986; Morrell, 1988; Stinson & Stinson, 1979). At least these parents can say their goodbyes to their child. As Taylor, DeFrain, and Ernst (1986) suggest, for parents who lose a baby to SIDS, there is no time for one last hug or kiss: "The sudden absence of the baby and the futility of the parenting role after the loss makes the situation seem more overwhelming" (p. 166). Additionally, a death due to SIDS shocks parents because they believe that "babies do not just die" (Arnold & Gemma, 1991, p. 53), especially apparently healthy babies. Therefore, right from the start this death makes no sense to the parents nor to anyone else. And that is exactly why the next unique circumstance of a SIDS death occurs.

Sudden and unexpected deaths must be investigated

In most places, "all instances of sudden, unexpected death are, by law, reported to the legal authorities, usually the medical examiner or coroner, who have the responsibility of determining the cause of death" (Guist & Larsen, 1991, p. 148). This requirement involuntarily puts the parents into contact with "a system with which they have probably never previously been involved, a system that generally investigates suspicious and criminal deaths" (Arnold & Gemma, 1991, p. 53). The professionals who represent this system and the "attitudes they convey to the family, that of blame or support, can have lasting effects on the parents" (Nikolaisen & Williams, 1980, p. 595).

Initially, the police may suspect that the parents abused the baby (Arnold & Gemma, 1991; Lowman, 1979). Because of this suspicion and because some police do not know how to distinguish victims of SIDS from victims of abuse, police may treat parents like criminals (DeFrain & Ernst, 1978). In fact, if "parents have a lifestyle that is at variance with that of middle-class America, they may...be accused of child abuse" (Weinstein, 1978, p. 832). To rule out any suspicion of child abuse and to establish SIDS as the cause of death, a medical investigation is conducted. Only a pathologist can conclusively diagnose SIDS, and the only diagnostic tool is an autopsy. Some parents react negatively to hearing that an autopsy is necessary for diagnosis (Smialek, 1978). Others welcome it, hoping that it will provide them with "an explanation for the death" (DeFrain et al., 1991, p. 66). Unfortunately, once parents hear the results of the autopsy, they often feel angry and cheated. Because the diagnosis of SIDS merely means that the medical experts can find no explanation for the baby's death, parents often continue to ask why their baby died. This takes us to the last and most unique feature of the SIDS loss experience.

The cause of SIDS is unknown

The "characteristic failure of the postmortem examination to provide a satisfactory explanation for the death" (Bergman et al., 1969, p. 102) significantly increases the pain and confusion of parents, siblings, and other family members (Arnold & Gemma, 1991; Cornwell et al., 1977; DeFrain & Ernst, 1978; DeFrain et al., 1991; DeFrain, Jakub, & Mendoza, 1992; Giljohann, 1993; Halpern, 1972; Mandell, Dirks-Smith, & Smith, 1988; Mandell, McAnulty, & Reece, 1980; Markusen et al., 1978; May & Breme, 1982; Rubin, 1985; Smialek, 1978; Williams & Nikolaisen, 1982). Because many people "need to believe in causes for human tragedy" (Lowman, 1979, p. 765) and no specific cause can be found for this one, everyone's belief in a "rational and/or metaphysical model of the universe" (Cornwell, et al., 1977, p. 657) is severely shaken. Until they can find an explanation that makes sense to them, like parents whose children have been murdered (Klass, 1988), parents who lose a baby to SIDS feel vulnerable and unsafe (Attig, 1996; Dyregrov & Matthiesen, 1987c). Their whole world is turned upside down since "the death of a child destroys ready-made directions and comfortable truisms. Suddenly, 'trustworthy recipes' for both interpreting the world and interacting with others no longer work [and] thinking as usual is no longer possible" (Brabant, Forsyth, & McFarlain, 1995, p. 81). To restore a sense of order and predictability, many people try to create their own explanations for why the baby died (Bergman et al., 1969; Cornwell et al., 1977; DeFrain et al., 1991; Williams & Nikolaisen, 1982). Most of the explanations reflect the fact that parents "almost universally experience a feeling of ultimate responsibility [when their baby dies of SIDS]" (May & Breme, 1982, p. 61).

When all four of these circumstances combine, it is no wonder that parents soon feel totally overwhelmed with grief and that they experience higher levels of psychological distress than parents who lose babies to stillbirth or neonatal death (Dyregrov, 1990; Vance et al., 1991). Some may even suffer from traumatic stress reaction (Raphael & Misso, 1993).

Parental grief after losing a baby to SIDS

Early individual reactions

Emotional reactions

Within minutes of finding their baby dead or being told that their baby is dead, most parents go into emotional shock (Bergman et al., 1969; Cornwell et al., 1977; DeFrain et al., 1991; Dyregrov, 1990; Nikolaisen & Williams, 1980). When the feeling of shock and numbness begins to fade, parents begin to feel many emotions, most commonly: "agonizing sadness" (Cornwell et al., 1977, p. 656); depression (Bergman et al., 1969; DeFrain et al., 1991; Dyregrov, 1990; Dyregrov & Matthiesen, 1987b; Price, Carter, Shelton, & Bendell, 1985; Rubin, 1993; Vance et al., 1991); anxiety (DeFrain et al., 1991; Dyregrov & Matthiesen, 1987b, 1987c; Raphael & Misso, 1993; Rubin, 1981, 1993; Vance et al., 1991); and anger, general irritability, and hostility (Bergman et al., 1969; Cornwell et al., 1977; DeFrain et al., 1991; Dyregrov, 1990). Many parents also begin to experience fear (Price et al., 1985). While some are generally afraid to be left alone in their homes, others specifically fear for the safety of their other children (Bergman et al., 1969; Cornwell et al., 1977). As their emotions fluctuate from moment to moment (Bergman et al., 1969), parents soon start to feel like they are losing control. Some fear they will soon go crazy (DeFrain, 1991; Dyregrov, 1990).

Cognitive reactions

Besides having trouble controlling their emotions, parents are disturbed by their thoughts. Troublesome thoughts in the early stages of their grief directly relate to the unique circumstances of death due to SIDS. Those who find their baby dead are often troubled by "intrusive thoughts of the discovery in the form of flashbacks" (Dyregrov & Matthiesen, 1987b, p. 109) and preoccupied with thoughts about their baby (Rubin, 1993). It is not uncommon for parents who have lost a baby to SIDS to experience intrusive thoughts, anxiety, and intense fear of further trauma—all indicative of a traumatic stress reaction (Raphael & Misso, 1993).

Obsessive reviewing is another common cognitive reaction. No matter who finds the baby, it is not unusual for both parents to carefully review every aspect of their child care to see if they did anything wrong or missed anything that might have caused or contributed to the baby's death (Cornwell et al., 1977; DeFrain et al., 1991). Parents are often overwhelmed by thoughts of self-reproach and guilt (Bergman et al., 1969; Cornwell et al., 1977; DeFrain & Ernst, 1978; DeFrain et al., 1991; l'Hoir & Wolters, 1993; Rubin, 1985).

Within a few weeks of the baby's death, parents may also be troubled by difficulties with concentration during the day (Bergman et al., 1969; l'Hoir & Wolters, 1993; Price et al., 1985) and with disturbing dreams about the baby at night (Bergman et al., 1969; Cornwell et al., 1977; l'Hoir & Wolters, 1993). At first, some just cannot accept that their baby is dead, but when the reality of the baby's absence hits them, grief overwhelms them (Bergman et al., 1969; DeFrain et al., 1991; Lowman, 1979). Fearing that they cannot control their crazy thoughts, some parents worry that they might be "going insane" (Bergman et al., 1969, p. 102). SIDS is beginning to take its "psychiatric toll" (Bergman et al., 1969, p. 99).

Physical reactions

In addition to feeling like they might be going crazy, parents may also feel physically ill. They may experience: dizziness, sleep problems, stomachaches, headaches, appetite loss, and fatigue (Bergman et al., 1969; Cornwell et al., 1977; Dyregrov, 1990; Dyregrov & Matthiesen, 1987b; DeFrain et al., 1991; l'Hoir & Woltman, 1995; Lowman, 1979; Price et al., 1985). Some parents also suffer from chest pain (Dyregrov, 1990) or what they call "heartaches" (Bergman et al., 1969, p. 102). As Dyregrov (1990) points out, these physical reactions suggest a highly aroused sympathetic nervous system. Additionally, breastfeeding mothers often experience intense pain as "their breasts fill with milk" (Arnold & Gemma, 1991, p. 50) for a baby that is no longer there. To relieve this pain, the mothers take medication or express their milk, only to pour it "down the kitchen sink" (Zagdanski, 1995, p. 300).

Spiritual reactions

When parents lose a baby to SIDS, life may lose all meaning (Wheeler, 1993–1994), making everything seems useless and pointless (Bergman et al., 1969; Cornwell et al., 1977; Dyregrov, 1990). Feeling overwhelmed and severely disoriented, some parents question whether life is worth living at all. Thoughts of suicide occur to some parents, more often mothers than fathers (Cornwell et al., 1977; DeFrain et al., 1991). Some parents lose their faith in God entirely; others lose their faith temporarily; still others rely heavily on their faith to get them through this crisis (DeFrain et al., 1991). Thearle et al. (1995) found that parents who were regular churchgoers before their baby's death experienced less anxiety and depression after the baby's death than nonattenders. This might explain why parents who possess some kind of faith or "preexistent reality structure [that] account[s] for a child's death" are less troubled by their child's death than those who do not have a ready-made explanation (Braun & Berg, 1994, p. 114). Nonetheless, even parents with a strong faith find themselves asking, "Why did God let this happen?" (Zagdanski, 1995, p. 300).

Behavioral reactions

Grief also affects parental behavior. Studies and personal accounts describe parental restlessness (Bergman et al., 1969; Cornwell et al., 1977; DeFrain et al., 1991; Dyregrov & Matthiesen, 1987b; Price et al., 1985). Some parents keep searching for their baby and doing things as if the baby still needed their attention (Bergman et al., 1969; Cornwell et al., 1977; DeFrain et al., 1991). Mothers struggle to stop thinking and acting like mothers, to stop "worr[ying] about [their] baby lying out in the cemetery. Alone. Cold. Afraid" (Zagdanski, 1995). To avoid the constant reminders of their baby and the intrusive memories of finding the baby dead, many parents just want to move away (Bergman et al., 1969; DeFrain & Ernst, 1978; Lowman, 1979). Over half the parents who participated in the Price et al. study (1985) moved shortly after the baby's death, half within the first month.

Some parents weep almost continuously; they cannot function effectively. Others perform all their duties without any sign of their inner pain (Cornwell et al., 1977). Many feel no interest in social activities; some begin to experience difficulties at work. Women often feel uncomfortable in the presence of pregnant women (Price et al., 1985). To deal with their insomnia, parents may begin taking sedatives (Vance et al., 1993). To block the pain, some parents increase their smoking, drinking (Vance et al., 1993), and "self injurious behavior" (Lowman, 1979, p. 674). Some actually attempt suicide (Cornwell et al., 1977; DeFrain et al., 1991).

Research issues

After reviewing these findings, what we have is a list of the ways in which grief affects parents emotionally, cognitively, physically, spiritually, and behaviorally. A list of reactions does not tell us how these parents cope with their grief. It does not tell us how parents make the transition from being overwhelmed by their grief to living a "normal life" again (Cornwell et al., 1977, p. 658). Finally, we do not know why some parents grow stronger while others never recover from their baby's death (DeFrain et al., 1991).

Parental guilt

The pervasiveness of guilt

Bergman et al. (1969) were among the first to notice the "pervasiveness of the parental guilt reaction" (p. 99) among SIDS parents. Their observation has been repeatedly confirmed by other studies (Carroll & Shaefer, 1993–1994; Cornwell et al., 1977; Dyregrov & Matthiesen, 1987b; DeFrain & Ernst, 1978; DeFrain et al., 1991; Halpern, 1972; Lowman, 1979; Mandell et al., 1980; Mandell & Wolfe, 1975; Markusen et al., 1978; Price et al., 1985; Rubin, 1985; Williams & Nikolaisen, 1982).

Although many grieving parents struggle with guilt (Johnson-Soderberg, 1983; Miles & Demi, 1986; Peppers & Knapp, 1980; Rando, 1985), parents whose children die suddenly seem to experience it more often and more intensely (Dyregrov, 1990). Johnson-Soderberg (1983) found that parents whose child died suddenly (some of SIDS) made close to three times as many guilt statements during interviews as parents who had known that their child was dying. When compared to mothers who had lost infants to a variety of other causes, guilt "penetrated the very core of the existence" of mothers who had lost babies to SIDS (Peppers & Knapp, 1980, p. 37). Guilt is "an overpowering and dominant feature of the entire grieving process" (Peppers & Knapp, 1980, p. 37) for parents who lose a baby to SIDS. It becomes almost "inescapable" (DeFrain et al., 1991, p. 77).

Sources of guilt

Many parents know it makes no sense for them to feel responsible for their baby's death, especially once they start to understand more about SIDS.

Nevertheless, many parents continue to feel guilty. Feeling guilty is "a source of dissonance" because it is "at variance with their intellectual knowledge of how they ought to be responding, and at odds with their knowledge of the syndrome itself" (Rubin, 1985, p. 350). Why then do parents continue to feel guilty, sometimes for the rest of their lives?

Bugen's (1983) two-dimensional model helps to explain variations in the intensity and duration of grief. Indirectly, it also sheds some light on parental guilt after a baby dies of SIDS. Bugen's first dimension concerns the centrality of the lost relationship. The more valued the lost person, the more intense the grief. The second dimension is belief in the preventability of the death. Bugen predicts that the most intense grief reactions will occur when people lose a special loved one and when they believe that somehow they "contributed to the death, either directly or indirectly" (p. 360). The determining fact is the "perception of preventability" (p. 357), not the reality of the situation. This describes the situation for many parents who lose a baby to SIDS.

Other authors support Bugen's preventability dimension. These authors (Carroll & Shaefer, 1993-1994; Cornwell et al., 1977; DeFrain & Ernst, 1978; DeFrain et al., 1991; Dyregrov, 1990; Lowman, 1979; Mandell & Wolfe, 1975; Markusen et al., 1978; May & Breme, 1982; Miles & Demi, 1986; Rubin, 1985) found that parents hold themselves responsible for the death of their baby, no matter what the realities of the circumstances. Additionally, Mandell et al. (1980) found that some grieving fathers feel guilty about being minimally involved with the baby while he or she was alive. When the baby dies, these fathers realize that they did not make the baby a central part of their lives; they also realize that they will never get another chance. This realization contributes to feelings of guilt.

The unique circumstances that surround a SIDS death also set the stage for parental guilt. Without an adequate explanation to prove that they are not responsible, parents examine and reexamine every aspect of their care, looking for the one thing that might have caused their baby's death (Cornwell et al., 1977; Dyregrov, 1990). Some parents experience "secret guilt movies'" (Johnson-Soderberg, 1983, p. 60)—a continual replaying of the discovery scene that makes them feel like they are going crazy. This is complicated by the fact that police may treat parents like homicide suspects. Since no one can prove who or what caused the death, parents often decide they must be guilty of inadvertently causing their baby's death (Markusen et al., 1978).

Bergman et al. (1969), Bugen (1983), Lowman (1979), and Markusen et al. (1978) believe professionals can prevent or reduce parents' feelings of guilt by carefully explaining to parents everything there is to know about SIDS.

Even after parents hear a detailed explanation, however, they may still say, "SIDS just isn't enough of an answer" (DeFrain et al., 1992, p. 169). What more do they need?

Parents' explanations

Parents seem to need a "concrete answer" (DeFrain et al., 1992, p. 169) to their question, Why did our baby die? They need an explanation that "makes sense" to them (Cornwell et al., 1977, p. 658). The baby's death causes the parents to have "an insecure feeling that [other] things can be taken away," too (Cornwell et al., 1977, p. 658). So, without a definitive or acceptable explanation from anyone else, parents begin to construct their own.

Many parents believe the real cause of their baby's death was suffocation (Bergman et al., 1969; Cornwell et al., 1977; DeFrain et al., 1991, Williams & Nikolaisen, 1982). Other concrete parental explanations include: choking, unsuspected illness, sibling caused death, hemorrhaging, brain virus, air pollution, atomic testing, freezing, reaction to shots, baby cried self "to death" (Bergman et al., 1969, p. 102); neglect, injury, birth defects, maternal error, and allergies (Williams & Nikolaisen, 1982); and the baby forgot to breathe, had a respiratory illness like a cold or pneumonia, or was born prematurely (DeFrain et al., 1991). Most of these explanations hint at parental self-blame or the need to blame another. But these are just physical explanations for the death; parents often look for other explanations as well.

Parents also look for metaphysical or religious explanations (Cornwell et al., 1977). Some decide that God took their baby (DeFrain et al., 1991). While this thought makes some parents question God's nature and wisdom (Cornwell et al., 1977; Zagdanski, 1995), others believe in a punishing God (Williams & Nikolaisen, 1982) or a God that would take their baby as a test of faith (Cornwell et al., 1977). Some parents choose to believe their baby was fated to die or died because of bad luck (Williams & Nikolaisen, 1982).

Research issues

These studies suggest that parents create many possible explanations for their baby's death; most explanations reflect the acceptance of parental responsibility. How then do they decide which one to accept? What criteria do they use to make this decision? Is this decision made just once or twice, or do parents keep changing their minds about why their baby died? And what makes them change their minds?

Cornwell et al. (1977) provide us with some clues about how to answer these questions. Fortunately, besides administering questionnaires, these authors also interviewed the parents three or four times during the first year after the baby's death. Rather than subjecting their interviews to rigorous analysis, however, Cornwell et al. merely summarize the issues. Nonetheless, the issues they identify are very telling. This study hints at the existence of an explanation-seeking and guilt-reducing process that parents work through over time. The following quotes from Cornwell et al. hint at this process:

> Parents often **initially** [emphasis added] felt guilty and thought that the death was their fault. (p. 657)

> Attempts were made to fit the event into a rational and/or metaphysical model of the universe. The parents **struggled with attempts to make sense** [emphasis added] of a sudden inexplicable disastrous event. In this country, parents expect their babies to live. When this confident expectation is shattered, a massive revision may take place in their understanding of what the world is about. (p. 658)

> Parents **attempted to maintain** [emphasis added] their belief in a benign God, and several **convinced themselves** [emphasis added] that the child would have been physically, intellectually or morally defective, had it lived. (p. 658)

This study suggests that parents work hard to construct their explanation: they construct several possible explanations over the course of a year; they struggle to decide which one to settle on; they have to resolve some inner conflict in the process; and parents feel stressed until they can resolve their conflict. The Cornwell et al. study provides a fresh perspective on parental guilt. Although this study was reported in 1977, no one has investigated this subject further. This important topic warrants further investigation.

Gender differences

There are many studies that examine the differences between the experiences of grieving mothers and fathers. On average, paternal grief seems less intense and shorter in duration than maternal grief (Bohannon, 1990–1991; Cornwell et al., 1977; DeFrain, 1991; Dyregrov & Matthiesen, 1987a; Irizarry & Willard, 1993). In their study of grieving parents (12% of the sample had lost a baby to SIDS), Lang and Gottlieb (1993) found that mothers experienced more difficulties and more intense reactions than fathers. One explanation for this might be that fathers seem to accept SIDS as the cause of their baby's death sooner than mothers (Williams & Nikolaisen, 1982). Another explanation might be found in the work of Dyregrov and Matthiesen (1991), who found that mothers who remained at home experienced more distress than either employed mothers or fathers. This finding suggests that perhaps gender is not the only factor at work here.

On average, fathers in the Cornwell et al. (1977) study took a little less than 4 months to feel like they had returned to "normal functioning" (p. 658), while it took the mothers just over 10 months. In contrast, Dyregrov and Matthiesen (1991) found that more fathers indicated that they were experiencing distress at 13 months follow-up than at 6 months.

In the DeFrain et al. (1991) study, 93% of the participants said that "their way of coping was different from that of their spouse" (p. 104). While personality differences may account for some of this variation, several authors suggest that sex roles may also affect how parents deal with their grief (Cook, 1988; DeFrain et al., 1991; Dyregrov & Matthiesen, 1987a, 1991; Fish, 1986; Mandell et al., 1980; Rando, 1985). Dyregrov and Matthiesen (1991) also suggest that, generally, our society focuses more on the mother's needs and reactions, leaving the father's needs "unrecognized" (p. 203).

Mandell et al. (1980) observe that grieving mothers appear withdrawn. In contrast, other authors (DeFrain et al., 1991; Nikolaisen & Williams, 1980) found that instead of withdrawing many women cry openly and want to talk about their experience.Women are more likely to take advantage of the opportunity to share their grief with others. In contrast, "fathers' grief often goes unarticulated [perhaps because] fathers have generally more difficulties in setting words to their emotions" (Dyregrov & Matthiesen, 1991, p. 202). On a practical level, most men seem reluctant to talk about their grief because they believe talking "won't bring the baby back" (Mandell et al., 1980, p. 223). Instead of talking, men are more likely to: concern themselves with their wives' well-being (Cornwell et al., 1977); increase their work involvement (Dyregrov, 1990; Mandell et al., 1980; Nikolaisen & Williams, 1980); assume the role of manager; suggest having another baby; and "intellectualize" their pain (Mandell et al., 1980, p. 222). Men are also less likely than women to participate in support programs (Mandell et al., 1980) or to ask for help from others (Dyregrov & Matthiesen, 1991).

Research issues

Sometimes what we learn about grief reactions in one gender stimulates questions about reactions in the other gender. Rubin (1985) found a "permanent presence of the child in the maternal experience" (p. 351). Do fathers also maintain an emotional connection to a "phantom child" (p. 351)?

If not, why not, and how and when do they let go of the baby? Price et al. (1985) found that the younger the baby at the time of death, the more difficult the mother's adjustment. Does the baby's age affect the father's adjustment in the same way? If fathers really do accept SIDS as the diagnosis more readily than mothers, why and how does this happen? What prevents mothers from accepting this explanation any sooner? And why might fathers return to normal functioning sooner than mothers? What contributes to this? Finally, why might women want to talk about their grief and why do men resist talking? Can we generalize to all men and women? Despite much research in this area, obviously many questions remain unanswered.

Grief and the parents' marriage

Incidence of divorce

"The death of a child may be viewed as a crisis point or pivotal point that either results in increased supportiveness within the marital relationship or in increased estrangement from one's spouse" (Price et al., 1985, p. 26). The baby's death changed 90 percent of the marriages in the DeFrain et al. (1991) study. Many couples experience a severe crisis in their relationship. Some separate or divorce within the first year or two after their baby's death (Cornwell et al., 1977; DeFrain et al., 1991; Mandell et al., 1980). Estimates about the divorce rate for these parents vary considerably. DeFrain et al. (1991) suggest the divorce rate is really no higher for these parents than for the general population, while Vance et al. (1995) found that after the death of a baby to SIDS, stillbirth, or neonatal death there is an increased likelihood of marital breakdown within the next 5 years. Parents who do divorce seldom blame the baby's death; other problems are given on the legal papers, making it difficult to estimate the real incidence of divorce or marital breakdown caused by the death of a baby to SIDS. To date, no one has completed a longitudinal study of the divorce rates for parents who lose a baby to SIDS.

Weakened relationships

While some couples separate or divorce, others stay together, although their marriage is weakened, more emotionally distant, or in a state of crisis within months of the baby's death. Vance et al. (1995) found an increase in marital problems over the 5 years following a baby's death. The percentage of weakened but intact marriages varies from study to study: 35% of the men and 22% of the women in the DeFrain et al. (1991) study felt their marriage had been weakened; 33% of the couples in the Cornwell et al. (1977) study, 30% of the women in the Price et al. (1985) study, and 21% of the couples in the Mandell et al. (1980) study felt the same way. The types of marital problems include increased fighting, emotional distance, and even "a defined need for marital therapy" (Cornwell et al., 1977, p. 657). Dyregrov and Matthiesen (1991) found that the differences between how spouses were handling their grief seemed to peak at about 6 months, making this a most stressful time for the health of the marriage.

Some marriages are in trouble even before their baby's death: "Anything that was wrong [with the marriage] before [may be] augmented one hundredfold" (DeFrain et al., 1991, p. 198). Young parents with few problem-solving skills may have had no previous experience with death and grief (Markusen et al., 1978). Consequently, they may not know how to talk about their grief and how to solve problems together. If a couple marries primarily because of a pregnancy and then the baby dies, then they may have little commitment to staying together (Mandell et al., 1980). But the death of a baby can strain even a solid and mature marriage.

Grief and marital strains

"Grief can be simultaneously both a shared and an intensely private experience" (Ranney, 1991, p. 59), partly because parents each experience (Lang & Gottllieb, 1993) and handle their grief in their own unique way. Many researchers assume that gender is at the root of this uniqueness (Cornwell et al., 1977; DeFrain et al., 1991; Mandell et al., 1980; Ranney, 1991; Williams & Nikolaisen, 1982). Riches and Dawson (1996) point to the difficulties that grieving parents have with sharing their grief since each has lost a unique relationship. To further complicate matters, some parents cannot understand or tolerate differences in the way people grieve. Instead, they try to change their spouse's behavior. This leads to increased fighting and more misunderstandings (DeFrain et al., 1991; Nikolaisen & Williams, 1980; Rando, 1985). For instance, Miles (1975, cited in Nikolaisen & Williams, 1980) says that some men consider their wives to be "uncontrolled and weak," while wives think their husbands are "uncaring" (p. 594). These kinds of comments may significantly increase marital tension.

Grief also affects the way couples function as partners. Writing generally about parental grief, Rando (1985) says that often both parents have simultaneously lost their major source of support: each other. If couples cannot get past this problem, the partners may feel abandoned and increasingly lonely (Riches & Dawson, 1996), leading them to give less than positive evaluations of their relationship. Thirty-eight percent of the parents in the

Cornwell et al. (1977) study said that their baby's death had negatively affected their ability to function as a marriage partner. Grieving parents also have little energy because it is "spent trying to cope with the death" (DeFrain et al., 1991, p. 198). Soon husbands and wives have nothing "to give anymore, and when you're not giving in a marriage at all times, that marriage can quickly fall apart" (DeFrain et al., 1991, p. 107).

Grieving parents may also experience communication problems (Rando, 1985). Irizarry and Willard (1993) found that women are better than men at predicting what their spouses are thinking and feeling about the baby's death and their grief. Although May and Breme (1982) suggest that couples should discuss their grief, many couples find it difficult to talk about their pain (DeFrain et al., 1991; Mandell et al., 1980).When one wants to talk, the other does not (Dyregrov & Matthiesen, 1987a). Couples may not even share their tears, perhaps because when one partner sees the other cry it causes both to cry. Cornwell et al. (1977) call this "resonating grief" (p. 657). Because of resonating grief, some partners start hiding their tears. It is difficult to tell whether this has a positive or negative effect on marriages. Dyregrov and Matthiesen (1987a) also found something similar. They called it "reciprocal emotional influence" (p. 12). These authors suggest that when parents trigger grief in each other it may be a sign that they need professional help.

Grieving may also affect marital intimacy. Fifty-two percent of the respondents in the DeFrain et al. (1991) study reported that their sexual relationship had changed. Some spouses felt they were not functioning well as sexual partners (Cornwell et al., 1977). Shortly after the baby's death, a woman's interest in sex may become almost nonexistent, while her husband's may increase significantly (DeFrain et al., 1991; Gottlieb, Lang, & Amsel, 1996; Irizarry & Willard, 1993). While men may find sexual intercourse provides them with a sense of release and a source of comfort, women may feel uninterested in sexual intimacy when they are grieving. This difference can certainly become another major source of marital conflict.

As couples try to deal with their grief, they may also be trying to decide whether to have another baby. This can be a difficult decision at the best of times. If both partners are feeling raw and overwhelmed by their grief, then it can severely strain any marriage (DeFrain et al., 1991; Mandell et al., 1980). Boyle, Vance, and Najman (1993) point out that although doctors and counselors frequently recommend that grieving parents delay getting pregnant for at least 6 months after a child dies this may ignore what the parents want to do, making the decision even harder for them. Possible difficulties with making the decision (Irizarry & Willard, 1993), getting pregnant, carrying the subsequent pregnancy (Irizarry & Willard, 1993; Mandell

& Wolfe, 1975), the birth of a new baby, and then trying to care for and love this new baby while fearing its death can put strains on any marriage (Bergman et al., 1969; Cornwell et al., 1977; DeFrain et al., 1991). And what about the mother's continued connection to her "phantom child" (Rubin, 1985, p. 351)? As yet, we do not know if fathers share in the memories and "bittersweet current relationship" (p. 350).

Strengthened marriages

While it is true that many marriages are strained to the limit by grieving, many parents have the opposite experience: this crisis strengthens their relationship. Many couples feel more closely tied to one another (43% of the sample in Cornwell et al. [1977]; 51% in DeFrain et al. [1991]; and 60% of the women in Price et al. [1985]). Although studies have identified the strains that might cause marriages to "fragment" (Mandell et al., 1980, p. 223) after the death of a child, there is little about how or why couples in the same situation might become closer and stronger. Riches and Dawson (1996) suggest that being able to "share intense feelings through conversation" may be what draws grieving couples closer (p. 6).

After a thorough review of the literature, I discovered only one reference specific to SIDS that presents some ideas about how families survive. Based on the comments and answers on questionnaires from individual parents (not couples), DeFrain et al. (1991) suggest that the following factors might make a positive difference: belief in God; "commitment, togetherness, and the ability to take turns being strong for each other" (p. 204); and the sheer will and desire to survive. These authors also suggest that effective communication within the family and with others outside the family makes a significant difference. Using individual and couple data from bereaved parents (SIDS parents included), Dyregrov and Matthiesen (1987a) found a positive correlation between a couple's ability to talk about "what happened" and a feeling of closeness in the marriage (p. 7).

To gather more information, I expanded my search to include studies about the marital issues of grieving parents in general. Again, most focus on the potential for problems and pain, not on the potential for strength and closeness (see Feeley & Gottlieb, 1988; Lehman, Lang, Wortman, & Sorenson, 1989; Valeriote & Fine, 1987). Riches and Dawson (1996) focus on the importance of talking about grief and the death as a key ingredient in reducing the sense of loneliness that often accompanies grief when a child dies. Although Schwab's (1990) study produced a very useful list and description of a variety of coping strategies used by grieving mothers and fathers, there was no attempt to examine how these strategies affected the marital relationships of these couples.

Research issues

There is an obvious and major gap in the research. To date, researchers have focused all their attention on identifying and listing the problems couples face when they lose a baby to SIDS. No one has studied couples who have successfully dealt with their grief while maintaining their relationship; no one has asked these couples to share their secret strategies. These couples must be confronted by the same grief-related problems as other bereaved parents. How do successful couples surmount these problems? How do they prevent grief from hurting their relationship? Why do some relationships become stronger and others become weaker? Couples whose marriages become stronger have much to teach us, and it is time someone asked for their help.

Grief and children

The death of an only child

Before discussing how older siblings might be affected by the death of the baby, a few words about parents who lose their first and only baby to SIDS. Although SIDS takes fewer firstborn babies, it does take some (Hillman, 1991). Thirty-two percent of the mothers in the Price et al. (1985) study and 29 percent of the couples in the Lowman (1979) study lost their firstborn babies. Parents who lose their only child "experience a complete cessation of parental responsibilities, as well as gratifications, [and they] are forced to contend with a total lack of experiences reinforcing their former parental identities" (Rando, 1986a, p. 32), or as Talbot (1996–1997) put it:

> [The death of an only child] presents a severe challenge.…A conflict arises between our wish to never forget our child, and the meaningfulness of our identity as a mother, and our reality of now living with no living child to parent. (pp. 178–179)

In contrast, parents who have other children still feel like parents, still have others treating them like parents, and still have someone needing them to act like parents.

Research issues

Most researchers ignore the differences that might occur in their findings when they do not pay attention to how many children bereaved parents have. In their discussion of their sample, researchers seldom specify whether parents in their studies have lost their only child or whether they have other children (see Bergman et al., 1969; Cornwell et al., 1977; DeFrain & Ernst, 1978; DeFrain et al., 1991; Dyregrov & Matthiesen, 1987b; Mandell et al., 1980; Nikolaisen & Williams, 1980; Rubin, 1985; Williams & Nikolaisen, 1982), or if they do specify that some parents in their sample have lost an only child, they do not use this information to explore how that might affect parents (see, for example, Carroll & Shaefer, 1993–1994). If researchers want to understand all the issues that contribute to the intensity and duration of the parental grief experience, the importance of birth order should not be ignored.

Older siblings

Since the "risk [of SIDS] increases steadily with increasing parity," most parents who lose a baby to SIDS have at least one older child (Hillman, 1991, p. 17). For example, 68 percent of the women in the Price et al. (1985) study had at least one older child. And some of these older children witness the discovery of the dead baby (Mandell et al., 1988).

Most children cannot comprehend the meaning of this event. They may wonder about other people's behavior; they may even wonder if perhaps it was something they said or did or thought that made the baby die (Mandell, McAnulty, & Reece, 1983; Mandell et al., 1988; Stahlman, 1996). Since the "unique characteristic of the childhood sibling bond is its sense of 'universal ambivalence'" (Stahlman, 1996, p. 150), children may remember times when they did not want their baby brother or sister or times when they felt angry (Halpern, 1972). This can contribute to feelings of guilt and, sometimes, a feeling of responsibility for the death. The problem is that no matter how parents handle this crisis the children may suffer. Children who are too young to understand grief may think their parents are upset because of something they have done wrong (Burns, House, & Ankenbauer, 1986).

Stahlman (1996) asserts that a child's response to a sibling's death is greatly dependent on how the parents handle the death and their own grief, but Baker and Sedney (1996) suggest that no matter how well the parents handle this crisis the children will experience "secondary losses," that is, changes in such things as parental functioning and routine (p. 110). Some grieving parents become so overwhelmed with grief that they do not realize the needs of their remaining children (Sanders, 1995). According to Price et al. (1985),

> With the emotional demands that the death of an infant places upon the parents the surviving siblings must often endure more than one loss. That is, the child experiences both the death of a sibling and the feelings of loss associated with the decreased emotional availability of the parents in their attempt to cope with their own grief. (p. 26)

Several studies show that parental behavior changes after the death of a baby. In addition to, or perhaps as a consequence of, feeling overwhelmed with grief themselves, some mothers withdraw from or reject their other children (Cornwell et al., 1977; DeFrain et al., 1991; Halpern, 1972; Mandell et al., 1983; Price et al., 1985). Halpern (1972) suggests that the very circumstances of a SIDS death contribute to the problem of parental behavior: the inexplicable and sudden death of the baby devastates and overwhelms the parents. They may be short-tempered and find it difficult to talk with or feel empathy for their other children. Some distressed parents overtly blame their older child for causing the baby's death. This can devastate the child (Halpern, 1972).

Instead of rejecting their children, most parents do the opposite: they try to get closer to their surviving children (Mandell et al., 1983). Seventy percent of the mothers in the Price et al. (1985) study reported that they felt closer to their surviving children after the baby's death. Many parents go beyond normal emotional closeness. Numerous studies say that parents grieving the loss of a baby to SIDS very often become very overprotective parents (Bergman et al., 1969; Cornwell et al., 1977; DeFrain & Ernst, 1978; DeFrain et al., 1991; Mandell et al., 1983; Rubin, 1981).

How does overprotectiveness translate into behavior? Overprotective parents commonly check their children continually, particularly while the children sleep (Cornwell et al., 1977; DeFrain et al., 1991). Parents may also overindulge their children and appreciate them more. They may become more permissive or worry about their children's health. Some parents become inconsistent with rules and discipline (DeFrain et al., 1991; Mandell et al., 1983). While 47 percent of the parents in the Cornwell et al. (1977) study felt that their parenting improved after the baby's death, 33 percent felt their parenting skills had suffered.

Most older siblings experience significant difficulties after the death of their brother or sister. Studies vary as to the number of parents who say their children seemed disturbed by the baby's death: 97 percent in Mandell et al. (1983) to 78 percent in DeFrain and Ernst (1978). Fifty-three percent of the mothers in the Price et al. (1985) study thought their children were "noticeably disturbed" in the first weeks after the baby's death (p. 26). The authors do not explain the nature or severity of these disturbances.

Most studies examine children's immediate reactions and then some follow them for the first year. According to the parents in the Cornwell et al. (1977) study, children's reactions varied with their age. After the death of the baby, toddlers rejected their mothers, had temper tantrums, and kept looking for the baby. Older children repeatedly asked questions about the baby's death and what had happened to the baby's body. They also worried about their own impending death. Children under 12 had trouble sleeping; they often felt afraid.

In the Mandell et al. (1983) study, 83 percent of the children aged 2 to 2.5 had sleep problems: these children resisted going to bed, then they had trouble falling asleep and staying asleep. In their nightmares, "monsters" pursued them, the same monsters that had "killed" their baby brother or sister (p. 654). Fifty percent of the 30- to 48-month-old children in the Mandell et al. (1983) study had significant changes in the way they interacted with other children. While some withdrew, others became aggressive to the point that schools and day care centers expressed concern (Mandell et al., 1983). Other problems included regression in toilet training (DeFrain & Ernst, 1978; Mandell et al., 1983), appetite disturbances (Mandell et al., 1983), bed wetting, crying a lot, and blackouts (DeFrain & Ernst, 1978).

Children's reactions varied over time (Davies & Segal, 1991). At first, the parents' reactions frighten and upset the children more than anything else. Gradually, as the children begin to comprehend that the baby really is gone, they react more openly. In the Price et al. (1985) study, after 6 months "only 10%" of the children remained "significantly disturb[ed]" (p. 26). Just over half the children seem to have difficulties beyond the 1-year mark (Burns et al., 1986). Some children still seem angry at the end of the first year, particularly with their mother (Cornwell et al., 1977). The three children described in the Halpern (1972) article were all seen in a child guidance clinic within 12 to 18 months of a SIDS death. Their reactions were so severe that they required the intervention of a child psychiatrist. And then there is the lasting legacy of losing a sibling to SIDS. Mandell et al. (1988) found that when some siblings become parents themselves they become afraid they will lose their own baby to SIDS.

Research issues

The issues come in the form of questions. Since the focus of the study is parental grief, my questions are about the parents in relation to their older children. What causes the parents to overprotect their older children? Is there a connection between the lack of a definite explanation for the baby's death and the parents' need to overprotect their surviving children? How long do parents continue to feel overprotective? How do they stop? Can they ever go back to being the kind of parents they were before the baby died? Do both mothers and fathers overprotect? How does this kind of parenting affect the parents' marriage and the parent-child relationship in both the short-term and the long-term? To date, we have no answers to these questions.

I have further questions. Why might some parents feel better and others feel worse about themselves as parents? And finally, what role does the child play in how the parents feel? Does the behavior of the child influence the parents' grief in any way? Clearly, this whole subject deserves further exploration.

Subsequent pregnancies and children

Most parents who lose a baby to SIDS eventually want to have another baby (Mandell & Wolfe, 1975; Price et al., 1985). While some want to get pregnant within weeks of the baby's death, others put off the decision until they feel less stressed and until they feel able to accept another baby as a separate person (Cornwell et al., 1977; DeFrain et al., 1991). Some parents decide not to have any more children (Cornwell et al., 1977; DeFrain et al., 1991; Mandell & Wolfe, 1975), often because they are "uncertain that they would be able to cope with further pain if they lost it" (Cornwell et al., 1977, p. 657). There is an important time element here though. DeFrain et al. (1991) found that, for some parents, this fear decreases over time, causing some parents to change their minds.

When researchers look at this decision, they usually treat it as a woman's issue (Mandell & Wolfe, 1975; Price et al., 1985). When the thoughts of both parents are studied, however, it reveals the source of possible marital conflict. While almost all the fathers in the Mandell et al. (1980) study wanted to have another baby very soon, their wives did not share this desire, mostly because they feared losing another baby. Because of their differences, "the issue of a subsequent pregnancy [became] a source of conflict between the parents" (Mandell et al., 1980, p. 222). Although many couples do eventually have another baby, little is known about how they deal with this conflict. Instead, researchers just report on the outcome of the parents' decision: the number of babies born after a SIDS death.

When parents decide to have another baby, it is either because they want a sibling for their other children or because they "need to fill the 'hole' left by the child who died" (DeFrain et al., 1991, p. 186). Once couples make the decision, some deliberately plan "for conception at a certain time so the baby could be born when there was a statistically lower chance of [a SIDS] death" (Cornwell et al., 1977, p. 657).

Despite all their planning and their desire to have another baby, some parents never conceive or deliver another baby. Others take far longer to conceive than they anticipated. In the Mandell and Wolfe (1975) study, 60 percent of the parents who wanted to conceive had "complications" (p. 77). Of those who had complications, 31 percent miscarried. Thirty-four percent did not conceive within the first year, and on average, it took parents 2.2 years to conceive again (the range was 1.2 years to 7 years). None of these women had any previous difficulties with conception or fertility.

Mandell and Wolfe (1975) suggest that the women's intense grief reaction may affect their menstrual cycle, thereby making it more difficult to either conceive or carry a baby to term. While this medical explanation makes good sense, it ignores the possibility that stress within the marriage might also contribute to the problem. The stress of first losing a baby to SIDS and then having difficulties conceiving or delivering the next baby is enough to strain any marriage.

If and when parents finally do have another baby, they begin to "suffer" from an intense fear that this baby will die from the minute they bring the baby home from the hospital (Cornwell et al., 1977, p. 657). At first, the new baby continually reminds the parents of the baby they lost: some call the new baby the wrong name occasionally. Parents check and recheck this baby to make sure it is breathing, especially during sleep. Some parents use a mechanical monitor to watch over their baby as well, although the use of these devices has decreased since the 1980s (DeFrain et al., 1991). Parents in the Cornwell et al. (1977) study took all kinds of specific precautions, such as taking a first-aide course, putting screens on the windows to keep the flies out, and giving up smoking. No matter what parents do to protect their baby from "the unknown force" that took the other baby, they feel stressed and afraid (Cornwell et al., 1977, p. 657).

Research issues

Stephenson (1986) writes about the "unhealthy coping mechanism" (p. 335) of having a "replacement child" to cope with parental grief (p. 336). He goes on to suggest that parents take "sufficient time" (p. 336) before having another child. He does not define how long they should wait. This illustrates a problem with this particular subject. We do not know whether having another child affects parental grieving; we do not whether the timing of the next pregnancy makes any difference. We also know little about how parents make this decision or what the next pregnancy might be like for parents. There is even less information about parents who decide not to have another child. Does this decision affect their marriage and their ability to heal from their loss? Obviously this is an important issue in the study of parental grief.

The changing nature of parental grief over time

Symptoms and consequences

Does grief "dissipate in time" as Lowman (1979, p. 673) suggests? The evidence suggests that grief does not neatly subside but that various aspects of it rise and fall somewhat like a rollercoaster. For at least the first few months, parents seem to feel either numb (Cornwell et al., 1977) or highly anxious (Vance et al., 1995). Then the acute pain of grief sets in, bringing with it all the many thoughts and feelings described earlier in this review. Some studies have found that within 6 months many mothers report a reduction in the total number of symptoms of grief (Lowman, 1979; Price et al., 1985). Within less than a year, most parents in the Cornwell et al. (1977) study said they could at least function again. DeFrain (1991) found that within a year after a baby's death parents reported that they were not as happy as they had been in the months before the baby's death but that their level of happiness had at least returned to average. But Price et al. (1985) found that although the number of symptoms decreases within the first 6 months, in almost half of the women in this study, "significant feelings of fear, sadness, and depression" persisted for well over 6 to 30 months longer (p. 28). Dyregrov and Matthiesen (1987a) had similar findings, while Vance et al. (1995) found that anxiety levels for mothers in particular stayed high for at least the first 30 months of bereavement.

Estimates of the proportion of parents who experience significant difficulties vary with the study, the methods used, and the nature of the sample. Vance et al. (1993) looked at very concrete evidence: use of sedatives and alcohol. They found that at 6 months grieving mothers used more sedatives than matched controls. As well, women who drank before their baby's death were more likely to increase their intake over the next 25 months. One quarter of the mothers in the Price et al. (1985) study had an "unsatisfactory adjustment" to their baby's death at the end of 6 months (p. 28). The authors do not define what they mean by this term. They also fail to describe how this adjustment problem manifested itself in the women's lives. Lowman (1979) also looked at adjustment in grieving mothers over the first 6 months. He assumed that a steady decline in the number of symptoms was equivalent to a steady decline in "significant mourning and disruption in [the women's] lives" (p. 673). When 35 percent of the women in his study did not report a lessening of symptoms, he labeled their grief "maladaptive" (p. 673). But it seems this problem is more common than people realize. Dyregrov and Matthiesen (1991) found that mothers who did not work outside the home experienced heightened and prolonged anxiety beyond the first 6 months. It was also at the 6-month mark that couples seemed to have the most trouble with asynchronous grieving. In the l'Hoir & Wolters (1993) study, 11 percent of the parents experienced delayed Post-traumatic Stress Disorder at least 6 months after the baby's death. Three women in the Cornwell et al. (1977) study sought psychiatric help for serious problems within the first year. Both mothers and fathers in the Vance et al. (1995) study reported that at 30 months they were still experiencing dissatisfaction with their life and that they were feeling both unhappy and miserable. It seems that the first few years do not produce a steady decline in parental grief.

The longer term perspective on the mental health consequences of losing a baby to SIDS is missing: we do not know how parents fare in the long-term because most studies only cover the first 6 years after the baby's death. Rubin (1981) compared the number of symptoms of grief in women whose babies had died between 2 and 6 years previously with women who had not lost their babies; the 2 groups were indistinguishable. Does this mean that parents are finished grieving within about 6 years and that most return to "normal life" again (Cornwell et al., 1977, p. 658)? The poignancy of the parents' stories in DeFrain et al.'s (1991) book shows that parental grief lasts a lifetime. DeFrain (1991) adds that "in our research we have found people who 30, 40, 50, and 60 years later describe the experience of losing their babies to us, and the descriptions are told so vividly that when the individual tells the story it sounds almost as though the death occurred just yesterday" (p. 224). As Rubin (1993) puts it, "Child loss [is] a major organizing event in an individual parent's life" (p. 293). This leads me to ask: How do parents organize their grief experience over time? What makes it better? What makes it worse?

Rubin (1985) found one aspect of grief that does not appear to decrease over time: guilt over the baby's death. He suggests that "persistent feelings of guilt" are characteristic of parents (particularly mothers) who have lost a baby to SIDS (p. 350). He further suggests that there is no relationship between the presence of guilt and the inability to resolve the loss successfully. This begs the question then: How can a parent feel responsible for the baby's death and resolve the loss at the same time? This is a subject for further inquiry.

Continued connection to the baby

For the first month or two after the baby's death, parents' "minds were attuned to perceptions of the baby" (Cornwell et al., 1977, p. 657). Some mothers respond to what they think is their baby's cry: they prepare bottles and frequently go into the nursery. While some just worry about their baby being cold or wet in the grave, others actively try to dig up their baby. Women in particular are often frustrated because they want "to go about their mothering tasks" (Cornwell et al., 1977, p. 657): their bodies and arms ache to hold the baby (Arnold & Gemma, 1991). But there is no baby to feed, no baby to hold and touch. Despite the passage of 6 to 30 months, 30 percent of the mothers in the Price et al. (1985) study reported "having difficulty with thoughts that [their] baby is still alive" (p. 26). Zagdanski (1995) worried about her baby being cold and afraid in the cemetery. It seems that although physical parenting becomes impossible, the emotional connection to the baby persists. Even if they have no physical body to care for, most mothers stay bonded to their baby for the rest of their life (Carroll & Shaefer, 1993–1994; DeFrain et al., 1991; Price et al., 1985; Rubin, 1981, 1985, 1993).

Rubin (1985) contends that parents can resolve their grief without "withdrawing all interest from the memory of the lost child" (p. 351). At first, this continued connection to the baby causes pain for the parents. One year after the death of their own infant, over 70 percent of the parents in the Cornwell et al. (1977) study were still "visually alert" (p. 658) for babies. Mothers "thought and dreamt of their babies and looked at mementoes" while fathers were less likely to do this (p. 658). Rubin's (1981) study shows that during the first year of bereavement the mothers' intense attachment to their baby "intruded a significant proportion of the time or interfered with functioning significantly" (p. 107).

What happens to this attachment after a couple of years? Mothers who lost their baby an average of 4.5 years earlier "demonstrated a more subdued, continuing involvement with the dead child" than those with a more recent loss (Rubin, 1981, p. 108). Stories from DeFrain et al. (1991) suggest that this connection continues for many parents, mothers more so than fathers. We have very little information about fathers and if they maintain a steady and private relationship with their baby. However, studies do show that many parents remember their baby at certain times of the year.

Many, but not all, parents remember their baby and perhaps experience a surge of grief on the anniversary of the baby's death (Cornwell et al., 1977; DeFrain et al., 1991; Halpern, 1972), on the baby's birthday, special family holidays, and missed milestone events such as beginning or ending school (DeFrain et al., 1991).We know little about how parents deal with these days.

Research questions

The importance researchers give to the passage of time varies: some make an issue of it, while others scarcely mention it. It seems important to ask whether the passage of time is an important issue for the understanding of the parental grief experience. Does the proverbial saying, time will heal, have any relevance to parental grief?

Although DeFrain et al. (1991) conclude that many parents continue to deal with their grief for the rest of their lives, many researchers examine only the parents' first year of grief (Bergman et al., 1969; Cornwell et al., 1977; Halpern, 1972; Lowman, 1979; Mandell et al., 1980). Others look at the first 3 to 5 years (Carroll & Shaefer, 1993–1994; DeFrain & Ernst, 1978; Price et al., 1985; Vance et al., 1995). While some studies look at how parents manage up to 6 years after the death of their baby (Dyregrov & Matthiesen, 1987b; Mandell & Wolfe, 1975; Nikolaisen & Williams, 1980; Rubin, 1981, 1985; Williams & Nikolaisen, 1982), only DeFrain et al. (1991) went beyond 6 years. They did not set a time limit for participation in their study. This provided the opportunity for readers and researchers to learn that grief for the death of a child is a lifelong experience. We still do not know how parents deal with their grief as the years pass.

We know something about the mothers' first 6 months of grief but little about the fathers' experience. Therefore, I have more questions. How does grief change over time for fathers? Is there a smooth reduction in symptoms? What does the trajectory of grief look like for both mothers and fathers over time? What influences this experience? Is it any different for fathers than mothers? Do fathers have difficulty at certain times of the year? If not, why not? Do fathers continue to have a relationship with their deceased baby like many mothers do? What transforms the parent-child relationship from an intense to a subdued connection? So many questions.

Critique of the Research Methodology

Research positions

Researchers studying the experiences of parents who have lost a baby to SIDS appear to approach the topic from one of two positions: as an interested student wanting to learn about the experience or as a distant professional wanting to analyze aspects of the parents' pain.

Bergman et al. (1969) were among the first students to ask what "psychiatric toll" SIDS exacted from surviving families (p. 99). In other words, these researchers just wanted to learn what this experience was like so they could find a way to help. Since little information about this subject was available at the time, Bergman et al. chose to learn directly from the parents themselves. The authors met with 225 families in their homes to listen and to learn. A quotation from Lifton (1982) helps to explain Bergman et al.'s approach:

> There are certain kinds of suffering that we as professionals don't understand and don't know about. A certain humility before suffering is useful....[Those who have suffered] have been through things that [we] don't know about; [we've] never touched them; they know things [we] don't know. At our wisest as professionals, we really just listen and give them the sense that they understand something that we don't know. (p. 226)

Bergman et al. (1969) did not attempt to systematically analyze their observations and interviews. Their article simply describes the nature of the parents' experiences and the factors that seem to contribute to their overwhelmingly intense and prolonged grief. I can feel the researchers' awareness and profound respect for the parents' pain as I read the studies conducted by Bergman et al. (1969), Cornwell et al. (1977), and Rubin (1985).

In contrast, other researchers write from a position of professional distance. Their primary goal is to measure, categorize, or correlate some aspect of the parents' experience. Although these researchers may ask much the same questions as Bergman et al. (1969), instead of meeting parents face to face, they study the experience from a distance by using questionnaires (DeFrain & Ernst, 1978; DeFrain et al., 1991; DeFrain et al., 1992; Irizarry & Willard, 1993; Nikolaisen & Williams, 1980; Price et al., 1985; Williams & Nikolaisen, 1982). These questionnaires are usually constructed after a review of the literature and, in some cases, a discussion with other professionals. Researchers then contact parents who have lost a baby to SIDS and whose names are on government and hospital lists to ask them to participate. If they agree, the parents receive a lengthy questionnaire in the mail with instructions to complete it by themselves. Many questionnaires consist of numerous Likert-scale, multiple choice, and closed questions about some specific aspect of the grief experience.

DeFrain and Ernst (1978) use two reasons to justify their use of questionnaires to study parental grief. First, they worry that interviews might interfere with the education and counselling services available to families. I fail to see how participation in an interview might interfere with any intervention program. In fact, Lowman (1979) actually used parents from an intervention program to complete his study; both researcher and parents benefited. Raphael (1983) suggests that parents might benefit from even one interview, even it is for research purposes. It could be therapeutic for parents to share their grief with someone outside the family, perhaps for the first time.

The second reason DeFrain and Ernst (1978) use questionnaires is because they want to avoid upsetting parents. This justification disintegrates when one reads a written note from one of their participants. She describes what it was like to complete their 13-page questionnaire: "I would write and I would cry. Put it aside a few days, and then write a page, and cry. If an interviewer had come to my door, I'd have broken down completely" (p. 987). Completing this questionnaire upset this woman for several days. At least if she had been interviewed, she would not have cried alone or perhaps for so long. Meanwhile, the researchers remain in their office, awaiting her response so they can analyze it, safe from direct exposure to her suffering.

DeFrain et al. (1991) continue to use questionnaires for their research to this day despite the fact that parents keep taking the initiative to contact them, seeking an opportunity to tell their stories their way:

> [The parents] call on the telephone to talk about their questions, their fears, their sadness. They invite us to meet with their family or their support group. They come forward after a presentation to tell their unique stories....These people, who have contacted us informally over the years, have each brought us insight into understanding the death of a baby. (p. x)

These parents are asking researchers to enter their world of suffering as students rather than standing outside it as professionals. They seem to be telling researchers to stop assuming they understand what it is like to lose a baby to SIDS and to start listening to someone who has. Maybe it is time someone listened to them.

Research instruments

The position researchers take towards their study influences the instruments they chose to use. The instruments then shape the kind of data that can be collected. As I have already mentioned, many researchers use questionnaires. As they are used in the studies under review, questionnaires produce lists, measure attitudes and intensities of feelings, find out if certain experiences are common, allow comparisons, and look for associations between various aspects of the experience. Results often come in numbers: averages, scores, number of symptoms, and percentages. While this type of information can be useful, it often quantifies and divides the parents' experience into pieces instead of promoting any understanding of the whole picture. For example, it does not help me to know that "the mean score of the parents' expressed feelings was 19.6 with a possible score of 7 to 28" (Williams & Nikolaisen, 1982, p. 59). Without basing this information in some kind of context, it is meaningless.

When constructing their questionnaires, some researchers include a few "open ended questions…when a range of different responses [are] expected" (Williams & Nikolaisen, 1982, p. 57) or when they want parents to add a few comments of their own (DeFrain et al., 1991; Price et al., 1985). Beyond completing the lengthy questionnaires, some mothers send the researchers pages and pages that describe their experiences in great detail and with great emotion (DeFrain et al., 1991). The "pain and sorrow…evident in [the parents'] responses" seem to surprise Williams and Nikolaisen (1982, p. 60). Instead of understanding that perhaps the questionnaire method restricts the parents' ability to tell their story, Williams and Nikolaisen (1982) conclude that their questionnaire must have reached a "special group" of parents, parents who chose to participate because they needed "a cathartic outlet for their feelings" (p. 60). What these authors fail to understand is that their open-ended questions may have released the "pain and sorrow" that the other questions merely tried to categorize and measure.

Some researchers use both questionnaires and interviews or observations (Carroll & Shaefer, 1993–1994; Cornwell et al., 1977; Dyregrov & Matthiesen, 1987a, 1987b, 1987c, 1991; l'Hoir & Wolters, 1993; Lowman, 1979; Johnson-Soderberg, 1983; Rubin, 1981; Vance et al., 1991, 1993, 1995). The questionnaires detect some issues; the face-to-face contact with the parents provides the researchers with the opportunity to explore these issues in greater depth.

Still other studies involve only face-to-face contact (Mandell et al., 1980; Mandell & Wolfe, 1975; Rubin, 1985). Most of these researchers asked semi-structured questions about specific aspects of the parents' experience (pregnancy problems, fathers' experiences, and maternal attachment to the baby) instead of letting the parents decide the topic. These studies contribute to the general store of information, but they still only present part of the picture.

Research samples

Once researchers choose their research position and instruments, they need study participants. Serious problems exist with some samples upon which SIDS grief research has been based. There are problems with mixing SIDS parents with other bereaved parents, and there are gender problems in the samples.

Some studies use heterogeneous samples of bereaved parents, ignoring the uniqueness of the SIDS-loss experience. The most blatant example can be found in the sample used by Videka-Sherman (1982). This sample consists of 194 parents: 110 parents who lost their child to sudden illnesses (57 percent of these were due to SIDS); 60 parents who lost a child to an illness such as cancer or heart disease; and 24 parents whose children died violently. The results of various objective measures were averaged across all groups, effectively ignoring the uniqueness of a sudden versus expected death, a gentle versus a violent death, an explainable versus an unexplainable death. Smialek (1978) also uses a heterogeneous sample. She observed parents who had come to the hospital because their baby had died suddenly. Only 75 percent of these babies were eventually diagnosed as SIDS babies. The other 25 percent of the babies died of other natural causes, accidents, or "homicidal mechanisms" (p. 160). In her description of parental behavior at the hospital, Smialek makes no distinction between the behavior of those parents whose baby died of SIDS and those whose baby was murdered, perhaps by their own hand. In view of the enormous guilt SIDS parents already feel, this is totally unacceptable research. Other researchers routinely use a sample of parents who have all lost babies to SIDS, neonatal death, and stillbirth (Dyregrov & Matthiesen, 1987a, 1987b, 1987c, 1991; Vance et al., 1991, 1993, 1995). For reasons they did not explain, l'Hoir and Wolters (1993) studied parents who had lost a baby to SIDS and parents whose child had experienced an APLE (Apparent Life Threatening Event).

The other major problem with samples concerns gender issues. First, mothers are overrepresented in studies that purport to be about grieving parents. For example, DeFrain et al.'s (1991) book about parental grief is based on a sample that is 83 percent female; the DeFrain et al. (1992) article on grandparent grief has about the same ratio. Articles by Nikolaisen and Williams (1980) and Williams and Nikolaisen (1982) are based on a sample that is 69 percent female. Chartier (1987), who studies men's grief, says this problem is not unusual. Either men's experiences are ignored totally, or when men do participate in studies, they make up only about a third of the total number of respondents. While this may be related to men's reluctance to participate, it is not good research practice to generalize from skewed samples.

The second problem is related to the first. Some authors acknowledge that their sample is so seriously skewed that they can only write about the maternal experience (see Price et al., 1985). Many others ignore this fact and write as if they have collected information from both mothers and fathers in sufficient quantity to justify using the collective term "parents." For example, Lowman (1979) writes about "SIDS parents," but all of his information comes from mothers (p. 674). Although DeFrain et al. (1991) admit that they have an overwhelmingly female sample, they bury this important fact on page 105 of their book:

> Most of the information in this study came from women who reported on their feelings and actions and on the feelings and actions of their spouses. As a result, our study is basically about women and their responses to the death of their child.

The DeFrain et al. confession points to a third problem: the use of one person (usually the woman) to speak for and about another's experience with grief. The only time that this is appropriate is when the goal of the study is to compare people's perspectives—but then both sides of the story are still needed. This is not, however, the reason many authors use the words of one family member to speak for another. Lacking male participation in their study, some researchers allow the women to speak for men (Mandell et al., 1980) or for the couple (DeFrain et al., 1991; Price et al., 1985) or even for the whole family (DeFrain & Ernst, 1978; DeFrain et al., 1991). While it may be true that men seldom participate in studies, researchers should not expect women to speak for them. Although not directly a gender issue, researchers ask mothers to describe their children's reactions to the baby's death (Cornwell et al., 1977; DeFrain & Ernst 1978; DeFrain et al., 1991; Price et al., 1985). No one thinks to ask the father about his children's behavior, or better still, no one thinks to observe or interview the children directly.

The last problem with sample selection is that few studies treat couples as the unit of analysis (see Carroll & Shaefer, 1993–1994 for an exception). Instead, they compare groups of men to groups of women, even if the sample consists of married couples (Williams & Nikolaisen, 1982). Although

Dyregrov and Matthiesen (1987a, 1991) do some within-couple comparisons, their study focuses mostly on gender comparisons. Although this study helps us learn about the similarities and differences between fathers' and mothers' grief, it does not help us learn how couples handle their differences within the bounds of their relationship. If this is our goal, then we must begin to include couples in our samples.

Research period

Besides choosing the sample, researchers must also decide on the period for their study. There are two issues here: over what period of time will the study take place? and how long ago will the parents have suffered the death of their baby? Both decisions have important implications for the results.

Although the death of a baby to SIDS may seem like a time-limited event to people outside the immediate family, it can feel like a neverending process to those inside the family. Many studies capture one or two pictures of this process, but these pictures are often frozen in time and have no context. This is a reflection of the use of single questionnaires or one-time interviews. In comparison, a longitudinal or retrospective study can capture changes in the parents' experience over time, changes in their thoughts about why their baby died, having another baby, the health of their marriage, and their grief.

For example, Price et al. (1985) asked mothers to look back at their experience and to compare how they felt just after the baby died and then 6 months later. This retrospective study shows the changes that occurred in the women's lives during a short time. Cornwell et al. (1977) began meeting with parents shortly after the baby's death and then 3 or 4 times over the first year. Their study has vitality, immediacy, and a recognition of the passage of time, even if it only covers one year. Rubin (1985) asked women about changes in their relationship with their baby over time. By recognizing that grief is a process and that attitudes and feelings might change over time, these researchers identified important issues that had gone unnoticed by researchers who had taken a narrower picture of the experience. Vance et al. (1991, 1993, 1995) takes a longitudinal perspective (up to 5 years), while Dyregrov and Matthiesen (1991) report on four interviews over the period of 13 months. Unfortunately, some researchers do not seem to understand the relevance of the passage of time. For example, Carroll and Shaefer (1993-1994) based their study on respondents who had lost their babies anywhere from 3.5 months to 39.5 months earlier. In their findings, it is obvious that they did not take this considerable range into account. L'Hoir and Wolters (1993) did not even mention how long ago their respondents' babies had died. Since the passage of time has been shown to have a significant impact on the parents' well-being, this is a significant methodological error.

The second decision about time is connected to what researchers already know about how long it takes to deal with a loss. If they believe that grief is time-limited and that it should be completed within 6 months, then they will only concern themselves with the first 6 months of the experience (see Lowman, 1979). If, however, they understand the neverendingness of the experience, they are less likely to set such rigid time limits (Rubin, 1985). The more grief time the study covers, the more we can learn about various aspects of parental grief over the parents' lifetime.

Analysis of data

My most serious criticism concerning data analysis has to do with research bias. There is a growing concern that "the measurement of grief itself is biased because of gender stereotypes" (Stinson, Lasker, Lohmann, & Toedter, 1992, p. 218). This position is shared by Chartier (1987), who says that much of the information about how people grieve is based on the study of widows. Cook (1988) concurs. She suggests that the study of "parental mourning may be shaped by a tendency to apply and operationalize concepts formulated through the study of grieving **mothers** rather than **fathers** [emphasis in original]" (p. 287). Without questioning the source of the concepts and the samples upon which they have been based, researchers and clinicians alike have accepted that talking and sharing tears is the right and healthy way to grieve. Anything different seems to be considered wrong and unhealthy. This makes some grievers, mostly men, appear deviant and in need of help.

For example, Mandell et al. (1980) found that grieving fathers coped with their baby's death by increasing their time at work, avoiding professional support, wanting another baby, and intellectualizing and explaining away their feelings. The authors (and the men's wives) say that these behaviors mean that the men are denying their experience; they are not working on their grief. The use of the term "denial" (p. 222) suggests that Mandell et al. believe that grief work must involve talking and crying. Cook (1988) found the same kinds of behaviors in the grieving fathers she interviewed. In her view, these behaviors are entirely appropriate and understandable, given the social pressure for men to be strong and to control their emotions in the midst of a crisis. We need to keep our eyes open for gender bias in the analysis of parental grief studies. It colors most of the early work in this area. Fortunately, there is evidence this is changing (for example, see Dyregrov & Matthiesen, 1991).

Beyond the gender bias, I have two other major concerns about data analysis. The first issue is what researchers consider usable data. A few studies seem to value the experience of the parents only for the statistics they create. For example, Mandell and Wolfe (1975) interviewed 32 mothers who had lost a baby to SIDS and who wanted to have another baby. Many of these women had difficulties conceiving or carrying a subsequent pregnancy to term. Mandell and Wolfe report only the ratio of women who had problems. Although the researchers interviewed women about their problems, nothing from the interviews is included in the article. It is as if the women's words do not count.

Other studies use the parents' words but not for research purposes. The researchers do not treat the parents' written and spoken words as usable research data. Instead, they scatter a few quotes throughout their articles to illustrate a point or to flesh out their statistical analysis (Dyregrov & Matthiesen, 1987a, 1987b; Williams & Nikolaisen, 1982).

Even those who seem to value the parents' experiences do not systematically analyze what the parents send to them (DeFrain et al., 1991) or say to them during interviews (Cornwell et al., 1977). Although Rubin does a masterful job of presenting information about maternal attachments to the deceased child, he does not explain what method of analysis he used to reach his conclusions (Rubin, 1981, 1985). This kind of approach creates a negative attitude toward qualitative research. It makes it look as if this kind of research involves nothing more complicated than writing down other people's stories.

Despite the wealth of information I uncovered in my review and critique of the literature, I found myself having more questions than answers. To ensure that as many of my questions could be answered as possible, I developed a very general research question and a few more specific ones.

The Research Questions

My review of the research lead me to conclude that there was still much to learn about the parental grief that follows the death of a baby to SIDS. My critique of the methodology used in previous studies lead me to conclude that this subject required a qualitative approach. To ensure that I captured as many aspects of the parents' experience over time as possible, the central and general question that I chose to guide this study is: **What is it like to lose a baby to SIDS?**

After collecting the parents' responses to this general question, I asked the following questions of the data:

- How do bereaved fathers and mothers deal with their grief over time?

- How do grieving parents deal with their grief within the context of their marital relationship?

- What factors influence the pervasiveness of parental guilt in the short- and long-term?

Chapter 2
Understanding the Parents' Experience: Loving A New Baby

Using only the stories of the 21 parents who participated in this study as my source, the next 4 chapters tell the story of what it is like to lose a baby to SIDS. As the parents try to deal with their grief, they also try to make sense of their loss and their experiences. Figure 1 (see next page) provides an overview of what the parents experienced over time. In subsequent chapters, I explore the nature of these experiences and develop a theory about how people cope with traumatic events in general. But first we turn to the parents' stories. It all began with the parents' **beginning to love their new baby**.

Making Room

Laying the foundation

Before choosing to have a baby, each couple in this study had laid a foundation for their relationship. This foundation consisted of their shared history, their communication and comforting patterns, and their feelings about one another and the relationship. Some couples were very happy. One woman described her marriage as "wonderful" and "so easy." Another said she could not imagine feeling any closer to her husband. Several believed

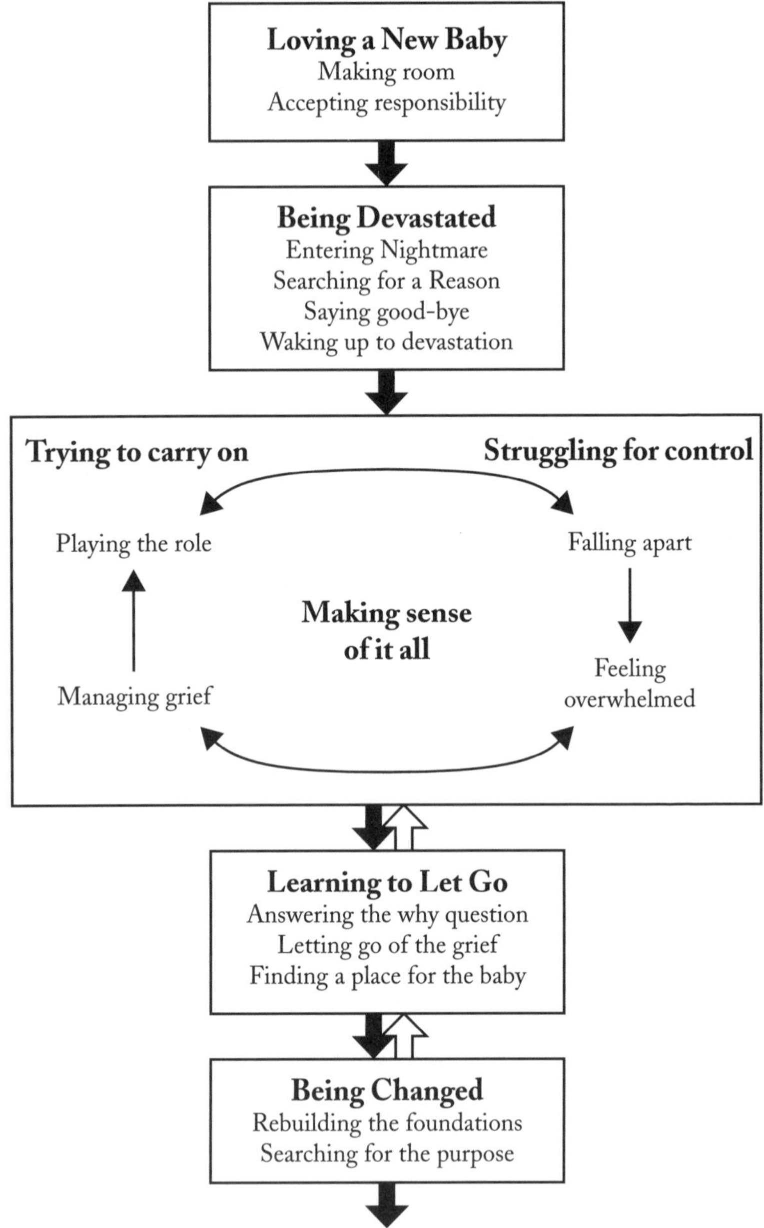

Figure 1 Overview of grief process

they could talk about anything with their spouse and that their relationship could withstand any problem.

Others felt less than satisfied. A few husbands complained that their wives was "very emotional and [unable to] reason." Wives were more likely to criticize their husbands for keeping their feelings private or for being too rational and practical. Some couples could not discuss or resolve conflicts. As one said, "We could talk about the telephone bill, but we couldn't talk about feelings." Because they wanted to stay married, these men and women had to try to accept their spouse, faults and all. Some had done so begrudgingly because they did not want to end their marriage. Others just tried to set aside their differences and make the best of what they had together. Part of either making the best of it or celebrating a happy relationship was deciding to make room in their lives for a baby.

Choosing to have a baby

Most couples felt they could control what happened to them. For instance, they could decide if and when they would conceive a child. Some wanted to begin their family; others wanted another child. In either case, receiving confirmation of a pregnancy made the parents feel happy and in control. For some, getting pregnant felt like a "natural thing," a logical step after getting married or deciding to have another child. For others, this pregnancy felt like a long awaited miracle. And so these couples celebrated the good news. Life was going their way, and they did not stop to ask why. As one man said, "That's Mother Nature, so to speak. That's the way things happen."

Birth control methods do not always work. Those couples who had not planned this pregnancy already had young children, some still in diapers. As a consequence, in the early stages of pregnancy, some mothers felt upset when they thought about how "very busy" they would be after the baby's birth. As the pregnancy progressed, most couples learned to accept what they could not change. In their hearts, they learned to make room for the baby. They also learned to accept that they could not control everything in their lives. Fortunately, this time they had months to adjust to this impending change.

Adjusting to the pregnancy

For women, "pregnancy is…from the first time you find out." All the women remembered the adjustments the pregnancy triggered in their lives. In addition to changing their bodies, pregnancy made the women think about their behavior. While some made only minor changes in their diet, behavior, or smoking habits, others monitored everything they did and everything they put into their bodies: "I didn't smoke, I stopped drinking coffee, and I didn't drink one drop of alcohol." Two women stopped working, and one reduced her work hours. Difficult pregnancies severely limited some women's activities.

In contrast, men had fewer obvious adjustments to make. Although one father remembers feeling "excited about the pregnancy," he mainly "just watched [his wife] grow." Men could feel the baby's movements, but only from the outside. Instead of adjusting to changes in themselves, they adjusted to changes in their wives. One reacted to his wife's moodiness, another to his wife's increased religious interest. No matter how "enthused" men were about the pregnancy, they fully expected that their wives would have a different and closer relationship with the baby "because they carried it." While some men could not get interested in tiny babies, others looked forward to becoming involved fathers.

Preparing for parenthood

During pregnancy, women, especially those who were pregnant for the first time, made room for the baby in their lives by preparing themselves for parenthood. They read and watched the media for information about babies. During her first pregnancy, one woman read an article about SIDS in a mother's magazine. Crying and feeling "awful" about what she had read, she convinced herself "this won't happen to me." And when it did not happen to her first baby, she forgot about it. Another mother learned about SIDS while watching a detective show on television. Wanting to protect her unborn baby, this mother tried to find out how to detect SIDS. When she learned that no predictive test existed, she tried to forget about it.

Men did not describe any exposure to information about SIDS during the pregnancy, how they tried to make room for the baby, or how they learned more about parenting or child development. A few, however, did describe how they prepared for the baby's arrival.

Preparing for the baby

Parents had months to prepare for the baby's arrival and the changes it would bring to their lives. Besides all the physical preparations, parents prepared themselves and younger children. Parents told older children about the impending arrival of the baby. Most older siblings seemed to look forward to having a new baby brother or sister. One little boy was "really excited."

During the pregnancy, parents thought a lot about their baby and wondered what he or she would be like. One mother thought about this baby's temperament, hoping it would be just like her first easygoing child. Some parents thought about the gender of their baby: some "wanted a girl so bad it hurt"; others wanted a boy. While one father just "wasn't into it," another felt very excited. He had "always wanted twins," and his wish had been granted. He looked to the future with excitement and thought about having "bunk beds...pillow fights and the same size and dressing them up and sort of getting them twin bikes and twin clothes." This father could hardly wait for his babies to be born.

While mothers waited, they "did a lot of those nesting and knitting kinds of things." Some made clothes and decorated bassinets. Friends and family helped by having showers for the expectant mothers, and mothers shopped for special things, too. Soon, parents started to accumulate baby things: "lots of beautiful clothes," "little shirts and T shirts and...sleepers," "toys," and "strollers and baby carriages and beds and cribs and high chairs." Some parents decorated a special room just for the baby. Others planned to put the baby in their room or to have the baby share a room with an older sibling. Once the rooms and baby things were ready, all the parents had to do was to wait for the baby to be born. They were ready to take on the responsibility of their baby.

Accepting Responsibility

Giving birth

The degree to which parents participate in the birth of their children has changed over time. At least 20 years ago, husbands were not usually present at the birth of their baby; instead, they sat and waited until someone told them the baby had arrived. In recent years, however, fathers have increased their involvement significantly. Most men now witness their baby's arrival, first cries, and first breaths of air.

Like the men, women's active involvement in the birth of their babies has increased over time. Women in this study who gave birth over 20 years ago were passively involved in the birth process. Some doctors administered anaesthetic and then delivered the baby with forceps. One doctor induced labor. The mother whose doctor induced labor remembers very little about the birth until the nurses gave her the baby. In more recent births, mothers participate fully and accept responsibility for the baby very soon after birth. That is, unless there are complications. One baby was delivered by Cesarean section. One woman had placenta previa. Still another woman gave birth to tiny twins. In all, 13 babies were born to these 12 families.

Welcoming the baby

Like most new parents, as soon as possible mothers and fathers carefully checked their baby by "unwrapping [the baby] and making sure all the appendages were there." Some parents had to discard their dream baby to make room for their real baby. For a brief moment, those who had hoped for one gender but received another felt disappointed, but as one parent said, "The minute you hold [the baby, that disappointment is] gone." Some celebrated the completion of their "perfect family": a boy and a girl or "two boys together." Most parents just rejoiced in their baby's safe arrival and apparent good health. The depth and intensity of their feelings for their newborn child surprised them.

Some mothers accepted the responsibility of caring for the baby, but they soon felt "overwhelmed." Others felt "ecstatic and scared at the same time." They wondered if they would ever become a good mother. Others tried to deal with a frightening premonition that something was wrong with their baby. One new mother "never felt right with [the baby]. I'd sit at night in the rocker and nurse him, and I'd cry. Instead of being happy with the baby....I just felt sad." Another mother also worried about her baby: "The second he was born, I kept saying, What's wrong with him?...I had this feeling." She repeatedly asked the nurses about her baby's condition. Both mothers tried to convince themselves that their fears were groundless. Worrying made sense for the parents of the twins; they needed to stay in the hospital for the first few months. Other parents felt they had nothing to worry about. They felt confident, and they thought their baby was "perfect." They could not wait to get home and begin caring for their "little angel."

First the baby needed a name. Names were important. Some honored the past or family traditions: "a family name that goes way back," a relative who died in the war, a sibling who had died. Other names celebrated special relationships in the present. Some parents named their baby after their own parents. And still others chose names that reflected a commitment to the future, names that were "strong," names that would continue into the next generation. Parents also thought about the sound of their baby's name. They wanted the name to sound just right. After all, they expected to be hearing it and using it for many years to come.

Caring for the baby

Once the baby came home from the hospital, parents accepted full-time responsibility for their baby. Mothers devoted almost all their time to feeding, changing, cuddling, and caring for him/her. One woman felt her "purpose" in life was to be a mother. Another "never went anywhere. I felt very close to [the children. The baby] was my whole life." After a few months, other women tried to balance the demands of motherhood with their jobs or careers. Both stay at home and working mothers occasionally felt overwhelmed by their baby's continuous demands. Like mothers everywhere, these women occasionally felt frustrated and angry: "My girlfriend asked me how [the baby] was doing, and I started to cry....'Don't even mention her name to me!' You know, because she had gotten to me. She was so colicky." Most of the time, mothers kept their frustrations to themselves. Sometimes they lost control and yelled at their fussy baby. Others shared their feelings with friends or their husband. Some women praised their husbands' supportiveness. One woman "couldn't wait for [her husband] to get home. He'd take right over." This gave her a chance to leave the house and regain her perspective. Others seemed angry that their husbands had not been helpful.

The angry feelings always subsided in time. Mothers loved their babies, and they devoted themselves to caring for them and "trying to give them everything." As one mother said, "I'm trying to give [my children] the love that I have. I'm trying to make sure that they have the best that I can give them."

New mothers learned how to care for their baby by trial and error. Over time and with increased experience, these mothers learned to read and react to their baby's signals. At first, they worried about whether they would ever "know what to do" or know "how to look after [the baby]." They had varying degrees of confidence in themselves as parents. Gradually, as their baby responded positively to their love and attention, these women began to feel increasingly competent and confident.

More experienced mothers often felt confident from the start:

> I was a very confident mother with [this baby] because everything had gone so well with [my first child]. I wasn't as worried. I didn't feel the need to check him every half hour. If he slept for two hours, that was fine. I didn't run up and check him constantly. I thought, "Well, two hours is a normal span to sleep." And I was very confident.

Mothers continued to learn all they could about parenting and child development. While recuperating from the birth of her baby, one mother watched a television program about SIDS in the hospital lounge. Although the program frightened her, she did not worry because "bad things that happened always happened to other people on the television." Another had a similar reaction. She read about SIDS shortly after her baby was born, but again, "it was something that I never thought would happen." Another drew her son close to her breast when she heard about a SIDS death in her community. Instead of worrying about SIDS, most mothers worried about more common problems: surviving the baby's sniffles, colic, and fussiness. Some fathers worried about these problems, too.

The degree to which fathers involved themselves in the actual day-to-day care of their baby varied considerably. As one father said, "Men might have all the concerns in the world [about the baby] but they are off to work and what not and they are not spending the same time [with the baby] as a mother is." Although all the fathers were proud of their new baby, some men were more involved in life outside the family home. One father just did not feel "ready for children…[and so he] really wasn't into it." His baby felt more "like a visitor" to him, so he "didn't have any experience with him." Besides, his career was just taking off. Some fathers believed that their primary responsibility was "bringing in the money for the food." Others felt torn between their financial obligations and their desire to spend more time with their family. Being the sole income earner, however, put pressure on some fathers to work longer hours. In addition, some men believed they had lots of time to spend with the baby—later, in the future. Besides, they wanted to "wait 'til [the baby got] older." One father explained it this way:

> Because when they are 6 months old, all they do is, they eat, they sleep, they cry, they burp, and, you know, like there's not a lot you can do with them, you know. They're too small; they're too young to do anything with.

In contrast, other fathers did everything with their tiny baby right from the start. They changed and fed and played with them whenever they could. In the interviews, some mothers spoke about their husbands with great pride, using phrases like "just a loving father" and the "father of the world." One woman felt her husband treated their daughter like "his queen." When asked to describe himself as a father, one man said he was "competent," while another talked about how "proud [he felt about]…being a father." He looked forward to playing with his tiny daughter after he came home from work:

> I know I'd come home from work and I'd be on the couch and [my wife] would come and put [the baby] on my chest and she could, at

that time, push herself up on her hands, and she'd lay there and rock and then fall down.

Besides playing with their baby, most fathers offered backup support when their wives needed help. When a specific decision about child care had to be made, however, fathers usually deferred to their wives' judgement. When the baby cried after being put to bed, one father wanted to "stay up and bottle feed [the baby]. [But] my wife told me that I shouldn't, so I didn't." Women usually had more experience with the baby, so they kept track of the baby's schedules: time for sleeping, time for eating, time to begin sleeping through the night, and time for immunization or teething. As a consequence, fathers usually relied on their wives to decide if and when the baby was sick. And this was not always a simple decision.

Over time and with experience, parents learned to read and respond to their baby's signals. At first, some less experienced parents turned to their own parents and other experts for support and information until they had enough knowledge and confidence in themselves to trust their own judgement. Once they felt they understood the reason for the baby's behavior, parents responded accordingly. Knowing what to do increased their feelings of competence. Still, there were times when caring for the baby felt like a trial and error process. Each baby, like all other babies, cried whether hungry or full, alert or tired, bored or overstimulated, healthy or unhealthy. The baby wriggled and fussed and smiled and snuggled. Eventually, most parents began to trust themselves to correctly read their baby's signals and to predict their needs. They also learned to recognize when something was wrong.

And some parents did wonder if something was wrong with their baby. Some mothers noticed unusual behavior, but they did not tell anyone. They just filed the observations away in their memory. For example, one mother noticed that after her son was pricked for a blood test "he was crying so hard that, you know how babies don't take a breath? He didn't take a breath for a very long time, and he was sort of turning purple, and I bent down and I shook him and then he took a breath." Others tried to understand the reason behind the behavior. One mother noticed that her baby "became stiff and almost panic[y]" when anyone unwrapped her or carried her down the stairs. When the doctor told the mother this behavior "was perfectly normal," she did not challenge him because she was "new at this mothering thing" and still lacked confidence as a parent. Another first-time mother who "had never been around babies" wanted the doctor to explain why her baby continually vomited. After repeatedly taking the baby to the doctor, the mother was finally told she was "just an overprotective mother." Similarly, when she pointed out that their son had stopped breathing twice, her husband told her she was "overreacting."

Even experienced mothers worried about their baby. One mother felt so anxious about her son's health after he had a convulsion that she dreamed he died. Worrying that the dream might be prophetic, she consulted the doctor. He tried to reassure her by making "light of it," saying, "Don't worry. That will never happen." Another mother reluctantly accepted the emergency doctor's explanation for her son's sudden limpness and fever. She wanted to believe that "Oh no, nothing serious [could] happen." To do this, however, she had to ignore the way she felt: "I knew there was something wrong with him." Confronted with problematic signals, these mothers tried to find logical explanations. When the experts did not agree with the parents' assessment of the situation, parents tried to make their own evaluations conform. Most, however, harbored doubts and continued to worry.

Besides dealing with actual causes for concern, some mothers experienced a frightening premonition that something was wrong with their baby. Premonitions came as vague feelings of uneasiness or specific dreams of death or abduction. These women tried to convince themselves that their fears made no sense. Instead, they tried to focus on how much they enjoyed their baby. Sometimes that was difficult because the parents always felt so tired.

The continuous demands on their time and the "disrupted sleep pattern" left the parents feeling exhausted for the first months of the baby's life. Getting up during the night to either feed or check on the baby took its toll on the parents. While some men complained to their wives about the lack of sleep, others kept silent or tried to ignore their tiredness. The women felt the weight of responsibility, whether they stayed home or went back to work. Breastfeeding increased their fatigue. Some had more than one child to look after: more than one mother had a toddler and a baby during the day and the baby again throughout the night. As one mother said : "I found it quite difficult with the two of them. And getting up through the night, I was turning into a zombie." One mother just felt "mad sometimes."

While they tried to cope with their exhaustion, some parents also had to deal with financial problems. To supplement the family income, some fathers worked out of town or worked extra hours; mothers returned to work, took in extra children during the day, or just settled for less income. Further complicating things, the financial, emotional, and physical demands of parenthood offered little time for romance or for enjoying family life. Some couples put off having a family picture taken. They were just "too busy."

Gradually, as the baby grew and parents felt more comfortable with the parenting role, life began to feel easier. Parents felt more confident and comfortable with their reading of the baby's usual signals. The baby appeared to be healthy and to be developing normally. Parents enjoyed watching their child grow and change: "I saw her grow, oh, a certain amount and learn to roll over....We had mobiles on top of her crib, and we'd spin them, and she'd watch'em. You could see the grin coming....Just, she started to laugh out loud and things like that."

Parents enjoyed playing with their baby. One father and mother played with their normally colicky son well after his bedtime one evening. Because the baby was more "laid back and easy going" than he had been for weeks, his parents just wanted to keep on "enjoying him." Another father took his two children to the community pool for an evening of fun together, while his wife went out with friends. Before putting her son to bed, one mother played with him "on the couch, making him laugh and giggle." Then, when he would not settle easily, she closed the door and let him cry for a bit. Another baby seemed restless when put down for an afternoon nap, so his mother sang "a song and just rocked the bassinet" until he fell asleep. Before leaving the baby with the sitter so they could go out for a romantic evening, a mother breast-fed their son: "He fell asleep on me, and I put him down, and he was happy, and he'd had a good day, and I was happy." A mother who was returning to work for the first time took her baby to the sitter. Before leaving, the mother talked to her daughter:

> I told her that I would be back at 5 o'clock to pick her up. I told her that mommy had to go to work to buy Pampers. And she just watched me. I just left her there, and she just seemed to understand what I was telling her and she just watched me walk out the door with a smile.

Instead of smiles on their faces, some babies had tears. They were sick. When babies had colds, had been vaccinated, or were generally fussy, parental fears and vigilance increased. Mothers and fathers "walked the floor," took "turns holding [the baby]," and "kept [the baby] with us." Parents watched carefully for signs of a serious illness, even consulting with doctors by telephone or at the office. One couple took their baby to the hospital because he seemed so limp. Although the doctor admitted the baby for observation for a few hours, he eventually discharged him to his parents' care, despite the mother' concerns:

> I didn't want to bring him home because I just had a feeling....[So] when I put him to bed, I was going to sleep in his room. And [my husband] said, "Don't be ridiculous! You will hear if anything, you know, should happen."

Both parents checked the baby several times during the night.

Checking the baby

Parents or sitters checked on the baby for one of three reasons:

- parents routinely checked the baby as part of their parental responsibility;
- parents felt concerned because the baby had not followed his or her usual routine; or
- parents were worried because the baby had been sick.

The reason for checking determined how the person felt when approaching the baby.

Routine checking

When parents decided to check the baby as a matter of routine, they felt relaxed and positive. They had no reason to suspect that they would see anything but their baby sleeping peacefully. Most parents routinely checked throughout the day and night, especially for the first few months. Most mothers and sitters checked intermittently, while fathers seemed to check at specific times. Typically, fathers checked before going to bed themselves or before they left home. One father checked "just in the process of getting ready to go play golf." In addition to checking during the day, one mother always looked in on her son before she went to bed herself. This time he was sound asleep:

> I went into [the baby's] room and checked him and there was this heating pad on the rocking chair. The babysitter had warmed his crib up and she'd left it on. It was dark in the room except for this little red light and I remember going and switching it off.

As healthy babies mature, they develop routines that influence parental expectations about on time and off time awakening. Newborn babies usually wake up for night feedings. Parents tried to adjust their schedules to adapt to this; for many, this was an exhausting time. They looked forward to the time when the baby would finally sleep through the night. If the baby was old enough to begin missing night-time feedings, some parents celebrated when they woke up in the morning. The baby had finally slept through the night. Believing their baby had reached a welcome milestone, one mother said to her husband, "Look at that. It's 8 o'clock. What a good baby!" Even if the baby had a daytime nap, parents often equated a long nap with good health. In either circumstance, if the baby was old enough to begin sleeping longer, then the parent or sitter went to check with a positive feeling.

Concerned checking

If, however, the baby was still too young to sleep through the night, then parents became conscious of the one big fear they could usually ignore: something had happened to the baby. Parents entered the room "a little scared":

> Usually [the baby] didn't sleep through the nights, and so when we did wake up, there was a definite tension because something was wrong because he hadn't awoke for the night feeding. You automatically had that in the back of your mind, and I always have had a little inkling, you know, if the child didn't wake up, there's something up.

While most keep their fears to themselves, others said something painfully prophetic to their spouse. One mother jokingly said to her husband, "I suppose I should go in and check him in case he's dead or something." Another lashed out at her husband because he had not checked the baby himself. The last thing she said before checking on the baby herself was: "You wouldn't even care if he was dead."

If both parents were home, then they negotiated to see who would check the baby, or the most fearful parent waited while the other parent checked the baby. Some mothers experienced a sense of foreboding; they were afraid to go to the baby:

> It was like something was holding me in bed. Like my chest was really heavy, and I just didn't want the day to start, you know. I can't explain it. I know it was there. I really believe I knew but didn't know. It's so hard to explain that. Like, if I knew, if I knew in the front of my head, maybe I would have gotten up, but in the back of my mind, something was saying, "You don't want to get up. Just lie in bed. Just let [your husband check the baby]. Let him do it."

In one family, the father had already gone to work, so the mother had no choice but to do the checking herself. Because she had slept in and she could not hear her children playing when she got up, she went to the bedroom with an "eerie feeling":

> They were in the same bedroom 'cause we only had two bedrooms and the door was closed. Now that was wrong already. The door was always open. I opened the door. I see [my daughter] sitting playing with her dolls on her bed and she was not a person to play with dolls really, she hardly ever did. The first thing she said was "Mommy, I tried to wake up [the baby] but I couldn't."

Worried checking

When the baby had been sick, parental checking took on a different quality. Parents either kept the child near them so they could monitor the situation continually or they increased the frequency of their checking. Some did both:

> We held him and kept him in the living room with us I guess until about midnight, 1 o'clock, something like that. Then put him in his crib. I checked on him, the last time was about 3 o'clock [in the morning].

If the baby had been sick, then parents often got up in the middle of the night just to be sure everything was all right. Sometimes parents slept through the night themselves; they had been exhausted. As soon as these parents awoke the next morning, they felt guilty. They felt like they had shirked their responsibility as a good parent. Hoping that the baby had slept in because the illness had finally passed, parents felt apprehensive as they walked towards the baby.

Chapter 3
Understanding the Parents' Experience: Being Devastated

Entering a nightmare

Discovering a problem

Within seconds of entering the room, those who went to check the baby sensed that something was wrong. Finders checked their baby in a variety of ways. One father described his feeling of terror:

> I didn't even turn on the lights. I couldn't find him at the head of the bed. So I felt around the covers, and he was at the bottom, all rolled up in the blanket, and I thought, "Oh, oh, we have a problem here." I thought maybe he was still alive, but then when I got him out, I was really frustrated and confused and very scared, very scared, yes. And I got him out at last and uh, he was uh, fairly. Well, well, he was really dead....He was cold and purple.

Others did not have to search for long; they could tell something was very wrong the second they saw or touched their baby. They soon realized they were **entering a nightmare:**

> And then I saw him in the same position, exactly the same position as the night before, and my heart just went to my feet, and then I kneeled down and his ear was discolored.
>
> He just didn't look right, and I touched him and he was cold, and then I rolled him over, and he was blue.
>
> I gave him a kiss, and he was cold.
>
> I took one look at the baby.... And I saw, you know, his one arm was sticking out.... He had turned blue.

Defining the problem

Within seconds of discovering the baby, the finders made a decision about the nature of the problem. Despite similarities in the babies' appearance, finders defined what they saw in one of three distinct ways:

- this baby is seriously ill;
- this baby looks dead, but maybe he or she is just really sick; or
- this baby is "really dead."

Then the finders shared their definition of the problem and their terror with someone else.

Sharing the terror

Sounding the alarm

Finding the baby was like entering a nightmare. It set off feelings of terror or panic. Finders had to tell someone. Most communicated their discovery spontaneously by making some kind of sound: groaning, screaming, or yelling, "Something's wrong!" or "Oh my God!" One man did not make a sound. He examined the baby, called 911, and then woke his wife to tell her.

Months and years later many finders still could not discuss the details of this experience with anyone. They carried the "burden" of that memory alone. One woman felt bad for her husband but admitted, "In a way, selfishly I'm glad it wasn't me.... Just the vision of finding [the baby] and I didn't have to do that, thank God."

Once someone else knew what they had found, some finders lost control: they screamed, threw things, or ran around the house. Others struggled to maintain control. As she tried to contact her doctor, a mother tried not to share her terror with her young daughter. A couple of fathers struggled to clear their heads; they needed to remember how to administer CPR. Others controlled their terror and tried to appear calm; they only screamed on the inside.

No matter how the finders shared their terror and their definition of the problem, the receivers of their message had to decide what to do with what they had just heard. Some parents offered an alternate explanation: "He's just asleep." Others denied the finder's assessment outright. One woman refused to believe her husband. While he called 911, she calmly cuddled their dead baby and got dressed, secure in the belief that the paramedics would, of course, revive their baby. A few parents tried to revive their baby themselves before calling for help, but without success. Despite his initial confidence that he could "fix this problem," one father finally had to accept that no matter how much he wanted to he "couldn't fix the situation."

Others instinctively understood and accepted the meaning of the finder's reaction. Somehow they knew that their partner's sounds, behavior, and facial expression could mean only one thing:

> He just said, "Oh my God!" and he started running up the stairs, and I was out of bed before he made it upstairs, and I knew, I knew what he was going to say. Even before [he] got upstairs to tell me [our baby] was dead, I knew what he was going to say. I wanted to scream at him, "Don't say it!" Even before he told me.

Although one man understood and accepted what his wife's screams meant, he still needed to see the baby himself; he needed to define the problem himself:

> When I heard her scream, I knew, I knew, I knew that he was dead. And I went upstairs, and [my wife] was on the bed sort of having a fit, just screaming and I says, "Stop!" She stopped, and then I ran into the bedroom, and I, I could see [the baby] and I could see that he was dead. I looked at him. I knew he was dead but I had to know, so I picked him up, and he was stiff. So I picked him up, and I looked at him and put him back down, like I found him.

Needing help

And then this father, like all the others who found the baby dead, had to decide what to do next. All the families eventually sought some kind of outside help. Some called for help that would come to them; others took their baby to someone for help. Although most asked for help within seconds of finding the baby, one family waited about an hour before taking their baby to the hospital.

Parents wanted help for one of three reasons:

- they wanted someone to save the baby's life;
- they wanted someone to try to save the baby or at least confirm the death; or
- they wanted someone to help them deal with the baby's death.

The decision about what to do and who to call reflected the parents' definition of the problem. Those who initially believed their baby could be saved eventually had to face the fact that the baby was "really dead." As definitions changed, so did needs.

At first, some parents steadfastly believed their baby could be saved. These parents moved quickly to call for help or to take the baby to the hospital:

> I wrapped the baby, he was very heavy in the blankets, you know, and the taxi was already there, and a few minutes later we were in the hospital....I have the baby, and I could hardly carry him and somebody, you know, I was kind of screaming, you know, "I want the doctor!"

Other parents alternately wanted someone to try to save their baby and to confirm the baby's death. One mother described the search for help for her baby. While one part of her prayed that the baby would be saved, the other part began to admit that he was already dead. Because her family still believed the baby could be saved, they did everything they could to revive him:

> And then we were in the car. Mom had put cold water on him to see if that would revive him or stimulate him. And my sister-in-law started mouth to mouth....We stopped at [the home of a neighbor who was a doctor]....They worked on him there for a bit, and then they decided that they'd get in the car in the back seat, and we'd drive to [the nearest hospital half an hour away]. It was hard to see...them working on my child.

Most parents just wanted some help to understand what had happened. These parents had no illusions: they knew their baby was dead. They just wanted to do what had to be done legally, and then they wanted an explanation and some support. One couple did not get these needs met at all. Rather than offering them any kind of support, the father's parents told them to call the police: "I remember being angry about that. Why in the hell would we want to call the police? I didn't kill my baby." Needing comfort rather than confrontation, they called a more supportive relative. Other couples had better luck. Because one couple decided they "didn't want an ambulance rushing and taking him away from me. I didn't want that because I knew he was dead. Nobody had to tell me he was dead," they called a sympathetic and nearby relative instead. She helped them by notifying the police. Then the mother called their doctor and their minister. Two families called members of the clergy. One minister said he "did not need to come, not if [the baby's] already dead" and not "unless [the couple] wanted him there." They did not insist. Despite the fact that the parents seldom attended his church, another minister came to their house almost immediately to help them "talk" and "understand everything."

In some cases, parents did not seem to know who to call for help. They could not think logically, so they did the first thing that came to mind. One father just automatically called their family doctor at home and blurted out, "Our baby's dead." Another father knew he had to call someone, but in his anguish, he felt confused about what number to dial:

> I picked up the phone and I thought, "I gotta do something" and I thought, I didn't know who to call. I looked at the phone. I looked and I didn't know which number to push and I looked, "Operator" and I pushed Operator, and I said, when she came on the phone, "My baby's dead." And she said, "Excuse me?" "My baby's dead." And she said, "Hold the line for a second." And then she said, "Yes sir, go ahead. What is your name?" And I told her my name and my address and I guess she had all the agencies or she connected me through to 911 or whatever and she said, "Okay sir." She says, "Somebody will be there right away, okay?" And I says, "Thank you" and I hung up.

And then this father, like all the other parents, began what seemed like the longest wait of his life.

Waiting for the nightmare to end

More and more, parents felt like they had entered a terrible nightmare. This just could not be happening to them, to their baby. They just wanted to wake up. But the nightmare would not go away. It just got progressively more terrifying as they waited for help.

Parents waited in their homes and at the hospital. Since each location presented unique stresses to the families, I describe them separately, beginning with the hospital experience. Although one mother remained at home with her baby, she had heard about the experiences of others whose babies had been taken to the hospital:

> I think [going to the hospital is] worse. When I hear these people that have had to go to the hospital, sit there, nobody talked to them, and they're there for like an hour or two and yet the baby's been dead when it arrived and yet nobody's told them. They've been sitting there for 2 hours hoping, you know.

At the hospital

Five babies in this study were taken to the hospital: one by the sitter, one by the firefighters, and three by the parents themselves. The reasons for going to the hospital varied. Some people believed the baby could still be saved. The sitter took one baby to the hospital. The mother refused to believe that anything was wrong with her baby. This whole nightmare made no sense to her because "there was nothing wrong with [the baby] when I left [for work]. There wasn't, she wasn't sick."

In contrast, other parents already knew the baby was dead. These parents went to the hospital to have the death confirmed, to notify other authorities, and to get help to deal with their nightmare. One couple held their son while they waited for the doctor to come and confirm the death: "Everyone [at the hospital] knew he was dead. He was cold and stiff so that was horrible because it wasn't like our own baby. It was awful. He was so cold." The firefighters took one obviously dead baby to the hospital, while the police drove the parents. Although this couple did not understand why their baby had been taken to the hospital, once they got there, all they wanted was a doctor to explain why their baby had died. They knew attempts to resuscitate were pointless.

Still others vacillated between feeling hopeful and hopeless. They were beginning to split into two parts: one part confronted reality, and the other part wanted to avoid reality. One part wanted to believe that the doctors could save the baby; the other part knew that was impossible:

> You always have the hope and you just keep praying. But somehow deep down, you know that things just aren't right. And different things

> go through your mind. You wonder, "Oh please give him back to me even if he is, you know, like a vegetable." Or you know because he went that long without oxygen, especially because he was so blue. You just keep hoping.

As soon as the parents arrived at the hospital, nurses or doctors immediately whisked the baby away, away from the parents' sight and control. Like other parents in this situation, one father was "turned…away at the door" to the examining room and "then [he, his wife, and extended family] sat in this room for 10, 15 minutes." The medical staff took another baby from the screaming mother and suggested she and her daughter sit in the public waiting room and read some magazines while they waited:

> And so you know, you are waiting there. Maybe it was good I had [my daughter] with me. I had to keep her busy, you know, reading stories to her and that. I don't know how long the doctor took, you know, and they were coming in and out, different doctors.

Most parents had no idea how long they really waited. Time felt warped. To most, it felt like they waited "forever." Parents felt lonely and terrified as they waited for news of their baby's condition. There was nowhere to go and, in some cases, no one to comfort them. They waited in unfamiliar surroundings with no sense of control over anything that happened. Officials restricted access to their baby and to information about what was happening behind the closed doors of the examining room. All the parents could do was wait. While they waited, they began to wonder what could have happened to their precious baby. What could have caused this?

Most parents left the hospital once a doctor confirmed their baby's death. For two mothers, however, this news did not end their waiting. Doctors refused to let either woman see the baby until their husbands arrived. They had to wait even longer while someone called their husbands and asked them to come to the hospital. When the men arrived, staff members told them what had happened.

At home

Parents who remained at home also had to wait, but they waited for the help to come to them. Only one mother who waited at home believed that her baby would be revived: "The thought [that he was dead] never even went through my mind until [the paramedics] told me that he was gone." All the rest of the parents who waited at home had already realized that their baby was dead.

At least these couples waited in familiar surroundings. Unlike parents who waited at the hospital, those who stayed home could do what they wanted to do, go where they wanted to go, and be with whomever they wanted. Some parents sat frozen to their chairs, some moved about aimlessly, and others tried to take control of the situation. Some chose to be with their baby: they looked at, touched, talked to, or held the baby. One mother "rant[ed] and rave[d] and carr[ied] the baby around." Another quietly held her baby while she prepared for the arrival of the firefighters. Those parents who could not bear to be near the baby often focused on watching for the arrival of help. Some parents tried to comfort each other. One mother took this time to reassure her husband: "This isn't anybody's fault. This isn't anybody's fault. This is that crib death." Others felt so devastated that they could neither give nor receive comfort. No matter how parents used their time, "it seemed like it took forever" for most outside help to arrive.

Those who had called family doctors or family members had the most control over what happened next. Two doctors invited the parents to be present while they examined the babies. While the mothers welcomed this opportunity, the fathers refused it. When family members arrived, they tried to offer their support, and sometimes they tried to take control. One sister tried to take the dead baby away from the mother's arms. A grandmother tried to go into the baby's room. The mother blocked her way, wanting to preserve happier memories.

Those parents who called 911 soon had to deal with the arrival of a whole series of emergency vehicles and first responders. Each service had its own goal and role to play in this kind of a call. In some cases, parents felt invaded by aggressive first responders; others appreciated their gentleness. First responders soon filled the house and driveway with their bodies, conversations, activities, equipment, and vehicles.

In most cases, two or three firefighters arrived first, usually with sirens screaming and lights blazing. One woman clearly remembers the arrival of the fire department:

> The next thing you know the house is full. I remember the firemen coming in, you know how they have to wear their fire outfit and they come, and they're lugging all this stuff....They went upstairs. [My husband] must have told them to go upstairs and stuff and then everybody comes, you know.

"Everybody" included, in the order in which they usually arrive: two or three paramedics, the police, and then medical examiner's investigators. Sometimes homicide detectives and police sergeants also respond to these calls.

Some parents tried to remain in control of their home, despite the presence of all these first responders. These parents tried to regulate access to their house and to the baby. One mother insisted on being present when her baby was checked by the paramedics:

> [They] don't want the parents there when they examine the baby. Well, nobody touched my kids unless I'm there. Like I'll be there! Simple, you know. And this guy said, "No, we don't want you there." And I said, "Listen, like I'll put it to you this way. You don't go upstairs without me. Like I don't give you the right to go upstairs without me. Simple." And he just looked at me kind of, you know, and I said, "No, you're not touching my baby unless I'm there."

Another mother controlled the entry to her whole house. She glared at the man who came to remove the baby's body. He took one look at her and somehow he knew he had better wait outside. He stood on the doorstep until the police handed him the baby's body.

Those parents who already knew their baby was dead reacted differently than those who still had hope. Those with hope welcomed the paramedics, firmly believing that the baby would be revived. Some parents who felt hopeless were angry. The presence of the police "outraged" them as did attempts to resuscitate the baby. All the equipment and rushing around angered them. It made no sense. One mother screamed at the paramedics as they arrived: "It's too late! We don't need you!"

Some parents just watched passively as a steady stream of strangers took over their home. They did not argue when paramedics demanded that they leave the baby's room and "shut the door" behind them. They did not argue as strangers "barged in, took over their home, and trampled mud across the carpet. [The first responders] are not going to worry about etiquette." A mother sat quietly on the couch while paramedics rushed to attend to her baby. Although their actions made no sense to her, she accepted their need to try everything: "I guess they have to try to revive them even though they knew he was dead and I knew. Like I said that intellectual part of my brain knew he's dead. They're not going to bring him back."

Even though most parents knew their baby was dead by now, while they waited for confirmation, they prayed for miracles and tried to bargain with God: "Making God those promises, like 'Just give [my baby] back to me and

I'll be a good person.' You know, 'Take me, but let [my baby live].'" But the parents' prayers went unanswered.

Hearing the devastating words

Hearing that their baby was dead "devastated" the parents. Few professionals used the word "dead." Instead, doctors and first responders often tried to soften the blow by using phrases like "There is nothing more we can do" or "We tried everything we could. It was too late." A paramedic tried to comfort one couple by sharing that he, too, had lost a baby to SIDS. Since these parents had never heard of SIDS, his words only confused them further. One mother will never forget the compassion of the doctor who tried his best to break the horrible news to her. Up until then, she had been adamant that her daughter had to be alive:

> There's something I have to tell you. He said, "It's very, I, I." He just didn't know what to say. He just and then the two nurses were there, and he said, "I hate to tell you this but," he said, "your daughter died.' I said, "She couldn't have." I said, "There's nothing wrong with her." He said, "Yes, she died. I'm sorry she died. There was nothing I could do." And he was crying, the doctor was crying.

Fighting the words

The severity and nature of the parents' reactions to the bad news depended upon their beliefs about their baby's condition at that point. For those who still believed that the baby would be saved, the news came as a great shock. Two women attacked the hospital staff: "I went nuts. I just went crazy. I fought with them because there was nothing wrong with [my baby]." Both women were given sedatives. Instead of lashing out, another woman just went into shock because she "thought they would save him."

Expecting the words

Those who already suspected that their baby was dead took the news as official confirmation. They tried to assimilate what was now a confirmed fact. The harsh reality of the words still shocked them, but they were not surprised. Instead, they had already begun to turn their attention to a new issue: Why had their baby died?

> The doctor checked him over and told me he found nothing abnormal. I remember thinking that was the strangest thing he could ever tell me. "He looks fine to me, except he's dead. Other than that, he's fine. You know, he's a perfectly normal baby. There's nothing unusual here."

Just why then would a "perfectly normal baby" die? As many parents and officials said, "There's got to be a reason." Within hours of the baby's death, the parents' **search for a reason** began—and for many parents, this search has never really ended.

SEARCHING FOR A REASON

Being investigated

The police and medical examiner's investigators began the official **search for the cause** of the baby's death. By carefully observing the home, the condition of the baby, and the behavior of the parents, police tried to rule out abuse or homicide. Some took photographs of the baby and the baby's room. Police questioned all but 3 of the 12 couples who participated in this study. Doctors intervened in two cases and prevented questioning. One reported the baby's death as a hospital death, thereby preventing any investigation of the parents. Another woman whose family doctor somehow avoided a police investigation was very grateful. She firmly believed that all his attempts to convince her that she was not to blame would have meant nothing if he had then called the police. The third couple cannot remember any police involvement at all, although family members did suggest that they call the police.

For those parents who were questioned, the obviousness of the police investigation varied. Some investigators casually asked about the child's medical history and checked the condition of the baby. Some were more obvious and direct, asking pointed questions such as "what we'd done the night before. They asked who found him, they asked what time, the last time I checked him, what time it was." A mother objected to being questioned twice: first, at the hospital and, again, as soon as she and her husband got home:

> Right now [the police] were there, wondering why. What happened, finding out where I was, where my husband was, who our babysitter was, where did we find her?...I thought he was very, very cold. Like no feeling, nothing. I don't know if that is what he was feeling. I don't know if that is what he was, but that is what I could see. He

> did apologize and explain it to me. "This is the reason why I have to be here. Because it is sudden death, and we have to know where were you and what were you doing, how long you've been working here, how long, when did you move here, where'd you find a babysitter." He said, "We have to find out all those things." So I was very angry about that because they had to, like couldn't they wait? But they said they had to do it right now.

The fact that the police had even considered the possibility that the baby had been murdered or abused shocked and upset parents. Hearing the words, "We don't suspect any foul play" upset one father. One mother felt angry that the police were even in her baby's room:

> Then the police go up there, and I remember wondering if they were going to charge me with something. This was just a thought. It wasn't my major thought at the time. My major thought at the time was that my baby had died. Like I thought, "I don't care" but my baby had died, and I think I knew what they were doing, the police. I just knew it. They were checking him over for bruises to see if we had beat him or something or killed him. I just knew it even though they don't tell you they're doing it. And I was just outraged at that because I would never do that.

The police questioning increased the guilt of those parents who felt responsible for the baby's death: "I found [being questioned] a little unnerving, especially when I was quite sure that I had, I was still really convinced that I was responsible still at that point, and I found that a little under pressure there." One mother had the opposite experience. She wanted the police to interrogate her thoroughly:

> As far as I was concerned, they didn't ask us enough questions....I wanted them to take pictures, I didn't want to be blamed. I wanted to be absolved from, you know, like I didn't want anyone to think I had done something wrong.

Most parents wanted to be absolved, but they needed an alternate explanation first. Those parents whose babies died over 10 years ago had the most difficulty getting a preliminary explanation or diagnosis. As a consequence, they either assumed responsibility for their child's death or assigned it to their doctor. Even if doctors told the parents they suspected viral pneumonia, and this was a common diagnosis years ago, this explanation did not make the parents feel any better. They berated themselves for missing signs of such a serious illness. Only one couple whose baby died over 20 years ago had a good experience with a doctor. The doctor at the hospital "explain[ed] in short details what had occurred. He explained right away what SIDS was." The father believed that this conversation "probably saved our bacon. [The doctor] did a pretty good job of, of taking any guilt away."

With most of the more recent SIDS deaths, paramedics, medical examiner's investigators, or doctors told the families minutes after examining the baby that they suspected SIDS. The amount of information they gave varied from a vague mention of the term without any further explanation to a supportive and clear explanation by a doctor:

> [The doctor] said, "She's perfect. She's very, very healthy. She's very clean, well-dressed." He said, "There's nothing wrong with her." ...[And then he said], "I'm sorry, it was crib death. There's nothing that we could do about it." And then he went on and explained what crib death was, that it was nobody's fault and everything else.

Although most parents were in no shape to ask the officials any questions, some doctors and emergency responders tried to encourage discussion anyway. The medical examiner's investigator gave one couple brochures from the Canadian Foundation for the Study of Infant Deaths (CFSID) to read. Paramedics gave another couple the telephone number of the local SIDS support group (unfortunately, the wrong number).

No matter how much anyone tried to explain SIDS to the parents, they could not absorb anything they heard. They were in shock. Nothing seemed real; it seemed like a bad nightmare. Even though one doctor carefully and sensitively explained all he could about SIDS, the mother just cried and asked again and again, "Why did she die?" This question haunted her and most other parents for years. They needed to understand the cause of their baby's death; they needed to find a reason to help them cope with this devastating loss: "It's tough to come to grips with something if you don't understand anything about it." Parents began their investigation by asking questions.

Asking questions

What did I do wrong?

Parents asked themselves, "What did I do wrong?" They examined their own behavior, beginning with the previous 24 hours and then expanding their investigation, in some cases, to even before the pregnancy. No thought, event, or action was too small or insignificant for scrutiny. Parents gradually created a list of possible wrongdoings: smoking, sleeping in, letting the baby cry too long, turning out the lights and shutting the door, laying the baby on his or her stomach, having a problem during the baby's birth, or going back to work too soon. One mother and one father each fervently believed that they actually had "killed" their babies; both believed they had given their baby too much medicine the night before:

> I was the one that was responsible the night before. I was the one that was with the baby.…I put her to bed, and I gave her some [medicine] before she went down, and I gave her the prescribed dose and maybe even, I think she was, I think it may have even been the dosage for a 1 year old. I just thought, "That's it. I've definitely killed her." I was absolutely, totally convinced and also the fact that I laid her down on her face. And that was, I am just absolutely stone cold convinced and even to this day, uhm, I do feel, I do feel that if I hadn't laid, it was a combination of factors and in retrospect, certainly had I not done those things, she would probably still be alive today. I do believe that…and certainly but unknowingly, you know, maybe I was responsible for her death.

What did I not do right?

Parents also asked themselves a second question: What did I not do right? They examined every child care decision for clues. Should I have picked the baby up when he or she was crying? Should I have checked the baby sooner? Should I have taken the baby to the hospital or to the doctor? Should I have insisted that the doctor admit my baby to the hospital? Should I have slept with the baby or at least in the baby's room that night? The list of "should I" questions had no end. Once parents found a possible lethal choice, they had to decide what to do about it. Some felt guilty: "I wish I would have got up at 3 o'clock in the morning.…I will never get over that. There was a lot of guilt there for the longest time." Some tried to forgive themselves and to let go of the feeling of responsibility, but they vacillated back and forth: "If I would have stayed up and fed him, maybe he would have been alright. Maybe he wouldn't have. It is hard to say." Because there was no proof of either innocence or guilt, parents could not absolve themselves, particularly this early in the experience.

What did I miss?

Parents also asked themselves one other type of question. It came from the belief that good parents should know when there is something wrong with their child. As one father put it: "What was there in front of my face that I didn't see?" They reviewed everything they could think of, looking for clues: "You're just sure you overlooked something, that there had to have been a clue there and you missed it." Some parents wondered whether they had missed signs that their apparently healthy baby had really been very ill. Those whose baby had been sick questioned their ability to differentiate between minor and major illnesses. If there had been any recent contact with a doctor, then parents sometimes questioned the doctor's skills and judgement. Whatever they decided, they began to doubt their competence as parents. One mother wondered, "Was it more than a cold? Should I have taken her back to the doctor?...Because I was a new parent and because I didn't know very much about babies. Was she sicker than I thought?"

Learning about SIDS

The parents' lack of knowledge about SIDS complicated their **search for a reason**. Most fathers had never heard of SIDS before, so this death made no sense to them at all. But two mothers recognized the signs and knew immediately that SIDS had taken their baby. One even told the 911 operator that it was SIDS when she phoned for help. Another tried to convince her husband that "this is that crib death." She wanted him to know this death was not their fault. Secretly though she still wondered if she had done something wrong. Other mothers who had previous knowledge of SIDS did not think about SIDS at first. When asked why they thought this happened, these women suggested that perhaps they had not fully understood what they had learned or that they felt too devastated to think straight. When they heard the first responders or doctor mention SIDS, some remembered having heard about it.

Parents who were not told that investigators suspected SIDS were most likely to blame themselves immediately. Those who were told SIDS was suspected but who had never heard of SIDS at all could not accept this preliminary diagnosis. Babies could not just die without a reason. It made more sense to blame themselves. Initially, some doctors and first responders gave an alternate diagnosis such as viral pneumonia. This made sense to those whose babies had been ill but not to those whose babies had shown no sign of illness. The presence of the police added to the confusion and to the guilt. Why had their baby died? Although the parents desperately wanted their questions answered, they turned their attention back to their baby. They knew they did not have much time left to spend with the baby. The questions would have to wait until their goodbyes were done.

Saying Goodbye

Beginning the transformation

The thought of "loving a dead baby" repulsed some parents and made no sense to others. Some felt uncomfortable with the body; some felt afraid of it. Other decided that their baby had already "gone," so there was no point in trying to touch, hold, love, or say goodbye to what was left behind. One couple decided that saying goodbye would be "too hard" for them. They gave up their only opportunity to see the baby one more time. By making this choice, they hoped that they could eventually replace the frightening image of their baby's mottled and stiff body with happier memories of a live, smiling baby. Others insisted on spending time loving their baby one more time. The parents' view or definition of the baby determined the choice they made.

To most parents, particularly the fathers, the essence of the baby was already "gone," causing the baby to look just "like a doll." Some mothers continued to see their baby as if he/she were still alive. One mother saw only her much-loved baby at first, but then, gradually, her perception of the baby changed. She eloquently and lovingly described the transformation:

> It was like an empty cocoon. From a butterfly. Like he was there but he wasn't. He just was not my boy anymore. It was just this little outside container that was there. It was really weird. I never really realized how that was. Even with such a small baby that doesn't have character lines, that, you know. He wasn't there. He was gone.

Holding on with love

In most cases, those who remained at home with their baby had more choices about what they could do next. Mothers carried their baby, held him/her, changed his/her clothes or diaper one more time, talked to him/her, and tried to pour a lifetime of loving into the baby:

> I got to sit in the room with [the baby for 20 minutes] and hold him and wrap him up and try and keep him warm and say goodbye to him my way, you know? I thought I was only in there a few minutes, but

> [my family] said I was in there about 20 minutes....[J]ust wishing I could take all the warmth out of my body and put it back into his. Like just breathe the life out of mine.

> We held him...and he was so cold...and I just wanted to warm him up. I remember holding onto his hand and wanting to warm it, and it was the only thing I could actually warm and keep warm. The rest of him was so cold.

Parents whose baby was in the hospital had to ask permission to spend time with their baby so they could say their goodbyes. Hospital staff forbid one couple to hold or even touch their baby. They could only look at the baby lying on the examination room table. Because of the way the nurses had wrapped him, all they could see was his face:

> I was allowed to go see him, but they told me not to pick him up off the table....I remember that, and it still bothers me to this day. [So you never got another chance?] Not really, no. Like even though he was cold, it would still have been nice to pick him up and to hold him. And I think my husband felt the same way, and then they had him wrapped in this wool blue blanket....I couldn't even touch his hands or nothing, eh? So I remember **being devastated** by that.

Another mother looked at her baby, lying on the table, dressed only in her diaper. She begged the nurses to let her take her daughter home, making promises to "look after her." Finally, she accepted that she could not take her baby home, so she asked, 'At least, let me hold her.' So they told me, they let me hold her. My husband and I just exchanged, take turns holding her. I just couldn't let her go."

Rather than actually participating themselves, a few fathers just watched while their wives held and loved their baby. One father never held his daughter again, but he remembers crying with his wife while she sat and rocked their baby for at least half an hour.

For many families, the need to love their baby did not stop at this moment, but they had to give up the baby's body, first to the authorities and then to either the earth or cremation. From now on, parents would have to find a way to love their baby from afar.

Giving up the baby

Giving up the body

Once more, the way in which the parents thought of the baby influenced how they handled giving it up to the authorities. Their location at the time, home or hospital, also affected the nature of this part of the experience.

Parents whose baby had been brought to the hospital had already given up their baby physically. As soon as the parents had entered the hospital, the staff had taken control of the baby. Then, even after the babies were pronounced dead, the hospital staff controlled access to and contact with the babies. They controlled how much time the parents could spend with the babies and told them when it was time to let them go. Then these parents had to leave their babies at the hospital. They went home with empty arms and heavy hearts.

Most parents who gave up their babies from home had more control over the timing and process. They could decide when they would give up the baby, to whom, and in what condition. Instead of telling the parents what to do, the doctors and most emergency responders involved the parents in each step of the process. Although the whole process seemed hurried for some parents, others were allowed to take their time. One couple thought they could supervise the baby's removal from the house, but the first responders tricked them:

> We were allowed to see him one more time. We went up, and he said, "Well, you go see him one more time." We did, and then he took us in the living room, and he talked to us, and uh, I said, "Well," I said, "can I go see him one more time?" And he said, "He's gone." [They snuck him out of the house?] Yeah. And I didn't want that. I just really wanted to see him go, to see that he was okay, that he was taken care of okay.

Fortunately, most first responders and doctors asked the parents when they were ready to give up their babies. This gave the parents the opportunity to hold their baby and say goodbye in their own way. Some, when given the choice, decided against doing anything with the baby before giving it up. Saying goodbye to a dead baby made no sense to them:

> [The doctor] asked me if I would like to go and get the baby ready to go, and I just gave him the baby, like right now, like, "He's dead so what do I, what's the use of me having it anymore?" I think I kind of

> shocked him, but that was my feeling. "Take it. It's not alive. It's not my baby any more. Just take it."...For me to just sort of give this over, you know, without, "I'm sorry, we have to take him" and all that kind of stuff and not even to go and change him or do something. I just couldn't imagine. It would be like dressing a doll to me.

Other mothers continued to treat their babies as if they were alive. They prepared their babies before giving them up by changing their diapers, dressing them, and wrapping them in warm blankets. One mother decided who would remove the baby from the house, preferring to give the baby first to a police officer who then gave it to the man who had come to remove the body. These mothers watched to see how people treated their baby:

> And I remember the man looking at me and saying, "Is this his head?" You know, he wanted to let me know that he was going to take good care of him, you know. Oh that's good. And, and uhm, I remember thinking, "That's good. At least he wanted to know where his head was."

One mother made sure her son's body would not be placed in the trunk of the car. She wanted him to be treated "just like a baby." The memories of how officials removed their baby's body still haunts one couple:

> Whatever the car is that picks up the body, they carried the body out in a black bag. Much like the shape of a doctor's bag but larger. I remember watching them walk to the car....It seemed so cold and so impersonal. I don't know what my expectation was. I guess my expectation was that they'd carry her out like a baby. Instead of a thing.

Planning the funeral

Once the parents had given up their baby's body, a series of difficult and related tasks and decisions awaited them. First, they had to plan the funeral: the formal goodbye ceremony: "[T]hat day, the very day, you're at the funeral home, planning a funeral. This was painful." Most parents had never planned a funeral before; some had never even been to one. Some could not face the task alone; others could not do it at all. One mother "didn't want to plan it. The last thing I wanted to do was look at all the books and pick out all the things they asked you to look at." One father made all the arrangements alone because his wife just could not face such a task. In some cases, friends and family helped with information and decision-making. This help was welcomed initially by some parents because it made them feel "supported." Parents regretted accepting help that ignored their wishes:

> You're not with it, and so what happens is a lot of times, you can't make those kinds of decisions. You get somebody else to make them for you, and after you get through it, you think, "I wish I would have done this [or] that."

Grandparents and the parents' siblings offered varying degrees of assistance with the funeral planning. While some made all the decisions, others merely carried out the parents' wishes. Problems arose when well-meaning family and friends tried to impose their beliefs or needs upon the parents. In some cases, parents who wanted to plan the funeral on their own had to fight others who wanted to do it for them. Arguments erupted. Other couples refused to argue, and instead, they just gave in and gave up, feeling "angry but too hurt to fight it." One family member tried to talk the parents out of having a funeral at all because he believed that "when a baby dies [you] don't need a funeral." When they insisted, he worried they would "be taken for a ride by the undertaker."

In addition to whether or not to even have a funeral, families disagreed on a variety of other issues: Who would pay for the funeral? Would there be a viewing? Would the casket be open or closed? What would the baby wear? Who could come to the service? Would there be a gathering after the funeral? Differences of opinion reflected family and ethnic traditions as well as people's personal needs and religious beliefs:

> When it came down to also making arrangements for the funeral, [a relative] was very upset because I didn't want an open casket.…It was all new to me but we weren't brought up with open caskets period, let alone a baby's.

In the interests of future family harmony, many couples set aside their own needs. They simply did not have the energy to fight; they just wanted the funeral to be over. One couple wanted to be the only ones present at their baby's funeral. Family members strenuously objected, insisting they had "a right to be there." After arguing about it briefly, the couple finally gave in to family demands.

Some parents, particularly the mothers, focused all their energy on making every detail of the funeral just right. They saw the funeral as "the last expression of love I could show." Making the decisions themselves also helped with "finalizing it, making the reality sink in."

And there were many decisions, big and small, to be made. First, families had to decide where the service would be held and who would officiate. One family had the funeral in the mother's home community rather than where they were living when the baby died. They drove for hours before they could even begin planning the funeral. Then parents had to decide who would officiate at the service. Those families who were affiliated with a church "had a priest [or minister] to turn to…a place to have the funeral [and]…God to draw strength from." Others had to make do with either a funeral director or a minister they had never met. As one woman said, "We didn't know any priests; we didn't know anybody." This made planning the funeral even more stressful.

Then parents had to decide when to have the funeral. One couple wanted to "shut the door" on the whole thing as soon as possible. Their desire "to get it over with" meant they were "squeezed in between two other funerals." Another couple had to wait for several days because their baby had died at the beginning of a significant religious celebration.

Parents also had to choose between burial or cremation. A quarter of the families chose cremation, all at the insistence of the mothers. They had a variety of reasons for this choice. For one mother, cremation was an ethnic and family tradition. For the others, cremation represented a way of caring for the baby and keeping the baby close to them. Some could not stand the thought of the baby in a box in the cold ground. Those who wanted a burial had to chose a tiny casket: "It was very hard, sitting in this nice little room, and then they open up the wall, and all these nice little caskets come out, and it just hits you, you know, the shock of it, the reality of it."

How parents made each decision reflected the way they were thinking of their baby at that time. Those who thought their baby had already "gone" seemed to pay less attention to every little detail. The funeral was just a formality. Those who had not yet reached that stage agonized over every decision because they were still loving their baby by continuing to think and act like parents.

Even the burial clothing became an matter of considerable concern. The parents' choice of clothes reflected their continued concern for the baby's well-being. They had not stopped parenting:

> [It] was the hardest thing to do…to buy an outfit for [the baby] to be buried in. Yeah, the people are kind of looking at [us] as we're crying in the department store. And you know what the funny thing is? Believe it or not, I'm looking for something warm. You know, it's so funny. You don't think right but I'm looking for something warm and…they had all the spring stuff. One of the sales ladies came over,

> and we found some, a wool thing, wool gown and wool booties and a whole suit, you know and everything, so anyways, like I said, it does not really make any difference now, but at the time, I felt he'd be cold, so I wanted something warm.

And then there were all the other details of the funeral. One mother insisted that the coffin "be carried by little children because that's what she was." Some parents chose special burial sites, just as if the baby would appreciate the view: "We selected the plot where we wanted [the baby] buried to make sure that she was facing the sunset. I love sunsets, and I thought she'd love sunsets." Another mother wanted her son to take his last ride in "a baby blue cadillac [rather than a hearse]....and I wanted him in the car with the priest." All these details reflected the parents' continued need to care for their baby.

Visiting the baby

Soon it was time for the viewing or visitation, the beginning of the formal goodbye ceremonies. Spending time with the baby before the actual funeral served four purposes. First, it forced parents to see, but only see, that their baby really was dead. It was far too early for parents to begin accepting this horrible reality. Acceptance took months or years, and for some parents, it just never happened. Some who still hoped to wake up from this nightmare found the visitation painful but helpful:

> A little thing inside of me was excited to see him. I don't mean that to sound morbid, but a little part of me was excited to see him. But then it hit home when you saw him 'cause they don't even look the same. It didn't look like my child.

Second, the visitation allowed parents to notice how their baby had been transformed from a person into "a shell." Some had seen this before; others saw it for the first time during the visitation:

> It was at the funeral home, [my wife] went over and she felt his cheeks and she says, "No, he's not there." She says, "You know, I think the soul is warmth." She says, "Because the soul is gone, so is, so is the smile, the warmth of the body" because the body was cold and stiff and lifeless and you know, like that, and the soul is gone. And she says, "Yeah, I didn't know what a soul was before, you know. You always hear people talk about, yeah, you know, your soul and what is that, you know?"

> And she says, "But looking at him, touching him," she says, "yeah, the soul is gone."

Some parents still could not see the transformation. They continued to see only their "beautiful baby." For these parents, mostly mothers, the visitation served a third purpose: to spend more time loving the baby. Some parents just gazed at their baby. Others touched, held, or kissed the baby; they put toys, special gifts, and even candy into the casket. Parents also talked to their baby. One mother said, "It was natural to talk to her. She was still listening somewhere." Others just used the time to "say my goodbyes."

Parents also used the visitation for the fourth and most practical purpose: to check on the details and to ensure that their instructions had been followed. This was both an extension of loving the baby and managing the ceremony.

Not all parents attended the visitation or even arranged to have one. To some parents, a visitation made no sense since the baby was "not there anymore." One father argued with the funeral director who insisted that the family needed a visitation. Neither parent wanted to see their dead baby. No one even told another couple that they could have a visitation. The father still has regrets: "It would have been nice to just spend maybe half an hour sitting there, but this is one thing that we never did or I never did." A mother who had no visitation described her subsequent anguish:

> I wanted to see him, I needed to see him, I wanted to see him and to hold him again. I know I couldn't have held him, but that need was there, you know, like you wanted to be holding a baby. You know, you wanted to smell him. You wanted to.

Saying the public goodbye

And too soon it was time for the funeral. As the parents prepared to go to their baby's funeral, many struggled with "the whole issue of, of parents attending their child's funeral. It's so wrong.…A child should be attending a parent's funeral, not the reverse." Parents could describe the funeral only by using comparisons. To one, it was "almost like an out of body experience." Others said, "I was in a daze" or "like I wasn't even there. It's like I was up here looking down on a TV screen and watching it all. Like you're numb.…It's almost like you're in a dream." Another said, "You just go through the motions."

To help themselves get through this experience, some parents tried to focus on what was being said at the service. One couple had worked for hours on an open letter to their friends and family. Having the letter read at the service helped them communicate to everyone at once just how they felt and how important their baby had been to them. One mother did not like what the minister said; his sermon did not reflect any of her beliefs. Another "was in agreement with everything that was said." Although it made her "break down" and cry, another mother felt comforted when her minister said,

> We are not here to pray for the little baby today. We are here to pray for the family that have lost a baby, for that family's loss. It is painful for them. The family has lost because the little baby had no sins or whatever. She was perfect; she is going to the right place.

Some parents cried during the whole service. Others, particularly fathers, sat "dry-eyed" and "like a rock." Some men controlled their tears because they believed it was expected of them. Others were just "in shock." Still others cried and did not care who saw them. And in most cases, there were many people there to see them.

The number of people who attended the funeral surprised some parents. One woman said she "didn't know that [she] had so many friends." One father was surprised to see his boss in the church. Most felt supported and comforted, but those who thought of the funeral as a private event felt embarrassed or overwhelmed. They just wanted to be left alone. Still others were upset because some members of their family had chosen not to come to the funeral. Particularly painful was the absence of their own parents and siblings. During the interview, they tried to make up reasons for the absences. Sending flowers was not enough because, as one mother said, it is "not how big your bouquet is but [being] there for you."

As the funeral came to a close, parents had another opportunity to be with their baby. One mother surprised everyone with her behavior at this point. She did not care what others thought of her; her only concern was her baby:

> My husband and I closed the coffin.We picked up the baby from the coffin first and kissed her good night and told her it was time to go now. It was good night, and one day I'd join her somewhere, I'd see her up there, and people were just watching me from the outside there as I was putting my baby away, to sleep. I guess some people think it was really strange that I would, how could I dare pick up this baby and kiss her. Jes, I mean, she is my baby.

Similarly, instead of having his son removed from the church by pallbearers, one father "went over to the casket and picked it up and took it out to the car." The funeral was over. It was time to finally "put the baby away."

Like the funeral, many parents had trouble remembering details of the burial. Most fathers did not describe this part of the experience spontaneously. Just arriving at the cemetery made one father "really realize that it's all over." One mother remembers losing control as her baby's coffin was lowered into the ground. She screamed, "Don't do that to her. Like, you know, she's scared of the, she's scared of the darkness. Don't put her away." She admits that "I lost it at the grave side. I didn't know what was happening." Another mother had a hard time because she could not see the coffin buried; the ground was frozen, so it would not be buried until spring: "But I didn't want to leave. They said they would call us when the grave was ready and everything, but I was just rooted to the ground, and I couldn't move. They got me to the car again, and I was just numb....I wanted to die."

Another mother felt relieved when the burial was over: "You've done what you had to do, and it's over with." Now she could perhaps begin to "deal with the fact that he died." First though, she, and all the other grieving parents, had to face "seeing people for the first time."

After the ceremonial part of the event ended, friends and family usually gathered in a hall or at someone's home to eat, be together and as one woman said, "catch up on all the old news." One father welcomed this opportunity to talk, "to try and tell people how I felt." Many parents seemed to have problems with this gathering. Some women "just didn't want all the people around." Some resented "all the laughter and the giggling and people were visiting." They felt angry when people attempted to "lift the spirits" with jokes or light talk. They were offended when people tried to make them "realize how lucky we were to have [the other children]" or when they "didn't feel comfortable asking anything about [the baby]." Some parents offered more comfort to others than they received themselves. One mother just could not stand it:

> And a whole bunch of people come over here after, but, like I was still numb, and I had taken a Valium that day, and I just, I just sat there at the kitchen table, not saying anything, not doing anything. If somebody was talking to me, I tried. I tell you I tried to take an interest, but I didn't and then I think I went upstairs afterwards, just to be alone.

Encountering the reminders

And then the gathering was over, and everyone went home. Gradually, the initial numbness wore off, and the harsh reality of what had happened began to surface. When the parents came home, they were confronted with the baby's "visible stuff," that is, the baby's things. Reminders of the baby filled the home.

Parents had to decide what to do with all the little things like bottles, blankets, clothes, toys, medicines, and pictures and big things like bassinets, cribs, and prams. And then there was the baby's room. Some parents wondered whether they could possibly remain in their home, surrounded as they were with all these visible reminders of their baby. The timing for decisions about the disposition of the baby's "visibles" varied. Some parents found the presence of the baby's things too painful. These parents put the "visible things" away or gave them away as soon as they could, some within hours of the baby's death. Others took their time with these decisions. Still others set aside their own "private stashes" of mementoes, things they just would not give up.

Those who had their baby cremated had one poignant reminder of their baby: the ashes. Only one couple scattered the ashes. Although they had chosen a beautiful spot, they just could not "do it" themselves. When the funeral home staff volunteered to do it for them, they felt relieved. Their baby was "safe now." Another couple did not bring the ashes home for many years; the mother could not handle having them in her house. The ashes presented no problem for the third couple; they still keep them in their bedroom. Parents who had buried their baby could choose if and when they wanted to visit the grave site. Although they were not subjected to continual reminders, some felt like they had lost their baby.

At first, the reminders hurt. For many parents, just seeing the baby's everyday things triggered strong feelings:

> [My husband] had tears running down his cheeks. It hurts to see a man cry. And then I asked him, I said, "What are you doing?" "Oh, I'm washing these bottles. I'm getting ready, I'm getting them ready for her when she comes home." I told him, I said, "She's not coming home. She's not coming home." And then he just said, "Oh." And then he just cried.

One mother had given up her baby in the "special" bassinet she had made for him. She did not want it back. Another "couldn't wait to get rid of, to get rid of the cradle, to get rid of all the clothes. I just, I wanted to do that the second I [got home from the hospital]." Following family tradition, one father calmly packed up his son's room immediately after the funeral:

> [He said to himself at the time:] "Hey, you know what you have to do." You know, that program was so strong in me that "Well, he's gone, he's dead, you know. He's gone." So we went home and…I took his crib apart and all his toys and all his stuff and put it in boxes and "Okay, that's it.'"And that's the way I looked at death.

Parents also gave some things away. Because the sight of all the matching twin outfits reminded her that she only had one live twin to dress, a mother gave away every matching outfit. Parents also put things like baby pictures away temporarily until they could handle looking at them again. Some made practical decisions: they put the toys and clothes into storage for the next baby.

And then there was the baby's room to deal with. Thinking they were helping, relatives cleaned out one baby's room within hours of the death. Another mother changed the baby's room into a play room for her daughter. Unfortunately, a change in function did not eliminate the eerie feeling she had every time she went past the room at night.

Some people never felt comfortable in their homes again. The memory of the baby's death overshadowed happier memories. Although one woman wanted to move right away, she could not; they had just made their first mortgage payment. In addition, she soon realized "it's just a way of running away from your grief, your pain, leaving the scene of the crime." A third of the couples did move over the course of the next year. Although one couple had planned to move prior to their baby's death, the woman felt "relieved" when they finally left the house. Another couple moved closer to family support. Some moved because one or both of them felt uneasy in the house. One man secretly felt so uncomfortable in the house that he avoided coming home and "couldn't stay in the house by myself.…I do not know why. Whether I figured there was some evil beings in the house or not."

Other parents had the opposite reaction. They could neither move nor dispose of the baby's "visible stuff." They wanted to remember that their baby had been "here." Some vowed never to move. A few parents left the baby's room and all that was in it undisturbed for emotional reasons. One mother kept the room exactly the same because "it was a place that I went to. It felt good to go in there." She refused to make any changes until 3 weeks before her next baby arrived. Although another mother "didn't touch [the baby's] room" for 8 months, it did not give her comfort: "All I could feel was my grief that he was gone." Only mothers described keeping special mementoes:

clothing that once smelled like the baby; a bottle of medicine; and the baby's special rattle:

> It's funny the attachment that you get to certain things. There's things that I won't give away ever....I still have the clothes that he died in. I just have them. They're tucked away. Some day maybe. I doubt it, I doubt it. I still have the quilt that we wrapped him in. It was a little bunting bag we wrapped him in when he died.

Pictures also played an important role in keeping memories alive. While some parents put the baby's pictures away, but in special albums, others integrated them into family albums. Still others displayed the baby's picture prominently, on top of the television set or in the entrance hall. A few displayed their baby's picture in special but much less obvious spots in their homes. Some families integrated the baby's pictures into the family photo display. No matter where they kept the baby's pictures, the pictures almost always aroused strong feelings and memories.

Other intangible or invisible "stuff" had the same effect. Baby smells triggered memories. One mother had a "really rough time" going by her baby's room because of the "Ivory smell" that stayed "for so long." Another had trouble notifying all the various government offices of her son's death: "You have to tell these people that your baby died at a time when you're having a hard time dealing with the fact that your baby's died." She also had to deal with a phone call from the health unit reminding her that she had missed an appointment to bring her son in for his shots.

Parents also had to deal with having time on their hands, time that used to be devoted to meeting the baby's needs. Mothers in particular had built their days and nights around the baby; they lost the rhythm of their "daily routine." Fathers missed coming home and playing with their babies; working mothers found weekends particularly painful because that was when they normally had time to enjoy the baby the most.

Nursing mothers had special problems. In addition to having extra time on their hands, their breasts were full of milk. Some mothers needed pills to help them stop the production of milk. Their swollen and painful breasts increased their emotional pain: "I wanted a baby to nurse to get rid of the physical pain that I was feeling as well as this sort of anguish." One mother produced milk only once after her baby died, and "it was the last time." Believing that drying up "should have been more painful," this mother decided that "maybe it was [painful] but what I was feeling [emotionally] was more painful than that." One father seemed more concerned about his wife's physical pain due to breastfeeding problems than how she felt emotionally.

Another painful issue involved the baby's name. One mother lamented that they had given their son "the perfect name and we could never use it again for anybody." Because some relatives never said the baby's name again, as if he or she never existed, parents missed hearing it. One mother kept her son's prescription bottle just so she could have "something that had his name on it." One father wanted his daughter to have her own head stone just so she could have "her own place" on earth.

As parents struggled to deal with all the baby's things, both visible and invisible, reality slowly began to sink in. This was not a nightmare. It was reality. They were awake now, and somehow they were going to have to learn how to deal with the devastation.

WAKING UP TO THE DEVASTATION

Hurting inside

The death of their baby devastated parents in many ways. Some felt it physically. One mother tried to describe what happened the first night:

> I remember [my husband] getting up in the middle of the night, and he was crying so hard that he started to, it was like he was throwing up, but it was dry heaves and, I mean, just horrible. You didn't sleep. You laid there and you were just stiff and you were trying not to, and...Hell doesn't even describe it. Because you want to say it was pure hell but then you think that doesn't even. You, you can't describe it. Words don't even come. All I can feel is my chest when you ask me to describe it, like you know. I can't describe it.

Another woman described how her husband experienced "pain in his chest...at night...like elephants standing on his chest." One mother suffered back pains; doctors told her to see a psychiatrist. She refused because "I was not crazy." Suffering severe stomach pains within weeks of her baby's death, one mother went to her doctor who promptly admitted her to the hospital for 10 days. The diagnosis was "emotional breakdown." Even parents' weights were affected. One father gained as much as "25 pounds" over the next year; one mother lost as much as "10 pounds in 3 days." A sibling also suffered digestive problems. While in hospital, this little girl looked everywhere for her baby brother. This was the last place she had seen him. She just wanted him to come home.

Feeling vulnerable

Trying to cope with the reality that their baby was "not coming home" severely challenged and devastated some parents intellectually. Nothing made sense anymore. They had to face the new and frightening awareness that tragedies can happen in the "perfect little family," that catastrophes do not just happen to "other people on the television." Their "safety net gone," parents began to fear that "if this can happen, anything can happen." They felt vulnerable and terrified, powerless and confused. Their world no longer felt safe or fair.

Questioning God

The feeling of unfairness and imminent danger can be partially connected to a new shakiness of some parents' religious beliefs in the early days of this horrible nightmare. Although some parents turned to their faith for strength and found what they needed, the death of their baby caused most parents to examine the most fundamental aspects of their faith. They even questioned the very existence and nature of God. As one father said, "If you're looking for ways to doubt religion, there's one right there." After all, "there can't be a God there because look what's happened." Others "had to try to think about [their baby's death] in terms of [their] understanding of God." Up until they lost their baby, most parents either consciously or unconsciously trusted God to be fair, loving, and reasonable. Their baby's death contradicted each of these beliefs.

One father wondered for a time how he could have trusted such a God to look out for his family. He struggled with feelings of "betrayal of God for taking [our baby]." Many parents began to doubt God's sense of fairness:

> [The death of the baby] made me question my whole religion because I thought, "Well, how unfair! Like how can He do this?"...It didn't seem fair to me that He would take a healthy, well-loved, and much-wanted baby.

After doing everything she possibly could to raise her children properly in a community where she saw other "women walking around, running around town...throwing their kids around, neglecting them, giving them up for adoption, throw[ing] them away," all one mother could do was ask God, "Why me?" The death of their baby just did not make any sense. It was not uncommon for parents to wonder what kind of God would take "much-loved" babies and leave behind children who lived in unfortunate circumstances. Because some members of the clergy tried to explain the baby's death by talking about God's will, parents replied with "Why was it God's will?" Until they could resolve their feeling of utter and complete confusion about their faith, they felt spiritually devastated.

Wanting to die

It is no wonder then that most parents also felt emotionally devastated as well. Several mothers wanted to die; some so they could join their babies:

> That first night was horrible. That first night, you can't. There is no word to describe that night, you know. That hurt, the feelings you're feeling.... When I think about it, I think I could have died that night, happily. You know, but I would have had to take [the rest of my family] with me. You know, but I wanted us all to be together again.

One mother could not bring herself to actively commit suicide, so she tried to think of another way to die. Sometimes she would think:

> God, I wish I could drive to work today and get into a bad car accident and just die. For the longest time, for months and months...I thought if I could die in an accident, not by my own hand, but in an accident some way like, then I will meet up with my baby.

Other mothers considered suicide as well but for different reasons. One thought about suicide occasionally because death offered an escape from her pain. Sometimes she wondered if she would ever again be able to "cope with tomorrow. How am I going to get up and cope with life?" Another planned her suicide many months after her baby's death. She decided she had been a bad mother and could no longer stand being alive. Fortunately, her plan did not work. Another considered suicide twice: early in the experience so she could join the baby and much later when she felt she could no longer endure the feelings of devastation. Part of this woman's problem stemmed from the lack of support she felt from her husband and family.

Straining relationships

Despite the myth that a death in the family brings people closer together, it strained some family relationships. For the families in this study, some relationships improved; other relationships deteriorated, temporarily or permanently. People's grief and their inability to understand the baby's death increased the strain of previous family tensions. Everyone felt edgy. During the first few hours and days after the baby's death, the stage was often set for future problems. There were problems within the extended families and within the parents' own marriages.

Many extended family problems began as early as the first few hours after the baby's death when parents notified family and friends about their loss. Naturally the calls caught relatives off guard. They found it difficult to comfort the parents. Some family members quickly made arrangements to be with the parents. Others lived too far away, could not afford to make the trip, or just chose not to come. Parents could accept some reasons for not coming but not others. A grandfather chose not to come to the funeral because he "couldn't face it." One grandmother said she would make the trip only if she was "really needed." For whatever reason, her son just could not tell her how very devastated he was. Her reaction had just added to his pain. Instead of coming in person to bring comfort, some people sent "a beautiful amount of flowers [but that] didn't bring comfort."

Some relatives lived in the immediate vicinity of the parents. Their nearness was an advantage for some and a disadvantage for others. Although relatives tried to be supportive, some did and said things that made the grieving parents feel worse. Some relatives did not offer any real support at all. For the men in particular, this lack of support from their own family increased the sense of loneliness they already felt. Some couples had the opposite problem: relatives who would not leave them alone, who came from all across the province, and who gathered at the couple's house, arriving as early as 7 in the morning: "There's tables of food everywhere, it drove me crazy." Another parent said, "It was like a wedding." And like a wedding, some grandparents argued over who would pay for what and who would be in charge of making all the important decisions. When family customs differed, making decisions about the funeral became very difficult.

Sometimes talking made things better, but sometimes it made things worse. Instead of offering comfort, one set of grandparents told the distraught parents to call the police when the baby was first found. Some parents were angered not by what was said, but by the total silence—the lack of acknowledgement of their grief and their baby's existence. Family members advised a few parents to move and sell their home immediately, asked about the existence of an insurance policy on the baby's life, and suggested suing the doctor. A grandfather had this to say as he entered the parents' house within hours of the baby's death: "What the hell happened?" Much later the mother understood the reason behind this question: "He [just] wanted to know what the hell happened." At the time though, all she thought was "Oh my God, he blames me." Parents who had strong and positive relationships with their relatives usually made excuses for insensitive comments and actions. Others could not justify the insensitivities and added them to the existing list of grievances. In some families, the death of the baby and the way relatives handled it left a permanent trail of interpersonal devastation.

The baby's death also affected the parents' marriages. While some drew closer to offer comfort, others withdrew. While some could share their words and tears, others could not "be there" physically for each other.

Feeling the total devastation

With almost all facets of their lives devastated, many parents felt like their whole world had been destroyed. They just kept "wondering when the hurt [was] going to go away. You keep hoping that tomorrow you'll wake up and you'll feel different, but you know, that never happens for a long, long time." One mother feared she would "never recover from this...**total devastation**." As one father said, "You think you're devastated for life and this will never go away." It was at this point that many parents began to ask themselves, "How am I going to carry on?"

Chapter 4
Understanding the Parents' Experience: Trying to Carry On While Struggling for Control

Playing the Roles While Falling Apart

Losing their baby to SIDS made parents think they might be "going crazy." It felt like they were "falling apart," splitting into two parts: an "outside" part and an "inside" part. The "outside" part took control in some parents. This practical part had almost "no feelings." Instead, it was concerned mostly with appearances, responsibilities, and obligations. When the baby died, the message from the "outside" part was simple: "This has happened. You have to accept it. You have to get through it." In other words, **try to carry on**. The "inside part, the part that really feels," took control in other parents. Grief overwhelmed them, causing them to fall apart. They **struggled for control** over their grief for some time before learning how to manage it.

Within a few days of their baby's death, "everybody goes home and life goes on and it's tough." Parents could see people going back to their lives and meeting their obligations again, almost as if nothing had happened. To avoid dealing with their own pain and in response to their own obligations, the grieving parents **tried to carry on.** They tried to play the roles of worker, parent, spouse, and community member. Each role offered the parents something different. Some parents went through the motions in one role and "buried" themselves in another. Some roles increased the pain; others facilitated healing.

Since each role has unique features, I describe how the parents tried to play each role and how they fell apart in each role. Although the process may look linear, it is not. Parents "yo yo[ed]" between playing their roles and falling apart.

Struggling to carry on as a worker

Playing the role of worker

Parents very quickly had to deal with the fact that after "the funeral ends everybody goes home and life goes on and it's tough." One of the toughest things for some parents was returning to work. A third of the working parents returned to their jobs within one week of their baby's funeral. As one father said, "There comes a time where you've got to put yourself back together, and you can't carry on like that." Another father was quite emphatic:

> One of the first things you're gonna realize is that life goes on. If you don't work, you're not going to get paid. If you don't get paid, you're not going to pay the bills, so they don't really care if you just lost a kid. I mean, society doesn't really care. I mean, the fact is the bills have to be paid, and you've got to carry on. Uhm, that's probably the first thing that you're gonna realize.

Reasons for returning to work

Feeling obligated

These comments reflect one reason parents returned to work: they had obligations. They felt obliged to continue supporting their families out of "economic necessity." Some men also felt obliged to do "the breadwinner thing." It was their role in the family. Besides the need for an income and to fulfill a role in the family, self-employed professionals also felt obliged to meet the commitments of their careers and clients.

Feeling time pressure

When the bereavement leave was up, some parents automatically went back to work: "They give you about 2 days bereavement and that's about it." One man "figured [he] was supposed to go right back to work after the funeral." He did not know his company offered bereavement leave. Professionals had no real bereavement leave; they had to make special arrangements so they could set aside their obligations at work to tend to their personal needs. Responding to their own need for more time, a few parents took sick time on top of their allotted bereavement leave.

Meeting a personal need

While some parents returned to work to meet outside obligations, others hoped working would make them feel better. Some men went back to work so they could at least appear to be "strong" and functional in the eyes of their wives and the community. Even if they did not feel like going to work, some men wanted to reestablish their family's routine. Going back to work made life seem "normal again." Some went to work hoping to be distracted from their grief, "thinking [they] could keep busy that way": "[Work] gets you off thinking of yourself and what might have been into something that you enjoy." A few parents "buried" themselves in their work; they "just wanted to work [the pain] off." Some mothers had quit work to have their baby. Those who "wanted to be a mom" again soon found new jobs or returned to old positions. They just wanted something to "fill that time in between" losing one baby and delivering another. In addition, working gave some parents a feeling of "satisfaction" and "importance." Working also restored feelings of confidence, competence, and control, feelings that the baby's death had stolen from the parents. And finally, there were a few parents who were just "anxious to get back to work," to get back to "the challenge" of having the "mind active," to feeling "centralize[d]" and focused. These parents had derived their identity primarily from their careers rather than parenthood.

Carrying on at work

When they first went back to work, most parents had a hard time setting aside their grief: "It was always on your mind, but there were brief moments during the day where it would drift out of your mind, and you could carry on." These moments offered temporary relief from the pain. Soon, some workers "had things to do, and [they] went ahead and did them." Then, sometimes out of nowhere, within days or weeks of returning to work, "[the pain] starts coming on to you. You can feel it." Some parents just could not hold back the feelings; they started falling apart at work.

Falling apart as a worker

Working in a fog

At first, many parents had trouble concentrating at work. Still numb from the shock and filled with questions about why their baby had died, these parents were "in a fog and you can't think. You can't put things together." A coworker told one father whose job demanded intense concentration, "You know, like this is not a very good place to be if you're not, if your mind's not here and you're not here." This coworker recognized that this father was not really at work. Only his body, his outside part, was there.

Not putting out

A few parents experienced job performance difficulties. After a few months, a supervisor criticized one bereaved father for "not putting out like you normally do" and for "withdrawing." Some parents just went through the motions at work. Previously dedicated workers now "just, I wanted to do my job. Put my head down and do [the work] and be gone." In jobs where income depended upon performance, some family incomes dropped. One woman was fired. Some parents had to leave work when they fell apart because they "couldn't do anything." They wanted to go home and "lie in bed and cry." Others took time off because they became physically ill. Later, some parents took time off work on the baby's birthday or the anniversary of the death. On those days, these parents just could not play the worker role. They just wanted to be with their baby, to be a parent again.

Trying to manage the feelings

For some workers, playing the role meant managing their own emotions to suit the demands of their job. At first, parents in people-serving jobs found it almost impossible to feel friendly or interested in their customers and coworkers. Some radiated anger instead. One woman glowered at her coworkers so much that "people were afraid to talk to [her]." An employer fired one woman because she was "taking [her anger] out on the customers." At least workers in physical jobs could put their anger to good use; their output increased on days when they were upset. They "worked it out" by exhausting their bodies.

Beyond having trouble controlling their anger, many parents often felt overwhelmed with sadness. Some fell apart and cried at work:

> The tears would be running down your eyes, and you couldn't look at the [customer or coworker] in the eye or look him in the face, but there'd be tears running down your eyes, and I'd just take time off from [work] and go to the washroom and sit there, and, you know, wash my face, and this happened a lot.

Most men worked hard to "keep it under control"; they isolated themselves when they felt upset, often crying in the privacy of their vehicles. Women seemed to have more difficulty controlling their tears. Fearing she would soon be a "basket case," one woman quit her new sales job because she could not control her tears at work.

Another woman had the opposite problem. She had such control over her emotions that she "just went into robot state" on the job. She felt nothing for the first 2 weeks. When she finally started feeling again, she fell apart physically. A doctor admitted her to the hospital for a "nervous breakdown." She, like several other parents, had returned to work "too soon." Some had made the decision while they still felt "numb." Others just felt pressured to **carry on**. All had "tried to grieve too quickly."

Conclusion: The struggle to carry on as a worker

One father had no trouble returning to work, but eventually, he began having trouble with family relationships; he had stopped feeling anything. Men who were used to compartmentalizing their lives seemed to have the fewest problems returning to work. When they were at work, they were "not thinking about home. That's, that's normal, right?" Parents who had the most trouble were those who could not stop feeling their grief and thinking about their loss but who felt obliged to be at work anyway. Working did not relieve their pain, nor did it offer them a reason to go on. Rather than providing them with an opportunity to connect with others, the job only increased their desire to be alone. Down deep, most working women identified more with being a mother than a worker. They had the most trouble returning to work.

Struggling to carry on as a parent

After the baby's death, both mothers and fathers tried to **carry on** as parents. Even those who had lost their only child still wanted to hold onto the image of themselves as "good parents." Reality challenged this image: their baby was dead. They wondered if perhaps they had unintentionally been "horrible parents." Combining this fear with the fact that they still did not understand why their baby had died, parents changed the way they related to children. While some coped by exaggerating the parental role, others rejected this role for a time.

Playing the role of parent to a dead baby

Even after the funeral was over, many parents **tried to carry on** some kind of relationship with their deceased baby. Over time, the intensity of the relationship changed, as did the activities that maintained the relationship. The way parents tried to care for their baby reflected how they thought of the baby. Those who had already "given up the baby" in their minds felt less need to actively parent the baby. Those parents who still thought of their baby as alive somewhere else tried to continue to show their love.

At first, parents wanted to care for their baby like it was alive. Because much of the mothering had involved physical contact with the baby, women quickly became frustrated by the fact that they were unable to touch and hold their baby. The baby's physical absence made the mothers fall apart. Fathers continued to play the role of family provider by going to work. Whenever they thought about their baby, they often fell apart.

Both mothers and fathers had to find a new way to care for their dead baby, either directly or indirectly. With varying degrees of success, parents **tried to carry on** a direct relationship with their baby. Because "a part of [them] will always be mothering [and fathering]," many parents tried to maintain a loving "connection" with their baby. It took awhile to stop parenting this baby; some never did stop.

Maintaining a personal connection

Parents maintained their connection both privately and publicly. At first, other people accepted the parents' need to maintain a public relationship with the baby. In particular, the parents wanted to display or look at baby pictures and to talk about the baby. Most people tolerated this need only for a short time. Then, by their actions and their words, they began pressuring the parents to release their connection to the baby. Some parents responded by becoming secretive, looking at baby pictures only when they were alone. When others found out about this, they told the parents such behavior was unhealthy. Even putting the baby's pictures in the family album upset some relatives who believed the parents "shouldn't have those pictures" there. A few parents insisted on displaying and looking at the baby's pictures no matter what others thought.

Parents also wanted the freedom to talk openly about the baby's life and death. Mothers wanted to talk about their pregnancy and delivery. More mothers than fathers wanted to use the baby's name in conversation and to relive memories of the baby's short life. Some needed people to listen while they relayed the story of the baby's death.

When parents tried to display their baby pictures or talk about their baby, they had to contend with others' negative reactions. Some people got uncomfortable when they heard about the baby's death. Others just felt the parents should "move on" and let go of the baby. Some parents reacted by becoming secretive; they kept their thoughts and memories to themselves. This secretiveness made them feel dishonest and ashamed for publicly abandoning their baby. If one parent hid the relationship from his or her spouse, it increased marital tension. Although some parents tried to play the role that others demanded of them, sometimes they could not carry it off, and they fell apart.

To avoid feeling split in two, some parents connected with their baby in private. They spent time at the cemetery, thinking about and talking to the baby, crying and praying, leaving flowers and gifts. Just visiting the baby's grave was not enough for some parents. Visiting frustrated some mothers because they "wanted to be holding a baby" instead of caring for it indirectly. Thinking about their baby "cold in the ground" made some feel even worse. They fell apart.

Some parents never went to the cemetery again after the funeral. To them, the baby "was not there." Instead, some believed the baby was "with God." Parents with this belief maintained their connection through their faith. One mother began going to church every day because she felt closest to her baby there. Believing in heaven helped some parents **carry on**. Other parents kept crashing into the thought that their baby was "dead. Just dead." This realization was enough to make them fall apart.

Other parents tried to be satisfied with a connection in their heads. They thought of the baby wherever they were. Some stayed home, thinking and talking about the baby, praying, looking at baby pictures, and spending time in the baby's room. For the first year after the baby's death, some remembered "every single week what we did with [the baby] last year at this time." They experienced the year after the baby's death as a series of "firsts":

> You live everything by firsts, you know. Like the first week you go, "Gee, last week Tuesday I was doing this and this with [the baby]. Last week Wednesday I was. Well, this is only a week ago, and he's not here

> any more. Well, how weird." You know and it was really tough and then you go to the first month. You know and then you go to anniversaries, birthday...like all those firsts. You remember to the day.

Many fathers thought of the baby while they drove. Sometimes thinking about the baby made parents feel good; sometimes it hurt. At first, parents fell apart whenever they thought about their baby. Playing the role of parent in their head did not satisfy them: they wanted their baby back in their "empty arms." They also wanted to tell others about losing and missing and remembering the baby. Often others let the parents know they felt uncomfortable about the continuation of this relationship.

A few parents tried to force their partners and others to allow them to continue to think and talk about the baby. They refused to "save somebody else's emotions or feelings for the sake of [my baby]. If they can't handle it, well, that's their problem." Some parents understood and accepted others' discomfort, and instead of forcing their needs on others, these parents went in search of a more accepting and willing "audience." Sometimes a sympathetic friend became the audience. In other cases, parents started attending a support group. There, other grieving parents understood the frustrations of trying to parent a dead baby. They understood the need to talk about the baby, to look at pictures, and to remember the baby's life and death. The group also provided a safe and accepting place for the parents to fall apart.

Falling apart as a parent to a dead baby

Although many parents tried to appear "strong" on the outside, inside they continually struggled for control over their sadness, anger, fear, guilt, and sense of powerlessness. In the beginning, other people tolerated it when parents, particularly mothers, "burst into tears" privately or in a "public place." As time passed, people grew less and less tolerant. Parents started hiding their grief from others. Even after months and years had gone by, they still sometimes lost control in public, often making other people feel uncomfortable.

Exploding

Embarrassed and trying to protect others from seeing their raw pain, some parents learned to "stifle it pretty quickly and contain yourself and get on with things." Others could not "contain" their pain "inside." After "crying for hours," one mother went to her family and told them it was the anniversary of her baby's death, hoping they would comfort her. Instead, they rejected her tears and ignored her pain. Another grieving mother lost control of her anger when someone told her she thought the bereaved should start "getting on with [their] life" after a year. This mother

> explod[ed] at this poor woman, [saying], "Who do you think you are? We've lost [our baby] for 6 months, and it feels like yesterday! If you think I'm going to be over it in a year and get on with my life, you've got another thing coming, and how can you be so callous and uncaring?"...By the time I was through with her, the poor woman was crying.

Yearning for the baby

Parents also could not "contain" their need to stay connected to the baby and to be "good parents." They wanted to hold, "smell," and "touch" the baby. One mother wanted to be with her baby so badly that she could not stop herself from going to the grave site, again and again:

> It would kill me to go to the cemetery. It was so cold. It would be minus 40, and I couldn't stand the fact that, you know, [the baby] was in that ground, and it was minus 40. That really bothered me. I could not stand it, but I would go a lot, and I don't know, I just would cry there. I just wanted [the baby] to know how much I missed her, and I guess I felt, even though I hated the cemetery, it would bring me closer to her.

Some parents could not stand the separation. One father had a nightmare about the baby floating away from him; a mother dreamt she could not find her baby's grave. A few wanted to be with their baby so desperately that they considered suicide. Their sense of obligation to their other children helped them **carry on** until this feeling subsided.

Parents also felt separated from the baby on special days. At first, the baby's birthday or deathday provoked a resurgence of the pain. Some suffered through the first anniversary of the deathday "minute by minute. This was the time I put him to bed; this was the time I found him; this was the time they took him away." Until they regained their balance and learned to let go of the baby and their grief, many parents just felt adrift in the "sea of grief."

No matter how badly these parents felt, most still had other children who needed them; they **tried to carry on** with their other children, first with their older children, and then with children who were born after the baby's death.

Playing the role of parent to the older children

Reeling from the death of their baby, most grieving mothers and fathers still had to carry on and be "good parents" to their older children. The baby's death had changed the way these parents looked at life and themselves. Many parents wanted to increase their commitment to their family life. At the same time, because these parents felt so defenseless and powerless, they feared for the safety and survival of their children. Their confidence in themselves as "good parents" had been badly shaken. They still wondered if somehow they had been responsible for the baby's death. All these feelings and thoughts affected the way parents played the role of parent to their older children.

Explaining the death

The other children ranged in age from 5 years to 4 months when the baby died. The average age was just over 2. The younger the children, the less likely they were to understand what had happened. Once the parents came home or the emergency responders had left the home, parents tried to regain their composure enough to explain to their children what had happened. Those with a strong faith usually gave a religious explanation: the baby "died and went up to heaven to live with God and that [the baby] was going to be a special angel in his Christmas choir." Families without a strong faith or whose children were too young to understand a religious explanation just told the children the baby had died, was "gone," or "was not coming back anymore." Most parents expected the children to ask more questions as they grew older: "For now [they] just say that [the baby] died and [they] miss him and that, you know, [they] always will remember him."

No matter what explanation the parents gave, these children "just could never understand where [the baby] went and when [the baby] was coming back." They seemed to accept and understand an explanation while it was being given, then they would play for a while and "come back 10 minutes later and say, 'Yeah, okay, so when's [the baby] going to be back?'"

Although parents had difficulty explaining what happened to the baby, they found the children's next question even harder to answer: "Why did [the baby] go?" Many parents had not answered that question for themselves yet. One couple was very honest with their daughter. In response to her "why" questions, they replied, "We don't know why. It's something that happens." They also said two other important things: "It's nobody's fault. It just happens" and "It wasn't going to happen to her. It only happened to little babies." Children who were not given this information were more likely to blame themselves for their brother or sister's death. They were also likely to be "scared that it would happen to [them]." The school-aged child who found her brother needed continual reassurance that no one blamed her, that her parents still loved her, and that she would wake up each morning. All the reassurances in the world could not make her feel better at first. She had lost her baby brother, and she was grieving.

Reacting

The older children's reactions to the death varied, depending on their age at the time, whether they witnessed events surrounding the discovery of the baby, if and how their parents explained the death to them, and how the parents handled the whole situation. The children's reactions also depended on how well their parents handled their own grief.

Some children witnessed some aspect of the discovery of the baby and the events that followed. The children who found the baby or who witnessed their parents' discovery were most negatively affected. They were frightened. A few children slept through the discovery or stayed in their rooms. A few parents took their children to a babysitter, while they accompanied the baby to the hospital.

In the short-term, children reacted to the death of their younger sibling by: becoming physically ill and requiring hospitalization; having temper tantrums; getting upset when babies cried; "clinging" to the parents or "rejecting" them; "running around" with "no sense of direction"; searching for the baby by asking questions or looking in places where they had last seen the baby; and asking if they could have another brother or sister. One little boy became very concerned when he could not match people up in pairs. In his mind, "everyone [should be] paired up with somebody." He was no longer part of a pair of children. He missed his baby brother.

The "blessings" of older children

The parents missed the baby, too, but having older children helped them deal with their pain. By their very existence, children provided parents with the reassurance and proof that they had, in fact, been "good parents." Parents could look at their older children and say to themselves, "I never did anything different [with these children than with the baby]." Older children also gave some parents a reason "to go on" each day:

> Physically, I had to get up in the morning, I had to make breakfast, I had to do all those things for [the other children], and in turn, it was, I think, getting me through the steps maybe a little faster.

Their love for and commitment to their older children gave some devastated mothers a reason to go on living. A few mothers who wanted to "join" their dead baby rejected the idea of suicide because "if I joined [the baby], then I leave [the other children], and that didn't make any sense." Some children made a special effort to comfort their parents with hugs, cards, and by being on their best behavior. Most parents just felt their spirits lifted by their children's spontaneous smiles and willingness to openly talk about the family's loss. Others enjoyed watching their children learn new skills. One mother felt that it was "just a blessing" that her older son "was at such an interesting stage and he was, you know, beginning to talk and get involved." He provided a welcome diversion from her grief.

Changing as parents

The parents' explanation for their baby's death affected the way they cared for their other children. Those who refused to blame themselves or anyone else for their baby's death continued to parent much the same, except they "clutched" (watched over and appreciated) their children a bit more than they had previously. Some still felt responsible for their baby's death. Others feared another tragedy would strike if they were not extremely careful. In both cases, these parents exaggerated their parental role, doing everything they could to become super parents. Other parents did the opposite: they reduced their involvement with their children, some temporarily, others more permanently. In some cases, grief overwhelmed the parents, making it impossible for them to function.

"Logically and rationally," most parents knew that the change in their parenting might negatively affect their children, but they could not help themselves. They found it difficult to meet their own needs and their children's simultaneously: "I know what's supposed to be done. Ah, but inside," in that emotional part, that was another matter. Sometimes the parents managed to **carry on** and function effectively in the parental role. They restrained their need to be "overprotective" or to pull away into themselves. Sometimes the feeling of devastation and fear took over and the parents fell apart.

The way the parents grieved affected the children. Some parents hid their grief because they knew children "didn't like to see [their parents] crying." One little boy would "scream, 'No!' if he saw [his mother] crying, so when he napped was the only time [she] would…really think about everything, and that was when [she] would cry." Many fathers and a few mothers controlled the public display of their pain, not because they did not want to scare their children, but because they always controlled how much they showed their emotions.

Other parents let their children see them grieving. These parents grieved openly. However, they managed to convey strength and stability to their children by making good use of each other, other supportive adults, and their faith. Their children understood that they were neither the cause of their parents' pain nor were they part of the solution. One little girl accepted that her parents were "very, very sad," but her parents made it clear to her that they could handle their sadness; she was free to be a child.

In contrast, a few parents did more than share their grief with their children: the children became their partners in pain. When grief overwhelmed these parents, they "leaned on" their older children for support.

Falling apart as parents to older children

Falling apart in this role meant that the parents did not effectively and consistently meet the needs of their children. Parents often "yo yo[ed]" back and forth between playing the role and falling apart. They fell apart by: becoming super parents and exaggerating their sense of obligation to their children; reducing their role and distancing themselves from their obligations; and reversing roles and leaning on their children for support.

Becoming super parents

Mothers and fathers who became super parents exaggerated their parental responsibilities; they dedicated themselves to parenthood and their children. Some children "got whatever [they] wanted." As one mother described it, the day after the baby's funeral, her husband began "really spoil[ing] my, our son after that. Took him out and bought him a tractor, a big tractor." When her son was in hospital for minor surgery, another mother "spent hundreds of dollars on toys." Some parents totally lost their perspective. Anything their children wanted they got.

Besides spoiling their children, a few parents had trouble with discipline. One woman lost control of her temper; she "abused" her older child. Others had the opposite problem. One mother was "afraid to discipline [the other children]." She could not control the children at all "because I felt that I'd be punished again. I just felt [the baby's death] was a punishment. And [so the children]...could do no wrong."

Other parents had "regrets" about the lack of time they had spent enjoying their baby. Feeling guilty about the missed opportunities for loving, these parents vowed not to make that same mistake with their other children. They devoted themselves to "spending time with" their children, "reading, doing whatever with [them]." Child-centered activities took precedence over almost everything else. Some parents made their children the sole focus of their lives.

By making their children the number one priority in their lives, parents increased the intensity of the parent-child relationship. Some parents "live[d] for" their children. Nothing else in their lives had as much importance. A few even set aside their marital relationship. The more important the children became, the more parents dreaded their children' inevitable independence.

In addition, many parents also exaggerated their desire to protect the children. Some parents saw danger lurking everywhere outside the house. They discouraged their children from pursuing normal activities. They continually reminded them of the dangers of walking to a friend's house or to school alone, skiing, skateboarding, playing hockey, or even just playing in the neighborhood. Some parents became chronic worriers, describing themselves as "basket cases" whenever their children were out of their sight or beyond their control. One mother worried when her children "let loose" and left the yard, especially "when he's on his bike and he's riding. Like you've got no control anymore. They go to school. You know, you think of these children [being] abducted." For this parent and many others, the possibility that something horrible could happen was "not at the back of [their] head like, you know, the normal [parent]"; instead, it was at the forefront of their thinking. Wanting to protect their children, these parents tried to keep them close to home.

For some parents, even home seemed dangerous. They worried that something horrible could still happen inside the home or that the child might get sick. One mother feared that someone would enter her house and "kidnap" her children; she was "afraid to sleep" and "afraid to let the kids out of [her] sight." Many parents were afraid to leave their children with sitters, so they seldom went out as a couple. While some repeatedly checked on their children while they slept, others could never check again, fearing a repeat of what they had found before.

Believing that they could no longer trust their own judgements about their children's health, some parents carefully monitored their children's well-being: "I think you watch them in a different way. You watch [for] small things." At the first sign of illness, parents took their children to the doctor or to the hospital:

> I never used to run my kids to the doctor. I used to think, "Why are these women so paranoid all the time?" You know, but yeah, my kids go to the doctor whenever there's any minute thing wrong and that's okay. You know, [the health care system] probably doesn't like me, but I don't really care. Doctors do and the doctors understand.

Although these parents knew that their behavior and their fears made little sense, they could not help themselves. They had to protect their children. The only way to reduce their anxiety was to exaggerate their protectiveness, to "try to make sure that nothing happens because, you know, you don't think you could ever cope again."

Parenting from a distance

Although they had the same fears, a few parents chose a different strategy. Fearing that another child might die, these parents felt "the defenses go up." They reduced their involvement with their children to protect themselves from the pain of another loss. Although they fulfilled their parental duties, they distanced themselves emotionally from their children.

Other parents had no choice about what kind of parents they would be: they were neither physically nor emotionally able to care for their children. They totally fell apart. One mother had to be admitted to the hospital for about 2 weeks, leaving her husband to care for their children. Another could barely function at all. Her husband called several times a day just to make sure she was still functioning.

Leaning on the children

Instead of being the strong adult in the children's lives, some parents became needy and dependent. Those parents who lacked emotional support from other adults were more likely to rely on their older children for support, comfort, and companionship. In the beginning of this devastating nightmare, some parents talked to the children about the baby. They sometimes mistook the children's curiosity or inability to understand what had happened as a desire to stay connected to the baby: "Sometimes she pulls out the [photo album], and we'll look at [the baby's pictures], and she'll often, again and again, say, 'What happened to [the baby]? Where did [the baby] go?'" Instead of seeing her toddler's behavior as a reflection of her need to understand what happened to the baby, this mother assumed that she "enjoys" looking at the pictures. This mother encouraged this activity, partly because her daughter was one of the few people who would willingly sit and look at baby pictures with her.

Some parents also communicated with each other through their children. The children received all the love and attention. The parents gave each other very little:

> Like [our older child was] the key stress reducer in the whole scheme of things. You know, it doesn't matter what's going on in terms of between us. Sometimes things, like in those initial weeks or months, things were very tense, and we could both relate to him, and we could both love him and give him affection and get affection back, which was a very important thing when you're feeling depressed.

In some marriages, as the husband-wife relationship weakened, the parent-child relationship strengthened and intensified. One mother and her child "were always together. We did everything together." Unfortunately, this left little room for the father. They shut him out.

Some children became their parent's constant companion. Children accompanied grieving parents while they drove aimlessly, shopped without any purpose, visited the grave site, and tried to find a place that felt safe. Besides never letting her child out of her sight, one mother started taking him to church every week, something she had never done before. This confused him because he thought God had taken the baby. His mother realized later that this experience "was tough on him. He never liked church."

As long as the parents continued to grieve and to rely on their children for support and understanding, the children had to act like adults. When the parent could not **carry on** and fulfill adult roles, the children could not safely **carry on** as children. The children were not allowed to set aside the loss until the parents did. In these families, the older children's long-term adjustment was negatively affected.

Older children were not the only ones who were affected by the baby's death. Parents played the role with a new baby and sometimes fell apart in that role, too.

Playing the role of parent to a new baby

Wanting another baby

After all the stress and pain of losing a baby to SIDS, why would these parents want to have another baby? Some parents wanted a baby as soon as possible. They did not take time to grieve or to work out what they thought about the loss of their baby to SIDS. They just wanted another baby. Their reasons for wanting a baby reflected their feeling of devastation. Devastated parents wanted a baby: to "get a part of [the baby] back"; to give birth again to the baby they had lost; to satisfy an "overwhelming sensation" and need; to replace the sadness in their life with "joy"; to take away the "guilt and anger" and "all [their] pain"; to restore their confidence as a parent; and to provide "the glue" to hold their marriage together. These parents were so desperate to have another baby that "if [they] could have gone to Safeway and bought a baby, [they] would have." Parents who used any of these reasons to decide whether to have another baby were more likely to attempt to conceive within a few months of the death. They were also more likely to fall apart during the pregnancy.

In contrast, some parents felt ready to have another baby just for its own sake. Others decided that they wanted to add another child to the family. Parents who used either of these reasons were more likely to wait awhile before getting pregnant. They had usually absolved themselves of any responsibility for their baby's death. Some couples had dealt "with the [SIDS] fear thing" and given themselves "lots of time to heal" before deciding to have another baby. Others decided they wanted more children right away and "that whatever would be, would be." They had never seriously held themselves responsible for their baby's death and could see no reason not to try again. They felt ready.

Some couples felt ambivalent and confused about having another baby. A reason that worked for them one day did not work the next. A few men set aside their own desire to wait only because their wives "wanted another child right away because...that was everything to her." These men hid the fact that they were "scared for a long time that something was going to happen" to this baby or maybe even to their wives. Other couples assumed that their desire to have another baby right away meant that they were ready to "go on" with their lives. It was not until months into the pregnancy that they recognized their confusion, ambivalence, and unresolved grief: "And then when you do make the decision and then you've got that 9 month wait and...you wonder, 'Did I do the right thing? Should I be having this baby? I don't really want it. What am I going to do now?'"

Making a "nervy" decision

Some couples experienced "controversy" when they tried to make the decision to have another baby. Husbands and wives did not always share the same need for another child, the same sense of urgency, or the same belief about why their other baby had died. In addition, since each person dealt with grief at a different rate and in a different manner, husbands and wives were not always ready to take on another pregnancy at the same time. Some men were ready far sooner than their wives. One man brought up the subject the day of the funeral. His wife reacted with anger. In most couples, however, women wanted another baby and men held back.

Fortunately, some couples could talk openly and honestly about their needs and how they were feeling. Other couples kept secrets from each other. One woman hid her fears about the next baby from her husband. She did not "think he'd let me have another baby if he knew how scared I was." Fighting about the timing of the next pregnancy increased marital tensions.

The decision to have another baby was, as one mother put it, "nervy." Parents' thoughts about this next pregnancy reflected their explanation for why their baby died and their belief about whether the death could have been prevented. Some gave up any feeling of control. These parents put all their faith in God and hoped everything would work out better this time. They prayed that "God wouldn't do it [to them] twice." Other parents tried to control the situation themselves by planning the timing of the pregnancy. They thought of all the ways they could reduce the risks of the baby catching a cold or getting sick. Others looked for the "magic [combination of factors] that would allow [them] to keep this child."

Finally, some parents just accepted the fact that they were taking a chance. Although they believed that "lighting can strike twice," they also realized that if they wanted more children they would just have to accept the risk. After all, as one father reasoned, the incidence of SIDS is "just 1 in 500 and that was our 1 in 500. And now we'll be one of the 499." One couple had no decision to make; they could not have more children. Eleven couples in this study decided they wanted another baby.

Trying to conceive

However they made the decision, parents set about trying to conceive another baby. They adopted one of three approaches. Some made getting pregnant the focus of their lives, so "every time I got my period, I'd be very upset." With this approach, women were more likely to have trouble conceiving or to believe that they were taking far too long to get pregnant. Some feared they would never conceive. Those who had lost their first baby began to wonder if they were meant to have children at all. Others wondered if they would have to be satisfied with the children they already had. A few women consulted doctors about the length of time it was taking to get pregnant. The doctors told them the problem was "psychological," that they just had to relax and "let it happen."

Rather than responding to the purely emotional and urgent need to have another baby, a few parents took a more calculated approach to planning the next pregnancy:

> Well, I read all the literature and basically I felt that we should have a child born late spring and then that meant, number one, it was past 6 months, from conception to the time of death, and I thought that was a good resting period, and then it reduced the incidence because if you look at some of the stats it seems like a logical time.

Although planners were more likely to wait longer to get pregnant than those who made it the focus of their attention, both approaches reduced sex to a goal-driven procreative act. Instead of spontaneously sharing their bodies for pleasure, comfort, and love, sex had to be planned. There were days they "were supposed to try," and if anything prevented intercourse on the right day and time, marital tensions increased.

Other parents took a more relaxed approach: they "let nature take its course." As a result, these parents could continue to think of sex as one way to offer comfort and to show love and affection for each other. Until they conceived, both husbands and wives **tried to carry on** with other areas of their lives. Their sense of well-being and healing did not depend solely on conception. People with this attitude had less trouble conceiving. Ten women conceived within 2 weeks to 3 years after the baby's death. One couple eventually gave up trying and adopted a toddler.

Some couples had problems early in this pregnancy. Two women miscarried soon after suspecting they were pregnant. Although their loss upset them, they each adopted a fatalistic attitude. They decided that something had been wrong with the fetus or that the timing was wrong for this pregnancy. Neither woman blamed herself, although both still wondered about their role in their other baby's death. Another woman lost three babies before carrying one to term. Although this woman maintained an optimistic outlook throughout each pregnancy, her husband seemed "scared to death," wondering if he could cope with another loss.

Doing the right things

To prevent the possibility of another loss to SIDS, some women changed their behavior during the subsequent pregnancy. Again, the choices these women made reflected their thinking about what might have contributed to their baby's death. Generally, this time some women "did all those things you're supposed to do and never did" in their other pregnancy. They tried to take "better care of [their] health" by "taking vitamins," "watching [their] weight," and "keeping more fit." These choices reflected the women's fear that "something that [they'd] done [or not done] during the pregnancy" had contributed to the baby's death. A few women wondered whether their smoking had affected the baby's health, so they quit. Although smoking was on her list of the "thousand guilts," one mother "still smoked as a kind of a test [and wondered], 'Now, was it my smoking?'" She had another theory about what might have caused her baby's death, and it was something she could not control. Besides changing some of their health habits, some women changed doctors, believing their previous doctor had somehow contributed to the baby's death.

Mothers did everything possible to look after their physical health for the baby's benefit. At the same time, they had to look after their own emotional well-being for the same reason. Women often worried about how their grieving might affect their unborn baby, thinking, "This can't be good for the baby." Despite their emotional pain, however, these women were "not about to take any sort of drugs like Valium or anything to dull the pain." Doctors also cautioned women about the potential dangers of grieving while pregnant. These women struggled to play the role of "good parent" to their unborn baby while trying to look after their own emotional needs.

Making room

Women who became pregnant within months of their baby's death or who were not emotionally ready to welcome this pregnancy had problems. One mother was "horrified" when she found out she was pregnant: "It was not a planned thing." She became "very, very sick" because she "was so stressed." Pretending to be happy about the pregnancy was hard on her. Although she **tried to carry on** in the role of the happy expectant mother, when people tried to congratulate her, "inside [she was] screaming at them, 'Don't congratulate me! This is not good. I am not happy. This is not good news.'" Another woman admitted she was "really anxious about the next baby." She tried to protect others from her nervousness because her friends were having babies at the same time. Both women succeeded in appearing to **carry on**, but inside they **struggled to control** their fear.

Some women had trouble making room for this new baby in their hearts. Many still yearned to hold their deceased baby. Grief preoccupied them; they still wanted an explanation for the baby's death. Then, on top of these concerns, they had to adjust to being pregnant. They tried to ignore their grief, and for the sake of the baby, they "tried to keep [feeling] up." They **tried to carry on** "just by basically not thinking about it and forcing [themselves] to act happy about things that [they] cared about." Sometimes these strategies did not work. Some days it became impossible to ignore either the baby they had lost or the pain they still felt. These mothers fell apart.

In the interviews, the fathers spoke with less openness about their own thoughts and feelings during the next pregnancy. Those who did speak about it admitted that they had also been nervous throughout the pregnancy. They had kept their fears a secret because they did not want to add to their wives' stress. Some men had always kept their feelings a secret; they seldom revealed their fears to their wives. They carried this emotional "burden" alone. Other men shared their fears freely. This helped the men feel closer to their wives.

When it was almost time for the baby to be born, some couples still had to make room in their homes and in their hearts. Those who had not yet put away the baby's room and who still identified the room with the deceased baby had to decide what to do. Pressured by her family to redecorate the nursery, one mother finally gave in during her eighth month of pregnancy: "If they hadn't pushed me to do that, I'd have left it exactly as it was." She could not let her dead baby go.

Welcoming a different baby

And soon it was time for the pregnancy to end and for the next baby to be born. Although a few women had "a heck of a time delivering," most had no problems. They looked forward to playing the role of parent to this new baby. When they held their new baby for the first time, they could not help but make comparisons. They compared this new baby with the baby they lost and with the baby they thought they would deliver. Many parents had some adjustments to make.

First, they had to accept that this baby was obviously not the one they had lost. This baby was unique and "different" in many ways. In most cases, this baby looked very different. Some babies just "felt so much different." Mothers thought this baby was "much healthier" than the baby who had died. The arrival of twins surprised one couple. Several parents also had to adjust to the baby's gender. They "went through a twinge of disappointment" when their prayers had not been answered.

Other parents celebrated: their prayers had been answered. Some had wanted the baby to be the same gender as the one they had lost. One mother who had lost a boy wanted to have another boy because she "thought boys were the cream of the crop to start with." However, most had wanted a different gender because "if she'd been a boy, I wouldn't have bonded to him. I would have thought, 'You're not [my boy], and you're not going to replace

[him].'" Parents also believed that having a baby of a different gender "[would not] bring up quite so many memories." Just giving birth made one mother fall apart. It reminded her of her other baby's birth. Instead of feeling great joy at the birth of her new baby, she felt overwhelmed by grief.

After a brief period of adjustment, most parents could see this baby as a new and unique little person. They began to "love [the baby] for herself [or himself]." That did not take away the "SIDS fear." Most mothers felt safe in the hospital, but the very thought of going home with this new baby frightened some parents. Despite this fear, mothers and fathers **tried to carry on** as "good parents." Although they tried not to let their fear control them, they could not stop monitoring this baby very carefully.

Monitoring against SIDS

Parents watched their baby in two ways: by using an actual mechanical monitor and by becoming a human monitor. They used their own eyes, ears, and presence to ensure the baby's safety. Before the availability of the mechanical monitors, parents had no choice but to be hyper-vigilant. One couple decided against using a monitor. The woman feared a monitor would make her

> even more neurotic. [She] just had visions of it malfunctioning and this baby going off, and there you are doing CPR or something on this kid that doesn't need it. And it would affect the whole family that way, too. Like [her oldest child] was old enough to know that there was some risk involved here, too. But I think it would have brought it really home to the rest of the family if we had [a monitor].

When parents tried to decide whether to use a monitor, they had several factors to consider. If both parents wanted the monitor, they had less trouble making the decision, but that was not always the case. Sometimes one parent wanted the monitor for "peace of mind" and to "sleep at night." Sometimes the other parent did not feel the need or was "kind of iffy on it." In some couples, the needier parent demanded the monitor, no matter how his/her spouse felt. Having given in to her husband's insistence that they get a monitor, one woman "didn't know how [she] was going to handle it and [she] didn't know if [she] could handle…the alarms going off." In other couples, the nonneedy parents recognized their spouse's stress and went along with the decision. Although one mother came to the conclusion that she "could have gone without a monitor," she fought to get one because her husband really wanted one: "He's in this with me, and if he needs it, we'll get it." This recognition of each other's needs helped bring couples closer together.

Besides making this decision based on their own needs, parents also had to consider the impact that the monitor would have on their older children. This caused a conflict for some parents. What the parents needed for their own sanity and what they needed for the new baby had the potential to increase the stress on their other children. Unfortunately, some parents did not realize this until much later:

> [The monitor] is a constant, constant reminder that [SIDS] could happen again and of your past child.... You see, here we are saying it won't happen again but we've got a monitor. You know. And also I think it made [our older child] think that maybe [the baby's] death was preventable. "Now Mommy's got a monitor. We won't lose this one." [So when the monitor went off], it frightened the dickens out of [our older child]. That night when the monitor did go off, I couldn't find him. He was hiding behind a chair in the living room with a book.

Children were not the only ones confused by the monitor's capabilities. Parents' understanding of its purpose varied. Until they learned otherwise, parents who did not know much about the monitor believed it "would save [the] baby." They hoped that this machine would monitor and regulate the baby's breathing. In fact, the monitor could only alert the parents if the baby stopped breathing. Even with this fact in their minds, parents assigned different meanings to the value of having their baby monitored.

Those parents who thought they could protect this baby from dying of SIDS thought of the monitor as their baby's guard or sentry. If the baby stopped breathing, then the monitor would sound the alarm, calling the parents' attention to the problem. Then they could try to save the baby by administering CPR. Men seemed more likely to want a monitor with this purpose in mind, believing that the monitor let both mothers and fathers sleep better at night.

Other parents believed that if this baby was a "SIDS baby," too, then he or she would die eventually, no matter what people did. Consequently, parents with this understanding thought of the monitor as their warning device, one that would alert them to their baby's impending death: "[The monitor] won't save our baby. This isn't so that it will save our baby. This'll let us know our baby is dying." Once warned, parents planned to make every effort to save their baby. This way they could reassure themselves that they had done everything possible for the baby. They did not want a repeat of their last experience: "I guess it's always in the back of your mind, 'Maybe we could have done something.' But we know now that we couldn't have.... I guess it's for your own peace of mind that we wanted a monitor."

Once they brought the monitor home, parents and children had to learn to "live with it." If they wanted to maintain their sanity, the family had to understand the reason behind each alarm. Initially, some parents "would go through [the alarm going off] six to seven times a day." While some parents felt it "saved" their sanity, others initially felt stressed by its presence. Over time, they learned how to deal with the alarm:

> I would be talking on the phone and the monitor would go off with [the baby] and I just, the phone would drop and I would be gone. And that was just the first beep, and it got to the point, we got to learn that it would beep, beep just because of his heart beat slowing. And so we would count the beeps, the alarms. And we'd go one, two, three, and on four, we'd start standing up, five, there, he'd go back on.

> One night [the alarm] went off, and it was real, and it was the only time it had gone off where it hadn't stopped by the time I got in her room, and she wasn't breathing. And her lips were a little funny colored. Uhm, but see, when you get the monitor, you also learn CPR.... I think everybody should know it anyway. It was amazing I knew what to do. [The baby was hospitalized] for 5 days just to monitor her plus they wanted to do EKGs. They did everything.... But she never set the alarm off once. She was the healthiest baby at the hospital.

In addition to learning to cope with all the false and genuine alarms, parents eventually had to decide when to stop using it. Taking the baby off the monitor scared some parents. They were "afraid to turn it off" for fear that "something [might] happen." Some parents stopped using the monitor a few months after this baby passed the age at which the previous baby had died. Others waited until the baby reached a year of age or until the baby grew old enough to play with the wires. Still others monitored their baby only during colds because they considered this baby to be "healthier."

Whether monitors were used or not, for the first year of the baby's life parents were "really cautious." They seldom left the house together. They watched over their baby all the time, continually checking the baby's breathing. In some homes, the baby "couldn't breathe without one of [the parents] being there with a hand on [its] back to make sure [she or he] was breathing." While some parents checked their baby frequently, others relied on their spouse to do the checking because this act still terrified them. Some regularly woke their baby to be sure he or she was still alive; others did this to prevent the baby from "go[ing] into a real deep sleep." One mother had the baby sleep with her. Others had the baby's bed right beside their own; they slept with one hand under the baby's body. Having been awakened to the fact that horrible things can and do happen to good people and their children, these parents just could not set aside their fears: "As frightening as it is, in the back of your mind, you know that it could happen. You think about it way more than any other parent that's never had it happen to them."

Counting the months

Within a few months, many parents felt exhausted. Some were on constant guard against the "SIDS fear." Some were still grieving: "We were still scared, and we lost a lot of sleep...because we were always crying, [feeling] angry, and [having] bad dreams." Looking forward to the day when this baby would reach some magic age, many parents "count[ed] the months." They could not wait until their baby passed a certain "milestone," either the age at which the first baby had died of SIDS or this baby's first birthday. Once the baby reached the magic age, most parents began to relax. They started to believe that this child just might survive. One mother stopped checking her son when he "fell down the stairs in his walker and when he didn't die, that was it. We didn't check him anymore!"

As the children grew older, parents could not help but be "overprotective," much like they had been with their older children. Most mothers and fathers justified their actions. Unlike parents who had never lost a child, these parents knew how precious the life of a child was. They knew the pain that could come if this life were taken away, too. Reasoning that they were not really "spoiling" their children, these parents told themselves they were just appreciating them more. Their children became a more central part of their lives. Some previously uninvolved fathers spent more time caring for this baby. They did not want to make the same mistake twice. Every time they thought about that possibility, they fell apart.

Falling apart as a parent to a new baby

Fearing pregnancy

Some parents began falling apart when they tried to get pregnant. Just the thought of having another baby so soon was upsetting to some. They were so full of grief and love for their deceased baby that they had no room for a new baby. On top of all that, there was the "SIDS fear." Despite her desire to have another child, one woman could not get pregnant. When she tried to understand why, she decided that she had been "too scared to have a baby, [fearing] that the same thing would happen again." To get around this problem, this couple adopted a toddler.

Other parents fell apart once doctors confirmed the pregnancy. Although they did their best to pretend everything was all right, some parents were in turmoil. Some men feared that this baby would die, too. Women tried to want this baby, but it took time to feel like playing the role of parent to a new life. Being pregnant made one woman feel like she was "cheating" on her deceased baby. She did not want this new baby; she just wanted her other baby back. Another woman "thought about [the baby she had lost] every single day right up until [the new baby] was born." She just kept hoping that her deceased baby would come back to her through this pregnancy. She had not yet begun to parent the new baby.

Fearing death

One mother spent most of her pregnancy worrying about how she was ever going to manage to control her fears once the new baby was born. She tried to plan practical solutions that would allow her to spend the maximum amount of time with the baby while minimizing any health risks. Despite all her plans, she panicked whenever she thought about the many months of stress that lay ahead. Because her husband could not tolerate hearing her talk about her worries, she felt totally alone. She had no one to turn to for help or comfort:

> Who can help you through those nights when you might be really nervous or whatever? There's just nobody.... The doctors aren't going to be able to handle your anxieties, and they're not going to have the time to deal with your worries, and they may care a lot, but you can't wake them up and tell them you're scared or you're worried. You can't phone the hospital every time you're worried. They're dealing with their work and their emergencies and the rest of it at night, and they don't have time to listen to you at night either, so I don't know. I guess I just have to learn to regain my confidence.

Sometimes the birth of the baby caused parents to fall apart. One mother "just cried and cried." She visited the ward in which she had delivered her other baby and that made her cry even more. She fell apart physically as well. She could not sleep; she "had fainting spells." When all the tests revealed no medical cause for her problems, she decided it was "just stress." She realized the source of her stress was fear: "I don't want to be taking this little baby home because what am I going to do if [this baby] dies?"

Having no faith

Fearing that this baby might die, too, most parents became very cautious. All the steps parents took to ensure the safety of their older children were also used with the younger ones. A certain amount of cautiousness was to be expected. Parents were reasonable about this most of the time. They **carried on** despite their fear. Sometimes the fear took over. Parents became irrational, and they fell apart. When that happened, parents could not always act in the best interests of their children. Instead, the parents tried to do things to make themselves feel better.

Even if their baby was on the mechanical monitor, some parents got up "five or six times a night to check." They could not even trust the monitor to protect their baby. One mother wondered whether she even trusted God. Because normally she had faith in God, she would "feel real bad when [she would] go in 500 times to check [the baby] and say, 'Sorry Lord. I don't seem to have a whole lot of faith here.'" One mother could not bring herself to stop using the monitoring device until her child reached the age of 2. Although this mother acknowledged that this was "too long," she could not control her fears. She lived in terror that something would take this baby, too. Even after the monitor came off, this mother watched over her child. Her practical self knew that this behavior made no sense, but her emotional self would not let her relax. Years later, she continued to be vigilant despite the protests of her husband and family. She never did regain her balance as a parent.

A few other parents felt the same way. They felt a surge of fear whenever they could not see their children, even children who were old enough to be attending school:

> I want to know where she is at all times....It's like if I don't know where she is and a half an hour's gone by, like I'm out there looking for her or I'm phoning around the neighbor's.

> I live in fear that something is going to happen to [my daughter]. Either she's going to die, get sick and die, or somebody is going to kidnap her or that she is going to become a teenager and run away from home. Something like that where she is going to leave me. I live in fear of that. That is my number one fear.

Instead of being overinvolved in their children's lives, a few parents, particularly fathers, withdrew. Some feared the loss of this child, too, so they protected themselves by holding back. Others could not connect to the next child. It was as if their hearts had frozen. Although they **tried to carry on** with their usual parental obligations, inside they felt distant. These children seemed to sense the distance; problems developed between distant parents and their children.

Conclusion: Struggling to carry on as a parent

Some parents could not understand why they kept falling apart and why they were having so much trouble with their children. They felt torn between their live children and their dead baby, between their own need to grieve and their family's needs, between their children and their spouse. With limited energy, parents found it difficult to meet everyone's needs and to play so many roles at once. The parents had no choice; they had many obligations.

Struggling to carry on as a marriage partner

Playing the role of marriage partner

Getting programmed

When these parents were children themselves, they learned what it meant to be either male or female in our society. Besides observing how their own parents treated them and each other, they noticed how society treated males and females and how the media portrayed men and women, husbands and wives.

Men learned how to be men from their own fathers. Many of their own fathers had been emotionally inexpressive and stoic. Toughness and emotional strength were "drilled into [the men's] heads all [their] lives." One man remembered the messages he received when he was still a little boy:

> You fall down...you're not supposed to cry. You're a man. You skin your knees, or, you know, you hurt yourself doing this, you know, get out and do it again, you know. You're not, uh, you get tough. You're supposed to be able to take that.

Cowboy movies, sports heroes, playing sports, and societal expectations further reinforced lessons from home. Little boys noticed that when cowboys "got shot in the arm or the leg, they didn't cry....They just, you know, kept on going, and I think that...was the man's role when he was growing up. You didn't show any emotion."

These ingrained messages helped to create the men's belief that "men are emotionally tougher than women." Refusing to believe they had been "nurtured to be like this," some men believed there was just

> a natural tendency among men to be more competitive. And if you're competitive, I think you have a tendency of keeping things in because, you know, like being competitive and opening yourself up like a book doesn't really make any sense. Just, it is counterproductive.

Everywhere most men looked they got messages that it was natural and right for them to "be strong" and to "keep [emotions] in." Those who were more expressive had to try to fit in with societal expectations of strength and silence. Men brought all these expectations and experiences into their marriages.

Women also absorbed some of society's messages. Some women grew up in homes where there was alcoholism or "where [their] parents argued a lot." To "survive," a few of these women learned to "shut down all feelings." They also learned that they should not expect other people to meet their emotional needs. A few women received the opposite message: people will look after you when you fall apart. Others learned to pay attention to feelings and to talk about their problems, sometimes even before they developed. A few women came from families that encouraged them to be emotionally independent. These women learned to be inner directed and to rely on their own strength in times of stress.

No matter how these women were raised, most grew up expecting to get married and to have children because that "was kind of the thing to do." They had learned to value intimate relationships and to be aware of their own and others' feelings. Most women expected others to value their ability to be nurturing in a relationship.

Reacting to the programming

When quiet men who believed they should "be strong" married women who expected themselves to be nurturing and aware of everyone's feelings, the expectations seemed to complement each other. When their baby died, many husbands and wives had problems with the way these expectations affected their relationship and their ability to deal with their grief. Sometimes one parent's needs conflicted with the other parent's needs.

Often role expectations conflicted with the need to grieve at all. Because that was all they knew how to do, husbands and wives **tried to carry on** by playing the roles they had learned during childhood.

In the beginning of the "nightmare," grief temporarily overwhelmed the parents, making it difficult for them to pay attention to each other's needs. Most "broke down" and fell apart. Some husbands allowed their emotions to show for as long as a month; others began to control the expression of their grief within hours of the baby's death. One man shifted from falling apart in front of his wife and "leaning on" her all the time to becoming "a completely different person all over again [at the funeral]. Because there were people all around and Mr. Macho had to be Mr. Macho." Husbands in general had a hard time ignoring the deeply ingrained messages about "being strong": they returned to playing the role of "Mr. Macho" or "the rock" quite quickly. Even when they were not feeling strong, these men decided they had "better play [at being strong]" for the sake of the family. No matter how they felt inside, they tried to offer strength to their wives, and they adopted a take-charge attitude in situations in which decisions had to be made.

Most men could not play the role of "Mr. Macho" and show their feelings simultaneously. Their "programming" was too strong. To these men, any display of vulnerability made them uncomfortable. They were not used to falling apart, so they had to guard against it. Playing the role of "rock" in this devastating situation deprived some men of the opportunity to fully experience their grief and to receive as much support as they needed from anyone, especially their wife.

Having to deal with the death of their baby also devastated the wives. Few women could set aside their own anguish to play the role of nurturing wife right away. Most wives wanted to "lean on" their husbands; they wanted to be taken care of totally. They offered little to their husbands, except their dependence and their tears. This reinforced the men's perceptions that they had no choice but to be strong in this situation. A few women became the "strong one" in the relationship because their husbands repeatedly fell apart; these women soon began to resent this position. They wanted someone to "lean on" themselves.

In general, playing the roles of husband and wife to the extreme became difficult after the baby died. If husbands were too strong and too silent, then they blocked out their own pain and usually that of their wives. If husbands paid attention to their own pain, then they fell apart and felt they could not offer strength to their wives. If wives were too concerned with their feelings and those of others, then they became overwhelmed with the pain. If wives blocked out their own pain to look after others, then they deprived their husbands of their role. This experience shook up old expectations and sometimes magnified preexisting marital problems. It took couples some time to learn how to handle their grief within their relationship. Until they found a strategy that worked effectively, they repeatedly fell apart.

Falling apart as a marital partner

Looking out for themselves

In the first few hours after the baby was pronounced dead, many husbands and wives were so devastated they could barely function. Some seemed barely conscious of each other. When describing various incidents, they would say things such as, "Yeah, I guess my [spouse] was there." Most were in a fog. They were "just looking out for [themselves]." And some could barely even do that.

Being broken

A few husbands were so full of their own grief that they could not be "Mr. Macho." They lost total control of their emotions, particularly their sadness, and their sense of power. Feeling overwhelmed with their grief, some men cried inconsolably for the first time in their adult lives. Although frightened at first by their husbands' emotional display, some wives welcomed this sharing and felt closer to their husbands than ever before. Although the women wanted this degree of emotional honesty to continue, if their husband came across as "broken"and needy rather than open with his feelings, then women felt angry and abandoned. They could not "lean on" husbands who wanted to "lean on" them. This was not what they had learned to expect.

Other women fell apart totally. They depended on their husbands for support. At first, most husbands tolerated this excessive neediness. Because of their upbringing, they expected women to be "more emotional" in this kind of situation. In addition, being needed for their strength made the husbands feel useful, strong, and powerful again. Some men eventually grew tired of being strong all the time. They began to worry that their wives' increased dependency would never end. They wondered if their wives would ever learn to control their emotions again.

Closing off

In contrast, some men went to the other extreme: they became so strong that they became "cold," first to their own feelings and then to those of their spouse. These men prevented their wives from talking about grief at all.

Some became emotionally absent; others left when they felt upset. In either case, the women were left wondering whether their husbands really cared at all. It felt like the relationship itself was falling apart under the strain.

A few husbands also worried about the future of the relationship and whether their wives really cared anymore. Instead of providing their husbands with love and support, some women feared they "would be crazy with grief over feeling somebody else's pain all the time." To protect themselves, they "close[d] off" emotionally to their husbands. They had to protect themselves from too much emotion, even their husbands' emotion.

Fearing the future

Although some men accepted their wives' sadness as "natural," the men found anger harder to accept. Most had never seen this side of their wife. A few did not like what they saw. One man became "scared" of his wife's emotional outbursts and her moodiness. He wondered about the future of their marriage. It felt like the whole relationship was beginning to fall apart.

Conclusion: Struggling to carry on as a marriage partner

Both husbands and wives "yo yo[ed]" between playing the role and falling apart. To regain some sense of control and order or to find a reason to go on at all, some parents tried other roles. Although eventually they learned how to manage their grief within their marriage, for awhile, most husbands and wives turned their energies elsewhere. Women with other children got more involved in parenting. Those who had lost their only child returned to work or to volunteer activities in their community. Men usually devoted themselves to their jobs, but most also tried some community involvement as well.

Struggling to carry on in other roles

Playing other roles

Parents who lost babies to SIDS were more than just parents. They were also volunteers, students, and friends and members of families, communities, churches, and teams. At first, some parents increased their commitment to playing roles outside the family and work environment to help them manage. Only one parent withdrew from all "incumbering things" like social commitments for a year. She decided to focus all her energy on grieving.

Keeping busy

Keeping busy outside the family helped most parents deal with their grief by providing an "escape" from the pain, a new purpose, and a way to deal with the stress and guilt. It also put them into contact with other people. To escape and to relieve the stress of their grief, parents took classes and participated in team and individual sports. In search of a purpose and in the hope that it would make them feel better, others became volunteers for the "SIDS bandwagon." They committed their time and energy to raising money to find the cause of SIDS, or they became involved in the support group. One woman tried to deal with her guilt by going to church "everyday for a long time"; another woman sang in the church choir. Visiting other bereaved parents kept one mother busy "for hours, crying and them crying with me." Another woman briefly volunteered on a hospital ward for seriously ill children. She thought being with children would make her feel better; it did not help.

Sometimes keeping busy made parents feel better, but the relief was usually temporary. Eventually, parents began to fall apart again. They realized that keeping busy would not make their grief go away.

Falling apart in other roles

Sinking in the sea of grief

No activity or distraction could remove the pain of losing their baby. Realizing this made parents fall apart again. A poignant example comes from a woman who tried to raise money to fund SIDS research. After hours and hours of "crazed" work, and with thousands of dollars in her hands, she began falling apart:

> Then it just hit me, and it was like this money was burning me. You know that, "What is this? This is nothing! This is going to do nothing! This hasn't brought [my baby] back!"...I remember feeling like that was blood money.

Another could not function as a member of the church choir because the choir kept singing a song from her baby's funeral. She "wouldn't show up for a couple of weeks, or [she] would walk out" of the practice. Soon the choir director asked her to resign. Many parents could not function in any role outside their family. They just struggled to survive in their "sea of grief." Two women had no choice but to participate in the role of daughter.

One lost her father suddenly within months of her son's death; the other had to deal with her father's serious illness and possible death. This overwhelmed both of them.

Conclusion: Struggle to carry on roles

Parents had problems when the roles they played interfered with each other. The worker role sometimes conflicted with parental or spousal roles. To function effectively at work, many parents had to "shut down" their grief completely. Workers then found it difficult to open up and express their grief at home. Some parents became so overinvolved with their children (alive and deceased) that they shut out their spouses; others could not function at work.

As well, the general inability to function effectively in any given role made some parents feel like they were "going crazy." This feeling seemed strongest about 6 months after the baby's death. Women seemed to have the most trouble with it:

> I was going out of my mind....I just felt like I was crawling the [walls]. It was just, it was just always with me. The room was there, you know. I felt claustrophobic. You know, one minute I, I couldn't stand the house and had to get out, and the next I wanted to be back home. Like I was just at a loss. I didn't know what I wanted. I was crying all the time. I was depressed, you know. I just, I felt like I was going crazy. I felt like I was going out of my mind.

Although parents found it difficult to keep playing the roles, this activity did serve an important function in their healing. Playing the roles

- fulfilled obligations to others;
- helped to suspend their pain;
- provided a reason to go on; and
- connected the parents to others.

Few parents could just **carry on** in their roles as if nothing had happened. Most fell apart occasionally, some more often than others. Although falling apart was a frustrating and frightening experience, it also served a purpose. It forced parents to confront their loss and to remember that they were more than mere role players in relationships and in society. They were people with "inside" pain and personal needs, too. In other words, falling apart made the parents realize they were "all human." They had to accept their pain and learn to deal with it. First, they had to let themselves feel the grief. They had to let it overwhelm them.

Falling Apart While Feeling Overwhelmed

When parents fell apart it was because their grief overwhelmed them. Feelings of anger, sadness, and fear and thoughts of guilt and powerlessness took control.

Overwhelmed by anger

Although some parents were unaware of feeling angry at first, most eventually began to feel their anger. The anger had many sources, and parents expressed it in a variety of ways. Some parents tried to hide the reason for their anger. A few mothers resented their own babies for dying, asking, "Why did you have to die on me?" Parents who blamed themselves for their baby's death went through a period of intense "self-loathing"; they found it hard to tell others why they felt so angry. Many parents secretly felt angry with God. If they talked about this anger at all, it was with other SIDS parents and a few understanding ministers. Parents who believed God took their baby were furious and confused. The fact that God had neither prevented the death nor protected their baby from harm also angered parents. A few parents also tried to conceal their anger at their spouse. They wondered whether they should blame their spouse for the baby's death. They also felt angry if their spouse had not responded to their need for comfort.

The source of another kind of anger was a secret even to those who experienced it. A vague kind of anger settled over some parents and became their constant companion. For a time, these parents just seethed, but they could seldom explain why, even to themselves. Most felt they had been "robbed" or that their baby's death was unfair. They felt like the victim of a crime, but they could not identify the perpetrator: "You hold a lot of anger because, of course, you don't know where to put this anger.... You're angry, but you don't know what to be angry at or who to be angry at." Sometimes, in an attempt to release this feeling of rage, the parents targeted more obvious sources. This usually meant their anger was out of proportion, misdirected, or destructive.

Some parents got mad at SIDS. They threw themselves headlong onto the "SIDS bandwagon," doing everything they could to raise money to help find the cause and everything they could to educate those who were "ignorant" about the syndrome. They got mad at parents who ignored or abused their children. Other parents who did not appreciate their healthy children also became a target for anger. Because some parents assumed a doctor had let them down or contributed to the baby's death, specific doctors or doctors in general became "convenient" targets for anger. Family, friends, or coworkers who had been insensitive or who had ignored their needs irritated the parents, too.

Some couples reserved the real fury for each other. While a few couples experienced occasional angry outbursts that cleared the air and identified problem areas, others lived in stony silence or in a war zone. The sheer fury these parents felt often frightened them. They feared the loss of their marriage. Some worried that they would lose control and hurt someone. Others wondered if they would ever have any "peace of mind" again.

Overwhelmed by fear

Like anger, parents kept some of their fears to themselves. When fear overwhelmed them, their behavior often gave away their secret. Several parents feared sleep: their own and that of others. They were afraid something else would happen if they let down their guard. They worried when others slept, fearing that other loved ones would also die suddenly and mysteriously. Staying home alone frightened a few parents. While some fully expected their home to be invaded by murderous strangers who would destroy their whole family, others sensed an "evil" presence in the house. The baby's room made one mother feel "panicky" every time she went past it. While some were afraid to leave their homes because the world outside seemed unsafe and threatening, others could not stand to stay home. Several parents vacillated back and forth: "If you were away, you couldn't wait to get home. You'd get home, and like half an hour after you were there, you'd just be stalking, you know, like a caged animal, like you had to get out."

Those who had other children worried about them incessantly. Thinking about having another baby was also scary. Those parents who had another baby worried constantly. Some mothers and fathers became anxious if they were even in the presence of other people's babies. This anxiety increased in intensity if the parent had to assume responsibility for another's child. Many did everything they could to avoid taking on such a job.

In addition, parents felt inexplicably vulnerable. Their "safety net was gone." Some felt abandoned by their God; others felt targeted by unknown forces or fate. The whole world felt unsafe. Nothing seemed to make sense anymore. It could all be summed up with this one sentence: "If this can happen, anything can happen."

Overwhelmed by sadness

Besides feeling angry and afraid, parents also experienced a sense of emptiness and anguished sadness. Parents did not need anyone to explain the source of this feeling: they missed everything about their baby. They cried for hours and went for long drives and long walks. They prayed, visited the baby's grave, and cried some more. One woman sat in her living room filled with flowers and sympathy cards and looked out her window:

> I'd look out that window, and it would rain and rain, and it would rain and rain, and it would rain, and I just felt like even the Lord was crying, you know. And it just, it was just, oh so depressing.

The feeling of sadness made the parents feel numb. It deadened any positive feelings they had and made it difficult to think clearly.

Overwhelmed by guilt

Besides feeling overwhelmed by troubling emotions, the parents were also overwhelmed with troubling thoughts of guilt and powerlessness. At first, most parents felt overwhelmingly guilty. They believed that they had failed as "good parents" because their baby was dead. Parents also experienced guilt just because, as one mother said, "Guilt and grief go together." Sometimes parents felt guilty about the way they handled their grief: for example, if they took "less time to come to terms with [their grief]" than their spouse, then they felt guilty. If they seemed to feel their grief less intensely than others, then they also felt guilty. If they hurt others with their grief, then they felt bad about it later.

Not thinking about the baby also caused parents to feel guilty. One father suffered intense guilt when he thought he had forgotten to acknowledge the anniversary of his son's death. Being pregnant again caused some mothers to feel guilty. Even laughter stimulated guilt feelings at first:

> The first time you laugh at something after you've lost your baby you feel horrible that you have just done the most sinful thing. Like how could you sit there and laugh at something when you're mourning your baby? There's all this guilt in every direction.

Overwhelmed by powerlessness

While guilty thoughts haunted many mothers, thoughts of powerlessness troubled fathers. The baby's death made fathers feel like they could not protect their family from harm. It also took away their sense of control. If given the choice, "as a parent, if it was put in front of you, you have to do this to keep your [child] alive, I mean, I'd do anything." The problem for this father and others like him was that "no one asked [them] if [they] wanted this baby dead." These parents believed they had to accept "the luck of the draw" or God's will. Some described themselves as "fatalistic," fully believing that "there's nothing you can do."

When all the painful thoughts and feelings overwhelmed the parents, they felt even more powerless. They could hardly even help themselves. Shifting their focus to thoughts of potency and power in the future, some parents wanted another baby right away. Then they had to confront the "SIDS fear," the fear that "it could happen again."

Conclusion: Feeling overwhelmed

It seemed as if all these painful thoughts and feelings would never go away. Parents began to wonder if they would ever enjoy life again. When they fell apart, grief overwhelmed them. Some days they just could not function. When parents had the strength to regain control, they tried to pretend everything was "fine." They soon grew tired of feeling one way on the "inside" and showing something else on the outside. They began to realize that they had to learn to manage their grief instead of letting it control them.

Feeling Overwhelmed While Managing Grief

Although most parents had some exposure to a previous loss, nothing in life had prepared them for the death of their baby. It was "like a bad dream." They felt lost, with "no mile posts...out in no man's land." They had no compass, no map, and no idea of their destination. They just wanted the journey to end. The journey would not end until the parents learned how to manage their grief. They needed to find a strategy that would help them cope with the devastating thoughts and feelings that this nightmare had unleashed.

Learning about loss

Parents turned to what they knew. Most had some previous experience with death before their baby died. These experiences led to certain assumptions.

The most common death was the death of grandparents. This type of death had usually occurred while the parents had been children themselves and, as one woman said, "Before [they] knew death." The deaths of their grandparents and people's reactions to the death taught the parents to assume that people should die in the "right order." Older people were "supposed to predecease you."

Before reaching adulthood themselves, a few parents experienced the deaths of other family members, notably a parent or a sibling. Although losing these people caused grief, death had usually been anticipated: "Cancer is a killer, and it wasn't a nice thing to have happen, but you sort of expect that will be the end result." This kind of death led parents to believe that some deaths made sense.

Some parents had also lost friends, and a few women had suffered a miscarriage. Other losses, although not death related, included divorce, moving great distances, and chronic family disruptions. These losses taught parents what to expect of themselves and others in a crisis. Parents forgot all these expectations until their baby died.

Learning about grief

Although parents did not believe that their previous experiences with loss had prepared them for the death of their baby, these losses had exposed them to family and ethnic traditions. One father saw more than his share of deaths before reaching adulthood. By watching how his own father stoically and silently handled each death in the family, this father learned to bury his thoughts and feelings with the body: "Whenever there was a death in the family, we used to go to the funeral or through the funeral really and then come home and pack everything up and psst! That was it. No discussions or anything. It was all inside."

While some families modeled the "stoic way to handle death and that is to carry on" and "shut down all feelings," others "talk[ed] more about it" and acknowledged their grief. Having been exposed to these significant role models, some newly bereaved parents just copied the strategies used by their own parents.

The parents' personal history also affected how they dealt with their emotions. As previously discussed, most parents responded to what they learned about being a male or female in this society. Most men subscribed to the belief that they should "be strong" and "in control" of their emotions during difficult situations. They tried to "contain" their emotions, especially those that suggested vulnerability. Because most men grew up in the presence of predominantly silent or emotionally absent fathers, few developed a broad emotional vocabulary. Although they became familiar with the powerful feeling of anger, they usually dealt with it physically, through fighting, exercising self-control, or channeling it through sports. Few men learned what to do with their sadness. Instead of "sit[ting] there and sob[bing] with your friends," most men believed in "fix[ing]" problems with logic and action. Only a few who learned about emotions from their mothers felt comfortable talking about them; they never developed the traditional male "poker face." For most men, friendships usually involved sharing activities, not feelings:

> [Men] can have tragedies happen around them and they are very kind of stern faced and they just don't ever let you know what is happening with them. You never know about nothing, like they just won a million dollars, or, you know, they just lost a parent.

Most men reserved the expression of their vulnerable feelings for the women in their lives. Even then, some could not share their inner selves. Early life experiences had taught them to "shut down their feelings." They "went through the motions" in relationships. Some jobs contributed to the suppression of feelings. These jobs forced men to be "competitive" and closed instead of being cooperative and open.

In contrast, most but not all of the women were used to expressing their thoughts and feelings. Most women wanted to talk about a problem until they felt it was resolved. Although most women were used to dealing with their sadness, some did not know what to do with their anger; they were used to turning it inward or hiding it. They based relationships with friends on sharing experiences through conversation, not just activities. Although all this talk about feelings and experiences usually gave women an extensive emotional vocabulary, many relied on this method of problem solving almost exclusively. Few women learned other strategies to relieve their stress.

The parents' temperament also influenced the way they handled stressful situations. While some parents were naturally very public or open about their thoughts and feelings, others were private or closed off. Parents also differed in their ability and willingness to acknowledge the existence of emotional issues in their lives. Some tried to head off the development of problems, while others ignored them.

Trying to manage grief alone

Parents needed to learn how to deal with their grief, that is, they needed to manage it instead of letting it overwhelm them. Parents had two basic tools available: their ability to feel and their ability to think. Some used both tools; some used neither. Others preferred to use one tool more than the other. When these two types of tools are combined, they produce four approaches to managing grief. I call them mourning strategies (see Figure 2).

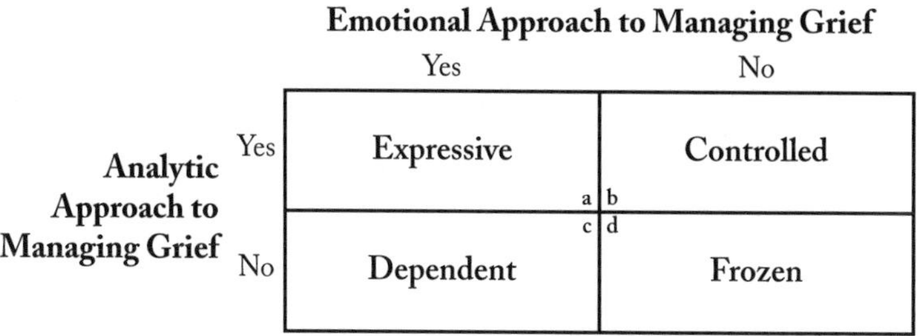

Figure 2 Typology of four mourning strategies based on emotional and cognitive approaches to managing grief

Mourning strategies

It took awhile for parents to find the strategy that worked for them. Some parents had trouble with other people telling them to use a different strategy. Over time and through trial and error, parents eventually discovered the strategy that suited them best.

Frozen mourning strategy

In the beginning of this devastating nightmare, many parents used the *frozen mourning strategy* (cell d), but not by choice. At first, they could not accept that their baby was dead. They felt so devastated that they could neither think nor feel. They were "numb": "I couldn't [cry]. I was frozen. I was in shock, more than in shock, I was frozen." Detached from their thoughts and feelings, they were almost unaware of their surroundings, their own pain, or the pain of anyone else: "And your body is working, but your mind really has been cut right off."

When adopted as a temporary measure to shut out the unbearable reality of the baby's death, this strategy served a useful purpose. It protected parents from emotional, intellectual, and spiritual overload; it allowed them to **carry on** until they had the strength to face what had happened. Staying *frozen* allowed the reality of the death to seep into their consciousness gradually. Eventually, the numbness subsided. Parents began feeling and thinking again.

Then, to cope with their painful thoughts and emotions, most shifted to other more active strategies.

Not all parents could thaw. Those who had experienced many losses in their childhood remained frozen. One mother froze her thoughts and feelings so she could **carry on**. Everyone needed her to be strong; they leaned on her for support. When she tried to express her pain and get others to look after her, they told her to "be strong." She did what she learned to do as a child. She "shut down," had "no feelings anymore," and "went into robot state": "[She had] to go to work; [she had] to be a mother." She did not begin to think and feel until 2 weeks had gone by and she had been hospitalized for a "nervous breakdown."

Another parent stayed *frozen*, too, but not because of a conscious choice. He had never been comfortable with emotions. Because he had experienced so many deaths as a child, he learned to "go through the motions" in life. The death of his son was no different than any of the other tragedies he had already survived:

> I was cold. Really, you know. He was here, he was our son, and he's gone, you know. And I didn't even think where he went, I, you know. It made no difference. He was just, he was just gone. Hmm, by me being that cold, I didn't talk about it. I wouldn't talk about it to anybody or, you know. It was just, well, he died and that was it.

Although the temporary adoption of this strategy protected the parents' sanity at first, adopting it permanently led to negative consequences. It affected the parents' health and their relationships.

Dependent mourning strategy

Within hours of the baby's death, several parents shifted from feeling frozen to feeling everything. All the painful emotions associated with grief overwhelmed them. In response to feeling overwhelmed, some adopted a *dependent mourning strategy* (cell c). They looked outside of themselves for strength and support. This kind of strategy initially triggered a comforting response from others. Some normally self-reliant and private spouses began to show their grief to others. Previously independent parents "wouldn't go anywhere by [themselves]." One wife describes the behavior of her normally strong and silent husband:

> I felt like he was depending on me....I couldn't leave him. He wouldn't lay down, he couldn't go and lay down unless I was lying beside him. He

> wouldn't eat unless I was eating. He wouldn't go anywhere unless I was there....I always thought he was leaning on me.

The pain of their loss overwhelmed the parents and made it impossible for them to think clearly. Every time they tried to think, their feelings clouded their judgement and they fell apart. They needed help with even the smallest decision. People usually responded to their pain by doing things for them. But with time, most parents gradually found a more self-reliant strategy to get them through this experience.

A few could not stop being *dependent*. They had always reacted to problems by letting their emotions overwhelm them. They always relied on others to make them feel better. When faced with any crisis in their life, they found it difficult to identify and take charge of the problem; instead, they let the feelings and the problem engulf them. If they started to cry, for example, they usually could not stop themselves without help from others. They routinely lost control.

Instead of trying to do something active about their pain, some parents just "waited for the pain to go away." Their baby's death made them feel helpless. Others tried to find a way not to deal with the pain, but to dull it. They "leaned on" their faith, other people, prescription medications, alcohol, and food. Even though this strategy did not make them feel better in the long-term, they did not know any other way to handle this problem. Raised in families in which emotional problems were neither discussed nor addressed, these parents did not know how to handle strong feelings. Consequently, they just wanted the pain to stop.

Controlled mourning strategy

Most of the parents had learned other strategies to help them deal with problems. After several days or weeks had passed, they went back to these strategies. Some parents were "control specialists." They used "mind control" to deal with their grief. Although men were more likely to adopt the *controlled mourning strategy* (cell b), a few women used this strategy as well. These parents took charge of their pain by actively working it through in their minds. Using "reasoning" and trying to think things through "logically," they examined all the "factors." One man described how he "process[ed]" the fear that he had contributed to his baby's death:

> I develop[ed] a concrete sequence of saying, "Okay, this is the thought process. This is how it works. This is really what is going on here. My emotions aren't telling me that at all, but I've got to make myself

> believe that." And you do that a couple of times and you don't believe it and you go, "Hey, this is logical." You go through logic, and then you've done the logical thing a number of times, and you're working it through, and then eventually you get to the point where you almost believe the logic, and eventually you do believe the logic, but then emotion takes over every once in awhile, and the more you reinforce the logic and it's the logical thinking that pulls you out of it, saying, and it's a big process. You have to think about all the different angles.

Another described how playing sports had taught him emotional self-control:

> [The grief] just basically stops right there [in my head], you know. It just sits there and it's like a temper, I guess. You know, it builds up and builds up, and then you've got to just take a deep breath and just, you know, think about it for a little bit, 30 seconds or whatever and calm down and deal with it.... You just simply take [the pain], you have to think about it, understand the logic behind it, you gotta, you know, back off and, you know, take a few deep breaths and calm down, you know, and deal with it. And I think that's basically the same way that I deal with most things, too.

Those who used "mind control" techniques usually did not like to talk about or show their pain. When they did talk about their experience, they used words and phrases like: "**making sense of it**," "looking for the logic," and "control it." To cope with their pain, these parents used the strategies they had learned from their parents, their sports heroes, and the cowboy movies. They seemed to believe that if they could block the thought, then they could block the feeling. By distracting themselves with work or having another baby, they made sure they were "so busy [they did not] have a great deal of time to think." Instead of expressing their grief with other people, some welcomed the challenge and "pain of exercise to cleanse" themselves. These activities were often solitary. While some preferred to be by themselves so they could think and work out their "reasoning," others wanted to be with people. They needed the presence of others to divert their attention away from the pain. When in the presence of highly emotional people though, these parents had to develop "barriers" to keep their own and other people's emotions "under control."

Although the adoption of this mourning strategy met the needs of most parents who used it, it caused some problems. After the first few months, some parents became so adept at "mind control" that they could almost prevent themselves from feeling any pain. Thinking it was all just a matter of being strong and taking charge of oneself, a few "control specialists" began to lose respect for those who continued to feel. They decided that those who continued to grieve were being "irrational" and "too emotional." This attitude had a negative effect on relationships. In addition, the more these parents turned inward to deal with their pain, the more they shut out their partners. Even a simple and caring question such as "How are you feeling?" would be considered "inane" and intrusive. It would trigger the raising of the "barriers," particularly if their spouse needed to express grief rather than control it.

Expressive mourning strategy

Some parents were accustomed to expressing what they thought and felt when they had a problem. Although more women than men adopted the *expressive mourning strategy* (cell a), one or two fathers did use this strategy almost exclusively at first. Expressive mourners "needed to talk"; they wanted to share their thoughts, feelings, and tears. Some felt they had no choice: they knew that if they wanted to feel better they "had to talk about it. [They] had these things that would go through [their] mind, so [they] had to voice them." Some described themselves as "just a crying person." They could not lock their pain inside; they had to let it out. Although these parents needed someone to listen to them talk, unlike the *dependent mourners* who expected others to make them feel better, *expressive mourners* did not need or expect other people to fix their problems.

Like any of the other strategies, however, when carried to the extreme, this strategy had the potential to create problems as well as to relieve them. Parents who communicated every hurtful and distressing thought and feeling sometimes distanced and frightened other people. Some expressive parents took their anger out on those they loved. This kind of behavior severely strained relationships. Some spouses resented being the target of the anger; they grew tired of all the tears. A few expressive mourners tried to force people to listen to them.

Over time though, these parents slowly learned the difference between a willing and an unwilling listener. Some parents learned to cry by themselves occasionally and to release their grief through vigorous exercise. Most expressive mourners also learned to share their grief with people who could tolerate their tears and hear the story again and again. They also made good use of the SIDS support group when it was available to them. The group provided them with a feeling of comfort.

Being comforted

No matter what mourning strategy parents used, they did not grieve in isolation. Other people responded to the death of the baby and the parents' grief by offering comfort. The kind of comfort people offered and the way in which they offered it either supported or challenged the mourning strategy that the parents used.

Forms of comfort

Comfort came in three forms: "physical support," "caring gestures," and opportunities to "talk about it." Unfortunately, actions that one parent found comforting might irritate another parent. Sensitive comforters learned the difference and adjusted their behavior to suit what the parents wanted. Insensitive comforters did not acknowledge the differences. Instead, they tried to change the way the parents grieved.

Physical support

When words could not express their feelings and thoughts, people often offered the parents "physical support," particularly within the first few hours after the baby's death. Physical support refers to the use of the body to give comfort in the following ways: "hugs," "cuddles," "holding," touching, and patting. This kind of comfort also included ordinary physical presence, that is, choosing to be with and near the bereaved. Comforters also offered their tears and eye contact. Physical support gave temporary relief by communicating warmth, affection, and connection.

Parents who adopted *dependent* or *expressive mourning strategies* usually welcomed this kind of comfort. Some *controlled mourners* wanted to be held; others did not. Some parents who were temporarily frozen wanted physical support, but they did not know how to ask for it. In contrast, those who were frozen permanently did their best to avoid being touched.

Caring gestures

Sympathetic people also offered the parents "caring gestures." Although these gestures took many forms, they can be divided into two basic categories. One set of gestures demonstrated an obligatory or traditional kind of caring. These acts reflected the recognition that because the bereaved parents had suffered a tragic loss they deserved special consideration and privileges. Obligatory "caring gestures" included: a sedative to calm the emotional outbursts; flowers, food, or sympathy cards; assistance with planning the funeral; attendance at the funeral; "a quick pat on the back" or a "shoulder to cry on"; "acknowledgement of the loss"; provision of bereavement leave; and "lenient" expectations at work. Although the parents appreciated these "caring gestures," they knew that such actions were offered to anyone who had suffered a loss.

Controlled and *frozen mourners* usually appreciated this kind of comfort because it did not invade their privacy. *Expressive* and *dependent mourners* usually accepted these obligatory "caring gestures" from professionals, coworkers, and distant relatives. They wanted more from close relatives, friends, and particularly from their own spouse. If these people offered the parents nothing more personal than "gestures," then the parents felt angry.

These parents wanted personalized comfort. They wanted comfort that met their specific needs and reflected that others really understood their pain. Examples of such "gestures" included: providing written and oral information about SIDS and how the baby's death might affect their marriage; anticipating the rough days and offering support; being available to spend extended periods of time with the parent just listening and asking questions; noticing when comfort was needed and offering it without being asked; and respecting the parent's privacy and mourning strategy.

Not all parents derived comfort from such personal "gestures." While *expressive* or *dependent mourners* appreciated people's attempts to offer this kind of support, most *controlled* and *frozen mourners* found such behaviors too intrusive.

Opportunity to talk about it

People also offered parents one other kind of comfort: the opportunity to "talk about it." Parents also felt comforted when others understood that there were times when they did not want to "talk about it." The "it" refers to three distinct but related topics: the baby's death, the baby as a person, and the parent's grief. *Expressive mourners* were most likely to want to talk about all three "its," while the others varied in their willingness to discuss each topic.

Talking about the baby's death

The most commonly discussed "it" in the first few hours and days of this nightmare was the baby's death. There were two parts to discussing the baby's death: the details surrounding the death and the death as an event in the parents' lives. In the beginning, most parents needed to review "every detail, every minute" of their child care practices and "go over [them] with a fine tooth comb." Other people varied in their willingness to listen to these details, both because of their own discomfort and because they thought such a review harmed the parents' healing. What people did not realize was that, in most cases, most parents needed to talk about their baby's death in order to heal.

Being able to review child care details and the circumstances surrounding the baby's death served three purposes. First, it helped parents investigate the facts surrounding the baby's death. This helped them understand what had happened. Reaching an understanding was crucial to their eventual healing because, as one parent said, "The biggest thing is, the quicker you understand that there is nothing you can do, then the better off you are." Second, the review also helped parents air the fear that they had contributed to the baby's death. Some parents needed to be talked out of blaming themselves and to be "absolve[d]" of responsibility. Third, the review also generated reassurances from others. Some parents needed others to tell them they had been "good parents." Most of the parents wanted to discuss the details initially. The few who did not want to discuss them publicly carried out their own review in their minds, although a few parents blocked all the details from their consciousness.

Some parents needed to talk about the death as an event in their lives. Talking generally about the death made the parents confront it as a reality. It also reduced the nightmarish quality of the experience. As one father said, "The more you talk about it, the more, the more you can put it in your mind as to what happened and when it happened." Talking helped parents acknowledge their loss. Discussing the event also had the opposite effect: it allowed parents to gradually distance themselves from the experience by putting it in the "past tense": "As time goes by, I think you talk more about what happened rather than what is happening or what just happened." Besides, when parents talked about what happened, they provided others with the opportunity to respond with comfort.

Controlled mourners usually wanted to talk about the details only until they understood them. Then they stopped initiating this kind of conversation. They had completed their review in their minds, and they had no need to talk about it anymore. *Frozen mourners* had even less need to talk about the event since they had totally blocked it from consciousness. For them, there was nothing to talk about. *Dependent mourners* often needed to talk, but this topic caused so much pain that they soon tried to avoid it. They could not achieve distance; no matter how much time passed, it seemed as if the baby had died yesterday. *Expressive mourners* who could not find a willing listener became frantic at first. They needed to talk to move away from the event.

Talking about the baby as a person

Beyond talking about the baby's death, some parents also wanted to talk about the second "it": the baby as a person. This topic included memories of the baby, concerns about the baby's whereabouts and condition in the present, and feelings about "all the potential that was lost [for the future]."

Although discussing memories was painful at first, some parents eventually began to feel a bittersweet joy when they recalled their baby's short life. Parents treasured memories of their baby's birth. They also tried to hang onto their last happy time with the baby. This was sometimes a struggle for those who had found the baby dead. Many tried to focus on the happy times, such as "dressing [the baby] up and taking her for walks." Parents cherished their memories of their baby's smiles, laughter, kisses, giggles, hugs, and smell.

Some parents needed to talk about baby memories to remain connected to the baby but not *controlled* and *frozen mourners*. They found the memories too painful, so they avoided talking about them. Many people in the parents' lives were only too happy to stop talking about the baby's life. This topic upset them, too. *Dependent* and *expressive mourners* were frustrated by this wall of silence; it made them feel like their baby had never existed.

Parents also wanted to talk about the baby in the present tense. For some, however, this meant talking about "the fact that [their baby] was in the ground." This was difficult for most. Those who had a strong religious faith "never thought about what was happening to the body after its burial." Instead, they talked about their baby being "in heaven" or "off with God." While some parents wanted to talk about their baby in the present, others could not. It upset them too much. Not having a psychic or heavenly location for their baby made parents think about their baby's actual earthly location. This topic also proved to be uncomfortable for other people, too. Because they did not know what to say, they sometimes said the wrong thing, particularly if they did not share the parents' religious views. To avoid saying the wrong thing, many people said nothing.

And then there was the third element in talking about the baby as a person: "all the potential that was lost." At first, fathers talked about "all the things [the baby] could have meant and done [and] been." While fathers talked about missed opportunities to "watch [this baby] grow up," mothers talked about missing opportunities to care for the baby and to develop a close relationship over time. Some couples discussed "what [the baby] would be like now…what [the baby] would have looked like, talked like," and what kind of personality their child might have had. Although many parents hungered to talk about their child's missed potential, this topic was painful for other people. They found it difficult to hear the parents talking about missing their baby and wondering what purpose their baby's short life and death had served.

Talking about grief

People in the parents' lives and the parents themselves varied in the degree to which they could talk about the third "it": grief. This topic included the parents' feelings of anger, sadness, and fear and their thoughts of guilt and powerlessness. While *expressive mourners* "needed to talk," *controlled mourners* chose to keep their grief private. They felt no need to share it. *Dependent mourners* had difficulty talking about their grief because it overwhelmed and frightened them. Nevertheless, they kept trying to find someone who could "take away the pain." *Frozen mourners* said little if anything about grief. They had not acknowledged their grief because they had successfully blocked it from their consciousness. As a consequence, they could not understand why people tried to comfort them, particularly by talking about the baby.

Characteristics of good comforters and good comfort

All three types of comfort had the potential to support, block, or modify the strategies that parents used to manage their grief. No matter how they managed their grief though, parents generally looked for comforters who were sincere, accessible, tuned in, and respectful. They also looked for people who could offer the kind of comfort that matched their needs, offered them some relief, and increased their sense of competence.

Sincere comforters

Parents looked for sincere comforters, people who gave from the heart, usually expending their time, energy, and effort. Grieving fathers appreciated the sincere efforts of other men who tried to express their condolences. They knew that men found it difficult to deal with this kind of situation. Parents appreciated comforters who brought food and who did everything they could to make the parents feel needed and loved. Sincere comforters made a special effort to show they cared for the parents.

In contrast, parents rated some comforters as insincere. These people offered comfort because they thought they should, not because they really cared about or understood the parent's pain. Parents did not feel comforted by comments such as "Well, it's a good thing [your child] wasn't 15 or 16 years old [when he died]." One father found that "a hard one to swallow." People told parents to appreciate the children they had or to have another baby right away. When people said they knew just how the parents felt or when they offered hurtful and unsolicited explanations for the baby's death, the parents did not feel comforted; they felt angry. Religious platitudes also upset parents who did not share their comforter's beliefs. One woman told a grieving mother she "should be happy for [the baby's death because] you're going to see him again [in heaven]...in 50, 60 years." This statement offered the mother no comfort at all. She just wanted her son back. Parents also wondered about the sincerity of people who sent flowers but did not come in person. Insincere comforters made parents question the very foundation of some of their relationships. If, however, parents could rationalize away the "insincere" behavior, then they felt better. For example, one father just "consider[ed] the source" and decided some coworkers were "not real genuine people anyways." When parents could not explain away the insincerity, then they realized just how alone they really were.

Accessible comforters

To combat the feeling of isolation, parents greatly appreciated comforters who made themselves accessible. The most accessible source of comfort for some parents was themselves. Those who were used to being self-reliant or who had never trusted other people with their problems tried to comfort themselves with vigorous exercise, reading, thinking, or crying. One woman "indulg[ed herself]" in her grief by "think[ing] about stuff and stay[ing] up late and then sleep[ing] in the afternoon and just go[ing] for walks" until she felt better. For other parents, the most accessible comforter was God. God gave them strength, a reason to go on, and constant companionship.

Most parents eventually turned to other people for comfort. Accessible comforters made themselves physically and emotionally available to the parents. When parents asked them for comfort, they did everything they could to help. One mother regularly visited her doctor to talk about the latest theories about the cause of SIDS; she felt comforted by these discussions. Years after the baby's death, a mother's friend continued to offer her a comforting ear and the opportunity to talk about her experience:

> I sat there from about 9:30 that night until midnight and that's all I talked about, was talked about from the time that [the baby] died until her funeral, [my] suicide plan, to the SIDS group, and everything. The following night I went back to her house and spent our entire evening and that's all we talked about. She just sat there and listened. She had the odd tear coming out, but I was crying.

Some parents also turned to the SIDS support program in their area. Some parents just called the SIDS Line. This service is staffed by volunteer parents who, in some locations, provide support and information 24 hours a day. Other parents attended the unstructured monthly meetings where they could talk about anything. In addition, some parents exchanged telephone numbers and called each other between meetings. Although more women than men attended the groups, some couples attended meetings together. Some fathers stopped going after one or two meetings because the group had "answered all the questions which could be answered." The women usually relied on the group and its members for both emotional support and information.

In comparison, some parents had no access to anyone they could rely on, not even themselves. Perhaps because they were so readily available, some parents turned to food, drugs, alcohol, work, and leisure activities. Some lost their faith temporarily; others felt angry with God. In either case, these parents could not turn to God for comfort. Other parents tried to turn to people, but not everyone could handle their pain. Some friends and family stopped talking about the baby or visiting. Hoping that at least her priest would listen to her pain or hold her while she cried, one mother discovered that he was inaccessible. Again, when confronted with behavior they could not understand, parents tried to find an explanation. Unless they could generate a positive explanation for people's lack of accessibility, the parents' sense of loneliness increased.

Tuned in comforters

To combat the intense natural loneliness of grief, many parents looked for comforters who could tune in to them and their needs. Tuning in meant paying close attention to the thoughts and feelings of the grieving parents, whether by listening, watching, or anticipating. By tuning in, comforters were really emotionally "there" with the grieving parent. One mother appreciated the flowers that various members of her family sent every year on the anniversary of the baby's death. This told her that they knew she was still hurting.

Not all grieving parents wanted the same degree of tuning in. *Expressive mourners* wanted a special kind of tuning in. They needed to be with people who could connect with and identify with their pain but who still felt strong enough to handle it. One woman described visits with a good friend: "She'd ask me questions...she'd say that she thinks about us often...and she'd start to cry, and she would just show me she cared, that she was hurting."

In contrast, most *controlled mourners* just wanted their loss acknowledged. This was a less intense kind of tuning in. To them, it was enough that people attended the funeral or patted them on the shoulder and said they were sorry about the baby's death. Anything more demonstrative felt like an invasion of their privacy. *Controlled mourners* could not tolerate much tuning in before their "barriers" went up.

Frozen mourners did not want any tuning in at all; they wanted people to forget the whole event. *Dependent mourners* needed to be around people who were very strong but not so strong that they could not feel with them. Too much tuning in by the comforter frightened *dependent mourners.*

Many parents reacted negatively to the extremes of tuning in. Some comforters were so tuned in to the parents' pain that they had nothing to offer. In fact, they often needed to be comforted themselves. Some grandparents fell into this category; they could offer little comfort because they were hurting too much. Grieving parents soon learned to put on a "mask" to avoid upsetting people. Having to pretend to be doing well or having to comfort other people angered the parents and created distance in their relationships, that is, unless they could find a way to explain away such behavior. If not, the sense of loneliness and frustration increased.

Similarly, at the other end of the continuum, parents had to deal with people who tuned out. Some people did not even try to understand the parents' grief. Again, if the parents wanted to maintain a positive connection to these people, they had to find a way to justify such distancing behavior; otherwise, tension increased in these relationships.

Sometimes people shifted from being tuned in to being tuned out. Within a very short time, some people who had been supportive, attentive, and comforting at the beginning began tuning out. Because they could **carry on** themselves, these people expected the parents to do the same. In particular, some parents had trouble with employers who had been understanding at first but who soon demanded that the parents get "back to normal."

Respectful comforters

Parents needed one last thing from their comforters: they needed their respect. First, parents wanted respect for the way they handled their grief.

Friends who let parents fall apart instead of insisting that they play the roles all the time showed respect for the parent's ability to handle the pain. Anyone who did not push the parents to grieve differently earned their respect. When parents felt accepted by others, positive feelings about the relationship increased. Parents also needed others to respect their grieving timetable. Wanting the freedom to grieve at their own pace, parents appreciated those who set no deadlines and restrictions. People also earned the parents' respect when they treated them as equals. Parents did not like to be pitied or thought of as "weak," "irrational," too "emotional" or too "cold." Respectful comforting meant there was no hint of superiority in what was offered. The doctor who willingly sat and talked with one grieving mother whenever she felt the need treated her like an equal. This made her feel important. Generally, comforters who treated the parents with respect built more positive relationships with them than those who were disrespectful.

Disrespectful comforters challenged the way the parents grieved. They tried to force them to "be strong," silent, or more open. People often disagreed with the parents' need or lack of need to talk about the "its": the baby's death, the baby as a person, and their grief. When differences became obvious, some parents withdrew from their comforters. Others tried to be assertive about their needs. Disrespectful comforters also pushed parents to stop hurting and "move on," often before the parents were ready. The lack of respect severely strained relationships.

Good comfort

Besides comforters who were sincere, accessible, tuned in, and respectful, parents also needed specific kinds of comfort. They wanted comfort that matched their needs, offered relief, and increased their sense of competence.

At first, parents did not know what would make them feel better, but they knew when something did not meet their needs. Feeling embarrassed by her inability to control her emotions and just wanting to be left alone, one mother did not want to have people in her home after the funeral. This did not meet her needs; it met the needs of her family. It was the socially correct thing to do. Another woman wanted to be able to "go with the flow," to feel all her pain, but others insisted that she take a sedative to subdue her reaction. Some men got angry with people who tried to make them share their grief. Unless these parents could find an acceptable reason for people's refusal to meet their needs, they felt isolated, misunderstood, and increasingly angry.

At first, the pain was so intense that some parents just wanted some relief. They did not care what kind just as long as it made them feel better. Taking a sedative, eating or drinking to excess, and abusing prescription drugs all offered temporary relief. Using these forms of comfort did not make the parents feel better in the long-term; instead, they just learned how to avoid pain. Avoiding any discussion of the whole nightmare also had the same negative effect. In fact, these kinds of short-term comfort measures impeded healing and growth. They also increased the parents' problems and created a new problem in their marriage. They needed something more: they needed comfort that also increased their sense of competence.

Parents needed the kind of comfort that not only made them feel better, but that also made them feel better about themselves. Constructive relief helped parents learn to cope with their pain, and therefore, it built up both their skills and confidence. Because of their attendance at a SIDS support groups, for example, some parents learned how to share their feelings more openly. They learned to see things from another's point of view, and eventually, they began to offer comfort to new parents. This helped them realize that they were healing.

Conclusion: Being comforted

In summary, the actions of comforters and the type of comfort they offered affected the parents' ability to deal with their grief. Most people let the parents mourn the way they wanted. Some people tried to tell parents they were doing it wrong. Nowhere was this more apparent and problematic than in the parents' marriages.

Managing grief within marriage

When the baby died, all the strengths and weaknesses of the parents' marriage became more obvious. Some parents became aware of their problems in retrospect:

> The problems that you're going to have stem from things that are already preexisting obviously. They're not things that are just brand new. If you want a good excuse for failure, you can blame it on the death of your child, but I think it just is probably like alcohol or drugs where it just amplifies the problem, and if you've got a big problem, you can think it was this, but it was something that was there all along. It's just made you more volatile.

Negotiating closeness

One "preexisting" issue proved to be crucial to the well-being of the marriage after the baby died: the level of emotional interdependence or closeness each spouse wanted in the marriage. Emotional interdependence can be stretched out along a continuum, with complete dependence on one end and complete independence at the other end. When couples married, they had to negotiate where they wanted to be along this imaginary continuum.

When couples married, each person contributed a dowry of experiences and expectations that eventually affected the overall tone and nature of the relationship. Each spouse came to the marriage with a personal history that included their experiences with love, loss, crises, and problems; ethnic and family traditions; and attitudes, behaviors, and expectations about what it meant to be male or female, husband or wife. These experiences and expectations were combined, along with each person's temperament and problem-solving style, to produce an inclination towards a certain kind of intimate relationship.

Spouses who wanted an interdependent relationship wanted to be able to lean on each other like "good friends." Some couples were so tuned in to one other that it was almost as if they had become one person: "I just think of [my spouse] as a part of me, like as my arm or leg or something like that and that we're connected."

Others resisted such closeness. At the first sign of dependency, they felt "crowded." "Once there [was] a bit of imbalance in the relationship" and one spouse needed support from the other, problems developed. Some spouses resented being needed and having to be strong enough to hold up the relationship. They resented it if their partner "leaned" on them too much. They also resented it when they felt like they received little in return. When this perceived "imbalance" could not be resolved, it created a persistent tension in the marriage.

Other couples worked out a relationship in which each partner could be emotionally independent. Being "quite different" from each other, this kind of marriage satisfied some couples as long as they continued to have enough "common ground" to keep them together: "We were always private. We still are. Things have changed, and that is the way we wanted to live our life." Couples in this type of marriage were practical rather than passionate partners.

What worked for one couple did not work for another. Some couples had to negotiate a compromise because each partner had different needs. Some reached a mutually satisfying compromise. Others could not reach an understanding about this issue. They continued to disagree and, in some cases, to fight about this problem. When couples reached a temporary truce, they usually felt vaguely dissatisfied with the arrangement. The baby's death severely tested and challenged all these negotiations and compromises. One other problem complicated things even more: the fact that parents seldom used the same strategies to deal with their grief. While some couples managed their differences well, others fought about them.

Managing differences

Parents seldom used the same mourning strategies, grieved with the same intensity, or grieved for the same length of time. They also differed in how they wanted to be comforted and how they comforted others.

As previously discussed, *expressive mourners* needed to "talk about it" and to share their pain with others. As a result, they felt comforted when their spouse encouraged them to discuss the baby, the baby's death, and their grief. Because talking and crying publicly made the grief of expressive mourners more obvious, spouses who mourned differently wondered when the grieving would stop. Because sharing grief made them feel better, some expressive mourners assumed others should use the same strategy. Some expressive mourners tried to force their spouse to talk: "You should want to talk about it still.... You know, people just clam it up, and you're going to have a big breakdown later."

Not everyone wanted to "talk about it." *Controlled mourners* usually wanted to be left alone with their grief. They did their best to avoid being around emotional people. Although many continued to "work through" their grief in their heads, controlled mourners looked like they had finished grieving within a few months. When trying to comfort their spouse, controlled mourners offered their silent strength and the facts of the situation. For example, when his wife tried to talk about her fears, one husband responded only with, "Did you hear the doctor? Listen to the expert." This was his idea of comfort. Another husband became increasingly upset by his wife's inability to reason her way out of her pain. Since logic worked for him, he could not understand why she insisted on being so "irrational."

Although *dependent mourners* wanted someone to lean on and to make them feel better, nothing seemed to relieve their pain for any length of time. In the eyes of other people, this grieving seemed to last too long and to be too intense. As a consequence, others found it frustrating to try to comfort dependent mourners. Their grieving seemed "irrational" and endless. Because dependent mourners were so overwhelmed by their own pain, they seldom noticed how anyone else grieved or offered comfort. Some could not describe how their spouse had dealt with their pain. They thought of their spouse as someone from whom they could "draw strength."

Frozen mourners looked as if they never grieved at all. Because they had frozen out both their own pain and that of others, these mourners had difficulty offering or receiving any comfort: "By me being that cold, I didn't talk about it. I wouldn't talk about it to anybody.…Not knowing what the consequences were to [my wife]." Frozen mourners just wanted to be left alone to **carry on** with life as if nothing had happened.

Parents used the strategy that suited them. Even when spouses chose the same strategy, however, misunderstandings still arose. Confusing behavior or attitudes triggered the need to make sense of it. Parents wanted to find an explanation for behavior they did not understand. Although the behavior did not differ that much from one couple to another, what made the difference was how the spouses explained the differences to themselves. In fact, the very act of trying to find a positive explanation for behavior they did not understand seemed to strengthen marriages. Those who found only negative explanations severely strained their relationships.

Impact on marriage

Several funeral directors and ministers warned parents that the baby's death could either strengthen or weaken their marriage. The choice was up to them. Couples had to decide whether they would deal with this crisis together or separately. Some reached a mutually satisfying decision about this, often based on their usual level of interdependence. Others could not compromise or discuss this issue; it increased "preexisting" tensions and conflicts about interdependence. Couples also had to decide if they could accept differences in mourning strategies. Some not only tolerated their differences, they benefited from them. When in doubt about behavior, these couples managed to find positive explanations. As a result, their marriage strengthened or at least did not deteriorate. Other couples argued about their differences and found negative explanations for behavior they did not understand. This weakened their marriage significantly.

When these two factors, emotional interdependence and the ability to find positive explanations for differences combine, they create a typology of four marriages: *isolated*, *conflicted*, *parallel*, and *connected* (see Figure 3).

		Emotionally Interdependent Relationship: Yes	Emotionally Interdependent Relationship: No
Positive Attribution for Mourning Behaviour	Yes	**Connected** (a)	**Parallel** (b)
	No	**Conflicted** (c)	**Isolated** (d)

Figure 3 Typology of marriages based on emotional interdependence in the relationship and positive attributions for mourning behavior

Isolated marriages

For the first few hours after the baby's death, several couples found themselves in an *isolated marriage* (cell d). They mourned independently of one another. They were so much "in [them]selves" that they were unaware of their spouse's pain. They could neither understand nor positively explain away their differences. The baby's death emotionally devastated one or both of them. To preserve what little energy they had, they withdrew from each other and from their relationship. They were in shock. Unable to understand their own or their spouse's mourning style or comfort needs, they felt alone, isolated, and overwhelmed.

One couple went away together after the funeral. Although they were together physically, they could not connect emotionally, nor could they talk about what had happened: "I really don't remember ever talking about this. These 2 days, 3 days that we had....We went for long walks and things." Once this couple returned home and tried to **carry on**, the isolation continued.

This sense of isolation passed for most couples. As the numbness subsided, most parents began dealing with their own pain and trying to respond to their spouse's needs. Then they tried to provide each other with support.

Conflicted marriages

Some couples developed a *conflicted marriage* (cell c). In this type of relationship, the partners were emotionally interdependent but unhappy about it. The relationship did not meet their needs. While one partner wanted more closeness, the other wanted more distance. When confronted with behavior they could not understand, particularly differences in mourning strategies, these couples used negative explanations. Therefore, most of the passion came from anger. Initially, the anger arose because of each parent's sense of powerlessness and guilt over their baby's death. Instead of sharing these feelings and supporting one another's pain, these couples argued about everything: "Just the smallest issue would just blow it totally sky high." Instead of compassion for each other's pain, tension filled the air. Sometimes they even thought about or brought up the possibility of "divorce":

> Actually, [my husband] and I were fighting a lot.... We were angry, and I didn't think, I really felt that he didn't feel the same way I did about [the baby] dying, and I would say, "You don't care." I would be, you know, like, "You don't care." And uhm, I was, think I'm a little selfish at times. I wanted him to hurt as bad as I did, and I felt he wasn't hurting enough.

Parallel marriages

Couples in *parallel marriages* (cell b) handled their baby's death much like they handled their other problems: they took a practical approach. Because they were used to "hav[ing] a private existence," they "got to get over [their grief themselves]." Part of the strength of these relationships came from the couple's ability to accept their differences. Each member of a *parallel marriage* respected the other's strength. Although they monitored each other's progress, neither felt responsible for the other's healing nor for talking that much about their grief. They found reasonable explanations for each other's behavior and moved on, their marriage neither strengthened nor weakened by the experience: "I can't remember it being a big strain on our marriage."

Connected marriages

Other couples developed *connected marriages* (cell a). These couples had found a mutually satisfying degree of emotional interdependence. Spouses could talk about, understand, and accept their differences to a mutually satisfying level. The most salient characteristics of *connected marriages* were the partners' flexibility and trust in one another. They took turns being strong for each other:

> When I was having my worse time where I just thought I couldn't handle this anymore, [my husband] would rise up and be there for me. And yet, when I was feeling really bad but I would see he was having a harder time, I would become stronger and think, "I've got to help him. He's having a tough time right now." And so you put your

feelings aside for [each other], and that really helps, you know, that you can.

This dance of comfort required the willingness and ability of each spouse to notice the other's pain, to set aside their own grief temporarily, and to offer comfort and strength. Underlying this was a sense of trust in the relationship. When the kind of comfort offered did not match what was needed, these couples discussed their needs. As they grieved, they learned more about each other, and their love and respect for each other grew. Because they accepted and understood their different mourning strategies, couples in *connected marriages* discussed how they handled their grief. For example, one couple attended the support group together, but they each had a different agenda. The wife wanted emotional support and information; the husband wanted only information. Once he "had the questions answered which [he] wanted answered," he decided to stop attending. She accepted his decision without question. She understood his need to "make sense" of their baby's death; he understood her need for outside support.

Trying to Make Sense of It All

Because everything seemed so confusing, somehow parents had to find ***a way to make sense of "everything that was happening."*** They became "preoccupied with why" questions, and they needed "an answer" to these questions. Raised to believe in science rather than magic, the parents believed that there had to be a logical explanation for their baby's death, for their own behavior, and for the behavior of others. In order to "move on," they needed to restore a sense of order in their lives. They needed to make sense out of the senseless. Until they found answers for all their questions, their world seemed chaotic, unpredictable, and unfair. They felt frightened, angry, and vulnerable.

Although the parents had already tried to find out why their baby died, ***searching for a reason*** continued for quite some time. The explanations that the parents developed for themselves affected their perception of themselves, their grief, and their marriage. Because grieving was a new experience for most parents, they also wanted to understand mourning behavior: their own and their spouse's. Like scientists, they kept creating and testing new theories until they found one that fit. Until they could finally ***make sense of it all*** though, parents "yo yo[ed]" between **carrying on** and **struggling for control**.

Trying to make sense of the baby's death

Asking questions

At first, the "biggest question" the parents had was what caused their baby's death. Parents began asking questions of themselves and the experts within minutes of finding out that their baby was dead. As the weeks and months passed, the need to ask questions continued. Parents continued to vigorously and privately interrogate themselves as they waited for the results of the autopsy. They reviewed and reexamined every facet of their relationship with the baby.

While parents anxiously awaited the results of the autopsy, they created their own theories about why their baby had died. Some assumed the autopsy would confirm that they had caused their baby's death. These parents fully expected the police to arrest them for the murder of their baby. Other parents assumed that the autopsy report would not only explain how the baby had died, it would also answer their questions about why the baby died.

Reviewing the evidence

Most parents received the results of the autopsy within days of the baby's death. Some reports took much longer. During the 2 or 3 weeks that it took for the report to arrive, one couple convinced themselves that they had inadvertently caused their baby's death. Once they started blaming themselves, it was hard to stop. Besides, what other explanation could there be? In their minds, all the evidence pointed to them. They had let him cry himself to sleep, and now he was dead.

Once the parents received the report, they had problems understanding it. Parents could not make sense of the words in the report. One mother described it as full of "mumbo jumbo." Even her own doctor could not explain it in words she could understand. She had to find a specialist to tell her "what it mean[t]."

One father had a problem with the contents of the report. He believed that this report was meant to "cover up" evidence of a doctor's incompetence. To this day, he is not sure his baby died of SIDS. In his mind, the evidence is just not there.

Hoping that the autopsy report would provide them with the answers they needed, some parents looked forward to receiving the report. They wanted to discuss it with their doctor or the medical examiner's investigator. They hoped the report would explain why their baby died, and they believed that once they understood their baby's death, then they could **carry on**. But this did not happen. Once they read the report, many parents felt disappointed and even more devastated and confused.

Even though the report certified SIDS as the cause of death, it did not explain why the baby died. Many parents had assumed that the autopsy would reveal a hidden and lethal physical abnormality in the baby or that it would at least explain the circumstances of the death. Unfortunately, the report did not always meet their expectations. One father remembered discussing the autopsy report with a medical examiner's investigator, who told him:

> I want to tell you about your son. He was, you know, he was in good health and the brain was fine, the heart was good, and good immunity system, the right food, and, you know, medicine, everything was perfect, you know. Good lungs, the whole bit.

This poor father was speechless for a minute, and then he responded,

> That's nice. It's good to know that he was healthy, but why did he die? Why?

A mother had a similar reaction. She had looked forward to discussing the autopsy report with her doctor because she thought it would answer all her questions. She expected to "come out feeling great, knowing that, you know, it was SIDS and that was that." Instead, she left the office "just howling." She soon realized that

> what it boils down to is they don't know what was wrong with [the baby]. Everything seemed medically fine.... [She said to the doctor], "You've just told me I had a perfectly nat, perfectly healthy, normal baby boy." And [she] wanted to scream, "Well then why isn't he still here?" You know? "Why don't I still have him? Why aren't I carrying him out of the doctor's office?"

The autopsy report did not help most parents **carry on**. Instead, it increased the **struggle for control**. The death still made no sense. Parents could not believe that a healthy baby could just suddenly die for no reason. It made no sense at all that a parent could "put your child to bed and you wake up the next morning and your child is dead." Parents needed a better, more comprehensive explanation. Someone had to be responsible. Even when they had been told repeatedly that no one was at fault, most parents could not accept this. If no one had caused their apparently healthy baby to die suddenly, it meant that horrible things such as this just happened randomly. Thinking about this possibility frightened them. Their world felt chaotic. To restore a sense of order, parents had to find out why their baby died. They had to find out who or what killed their baby.

Launching their own private inquiry, most parents treated themselves as the primary suspect first, moving on to other suspects only when they had "absolved" themselves of any responsibility. In a few cases, it took only an hour or so for parents to decide they were not responsible. In other cases, it took months. Some never stopped blaming themselves.

Like detectives looking for evidence, the parents questioned themselves, asking the same three questions they had asked soon after the baby was found dead: What did I do wrong? What did I not do right? "What was there in front of my face that I didn't see?"

Trying to assign the blame

Rejecting responsibility

After carrying out their investigation, a few parents refused to blame themselves. To "try to understand what the hell happened" and to learn as much as they could about SIDS, some parents talked with their doctors, attended a SIDS support group, and read everything they could find about SIDS. They concluded that no one could be blamed for this death because SIDS "just happens and there is nothing you can do about it." Although these parents continued to feel sad about their baby's death, they soon stopped searching for someone to blame. They accepted that they had lost "the luck of the draw." Only parents who could tolerate uncertainty and a lack of control felt comfortable with this explanation in the long-term. Others tried this explanation and rejected it when it made them feel uncomfortable. In their minds, there just had to be another explanation.

Accepting responsibility

Although they had no hard evidence to prove that they had caused their baby's death, some parents continued to blame themselves. It made the most sense: "I was the one who was responsible for [the baby]. I was the one that was with [the baby]. I just thought.... 'That's it. I've killed him.'" Many parents needed a concrete explanation. They reexamined all their original explanations. Sometimes they remembered something that might have caused a problem. Even though it was painful to "assign the blame" to themselves, it made them feel better somehow. At least this way the death was not random; it made sense.

Once parents accepted the blame, it affected how they felt about themselves. Some were "filled with self-loathing." Feeling like this made it particularly difficult for them to **carry on** as a "good parent." If they believed they had accidentally caused their baby to die, then they had to become super parents to prevent SIDS from taking the next baby. They also had to try to forgive themselves. And this was not easy because "that was just so hard to think that I might have killed our own [baby]." Parents "yo yo[ed]" between accepting responsibility and wanting to find another explanation. If they rejected an explanation without having another to take its place, they felt anxious and vulnerable. They fell apart. They needed an explanation to **carry on**.

Even though they wanted to blame themselves, some parents could not find any specific or conscious act that might have caused the death. They decided to blame themselves anyway because they believed they had unintentionally caused the baby's death. For instance, after hearing a doctor talk about the greater incidence of SIDS in boys, one father wondered if he had passed on a lethal chromosome to his son. A mother began to wonder if her baby had chosen to die because "there were days I didn't like [the baby]. And you know, that haunted me for months. Like, you know, did [the baby] hear me thinking this?" These accounts were harder to deal with because the parents did not know how to protect their other children from future harm. Therefore, accepting this type of explanation increased parental anxiety instead of reducing it. Still, having no one to blame felt worse. Without someone to blame there was only chaos.

Blaming others

Because they "needed to blame someone" and they "couldn't blame [themselves]," some parents tried to assign blame elsewhere. A few blamed their spouse; one even blamed her mother for not helping after the baby's birth. Parents made these accusations when they felt desperate and frustrated. Rationally they knew they should not be blaming family members, so they had to look elsewhere: "I didn't want to blame my husband, so I had to blame the doctor."

Blaming the doctor did not always make the parents feel relieved. They had chosen the doctor; they had chosen to accept the doctor's advice. Blaming the doctor caused them to return to blaming themselves, a position they wanted to avoid. At least blaming the doctor restored a sense of order and control. It made another death seem preventable. All they had to do was avoid that particular doctor and be very careful about taking any doctor's advice. Parents could **carry on**, secure in the belief that they had found the guilty party.

Some parents could not find anyone specific to blame, and that frustrated them. A couple of parents said they thought it might have been easier to lose their child in a car accident. At least then they could understand the circumstances of the death, particularly how the baby died. In addition, they would know who was responsible so they could at least "be angry at that driver."

Suspecting God

Some parents began to wonder about God's role in the death. Many parents considered the possibility that the death had been an "act of God." A few parents rejected this idea outright, refusing to believe that their baby had died because of "God's will." They did not "think that God [was] instrumental in picking this person for one reason or another." To these parents, there was no "logic in creating, creating a life and taking it away." It just made no sense to them. There had to be another explanation.

Other parents very carefully considered the possibility that God "took [their baby] away." After all, many parents already believed that "God gave [life] and God takes away [life]" and that "[God is] responsible for everyone's death. There's a time and a place for everyone to die." These parents had not questioned this belief until their baby's death. The minute they began to suspect that God might have taken their baby, they started asking questions again. The big question was: "Why would He do this to me?" They needed to uncover God's "reasons so that [they could] understand."

The baby's death severely challenged some parents' faith. Like hundreds of theologians over the centuries, parents had to somehow explain the following problem: "God is all powerful. God is all good. [But] terrible things happen." One father said he "didn't blame God. The only thing I did do is I kept asking why." If the baby really had died because of "God's will," then what was God's reasoning? Would a loving God really take their baby, knowing how much suffering it would cause? Or was there such a thing as a loving God?

Some parents tried to stop asking such questions, but they found it difficult: "If you have a strong enough faith, you do set that aside, too. But you just wanted the reasons for this." Until they could figure out God's reasoning, some parents "felt not really angry at God. Just confused." Others allowed themselves to "get angry at God" for "taking [their] baby." As long as the parents struggled with these faith questions, however, they could find little comfort from God or their religion. Even their minister's explanations rang hollow somehow. With no solid explanation for their baby's death, it seemed even their faith was falling apart:

> I can't accept someone just saying, "That is God's will and you must accept it." To me, that doesn't help me at all. I still question the whole Christianity issue again now because of this. It's really made me confused, and I've been rereading certain parts of the Bible, even the chapter on James. It's all about trials and tribulations.

Conclusion: Trying to make sense of the death

The more unanswered questions the parents had, the worse they felt. Sometimes they found temporary answers that made them feel better; at least then they could **carry on** for a little while. Other times the answers crumbled under scrutiny, causing the parents to struggle for control. If they were ever going to heal from this devastating loss, then they needed a solid, comfortable, and sensible explanation for their baby's death. They continued searching for the logic behind their baby's death. While parents were trying to make sense of their baby's death, they were also trying to make sense of their own grief and that of their spouse.

Making sense of differences in mourning behavior

Because most parents had never suffered such a devastating loss before, they did not understand either their own reactions or those of their spouse. When confronted with behavior they could not understand, the parents tried to make sense of it. In particular, they needed to understand why sometimes they could play their roles and sometimes they fell apart. They also needed to understand why they mourned differently from their spouse. Their explanations enabled them to **carry on**.

Asking questions

To uncover the reasons for confusing behavior, most parents continually asked themselves questions: "Why did I do that?" Those who could discuss their grief with their partners sometimes asked each other questions, such as "Why are you doing this?" They also compared their mourning behavior to their spouse's and asked more questions: "Well, you must be doing better. Are you doing better than me? What's wrong with me?" Instead of asking questions of people directly, others looked for their answers by reading books and pamphlets about grief. They "read the stories about how [they] should feel." When their behavior and feelings did not match what the experts said, the parents asked, "Is something wrong with me because I'm not acting normal?" Parents needed to find answers to all their questions so they could **carry on**. Whenever they lost control, they looked for a way to make sense of what was happening to them. Finding an explanation helped to restore a sense of order and predictability in their lives.

In particular, parents wanted to understand why their mourning behavior differed from their spouse. They wanted to understand differences in: the length of time it took before each parent could effectively and continually play the roles, the apparent intensity of grief, mourning strategies, and what each needed to feel comforted. Few couples openly discussed their differences; instead, they secretly made up their own explanations based on evidence from the past.

Reviewing the evidence

When confronted with behavior they found confusing, parents reacted by trying to find an explanation. Some parents always managed to find a positive explanation. These parents generally seemed to have a positive attitude about life, themselves, and their spouse. When the same confusing behavior confronted other parents, they provided only negative explanations. Some of these parents seemed to have a history of seeing themselves, their spouse, or their marriage in a negative light. The baby's death destroyed the ability to see things positively. The use of positive and negative explanations to explain confusing behavior affected marital relationships and the parents' ability to heal.

Assigning responsibility

Common explanations for differences in mourning behavior included: previous experiences with loss and with their own family upbringing; differences in gender, personality, and the intensity of the parent-child relationship; and unique circumstances. Positive explanations were based on the assumption of positive intent. These parents wanted to believe that people always did the best they knew how to do. Negative explanations were based on the assumption of negative intent or a lack of caring on the part of others. These parents focused on people's faults rather than on their confusion about how to handle this whole experience.

Being positive

Some parents had no previous experience with such intense grief, while others had varying amounts of grief-related experience. Experienced mourners at least understood what to expect of themselves. In some cases, they forgave their partner's upsetting behavior, saying to themselves, "I've dealt with grief....[My spouse] didn't know what to think, what to do." Instead of judging or trying to change the way their spouse mourned, experienced and compassionate spouses acted as teachers. They explained the grief process and what to expect. Then they did what they could to provide comfort and support. When one or both members of a couple adopted this forgiving and caring attitude, it helped draw them closer.

Some parents also realized that people learn how to handle their emotions while growing up in their own families. When trying to explain to herself why she could not show her feelings to anyone, not even to her husband, one woman traced it back to her upbringing: "Nobody in our family talks about their deep feelings really." Once she accepted this fact, she forgave herself for not sharing her pain with anyone. Other parents accepted the way their spouse grieved for the same reason: they believed people learned how to handle emotions at an early age. This explanation meant they did not take their spouse's behavior "personally."

Some parents believed that the way people grieved reflected the "male/female sort of thing." Differences did not arise because one parent cared more or less for the baby or their partner. Instead, these parents believed that because "men and women are just built differently" they would naturally mourn differently. Men said women were naturally "more communicative," "more sentimental," and "more emotional." They also talked about men being "private" and closed with their feelings because of their innate competitive nature and because they were naturally the stronger sex. The most important element of this explanation was the recognition that one's gender might affect mourning behavior. In their minds then, no strategy could be considered inherently right or wrong. This explanation allowed for a sense of partnership and an acceptance of differences. With this approach, differences could complement each other. Partners could help each other because they experienced things differently. Their relationship could be strengthened.

Another aspect of the gender explanation related to men's perception that their job was to "be strong" for their wives. Even if they were falling apart inside, these men believed that they had to pretend to be coping so that their wives had someone to "lean on." These men also stopped talking about their own grief sooner than most of the women. Keeping their grief under control was easier when it was private. Keeping silent was also the men's way of caring for their wives. Many men believed that sharing their own pain would just increase their wives' suffering.

A few women understood the reason behind their husbands' silence. Instead of criticizing her husband for withholding his feelings, one woman loved him even more for his quiet reserve. She believed that "he was keeping it in because he didn't want to upset [her]." She chose to look for positive intent. Her explanation increased the loving connection between them.

Besides the gender explanation, some parents believed that differences might have arisen from basic personality traits. One woman realized that her husband was naturally "a very calm person, rational" and that, in contrast, she was "very irrational, very impatient." Instead of seeing their differences as indicative of a problem, however, this woman treated it like a strength they could offer each other. Her husband helped her to "look at things in a different way." She provided him with the opportunity to deal with his emotions. Although another woman would have felt better if her normally quiet husband had shared more of his feelings, she had long ago accepted his quiet reserve. When their baby died, she accepted what little he said about his feelings: "For as talkative as [he was], that was good." She did not expect him to change just for her. Another woman accepted her husband's need to be alone shortly after the baby died. She knew him to be a very private person, so she chose to believe that his departure had nothing to do with her. These partners accepted each other's mourning strategies. They believed that "because you do it one way doesn't mean it's right for that person." They accepted their differences and tried to turn them into something positive.

Parents also explained their differences by believing that their experiences with the baby had been very different. Although women referred to this fact, too, men used it more frequently to explain why they returned to "normal" sooner than their wives:

> Women are a bit more emotional about it [because] a woman is closer to the baby than a man is. I mean, the woman carried the baby for 9 months, you know. She gave birth to that child. She's the one that's washing it, feeding it, clothing it, uh, caring for it, getting up in the middle of the night, doing everything. I mean the father may be there, you know, and he might have all the concerns in the world, but he is off to work and what not, and he is not spending the same time as, as a mother is.

Some parents also used the existence of unique circumstances to explain their own behavior. A few parents had to deal with the serious illness or death of another family member shortly after the baby's death. By giving themselves permission to get lost in the "sea of grief," they reduced their expectations and accepted that they were under tremendous pressure. One mother needed an explanation for the opposite problem: she could not understand why she did not feel the intense emotional pain the books told her she should be feeling. Then she realized that though she missed her baby, she still had her twin to hold and love. This realization helped her to accept her own behavior and to stop wondering if she was "normal."

Parents who adopted a positive approach to explaining their own or their spouse's behavior tried to be understanding and accepting. This attitude increased their sense of connection and empathy. Instead of blaming people for not acting a certain way, these parents assumed that behavior was a combination of people's innate tendencies, learned approaches to problems, and different life experiences. They also chose to assume that everyone was doing the best they knew how to do in the middle of a terrible situation. This approach helped these parents take the next step together: **learning to let go**.

Being negative

Unfortunately, not all parents could be so positive. Some looked for and found negative explanations for mourning behavior they did not understand. These parents could not accept that people needed to grieve in their own way. Instead of understanding that people's behavior had been influenced by a variety of external forces and was not always a matter of choice, they attributed behavior to negative intent or character faults. In addition, parents who adopted this approach seemed more concerned with how their spouse's behavior affected them personally than how their spouse might be feeling. This approach led to the development of or an increase in marital problems.

One of the underlying assumptions of almost all of the negative explanations was that people chose their mourning behavior intentionally. For example, several wives knew that their husbands had come from families in which the "family's way of coping" was to avoid talking about problems. As a result, they knew their husbands did not feel comfortable talking about feelings: "Although [these women] understood it, [they] still kind of resented it." They assumed that if their husbands really cared they would find a way to share their grief. Some women demanded that their husbands share their grief more openly. When the men did not comply, the women took this as a "personal insult." They ignored the possibility that the men were silent because they had never learned how to talk about their feelings and that they had spent their whole lives learning how to control their emotions. By choosing a negative explanation for the silence, these women increased the likelihood that their husbands would continue to be silent in the future. The men could sense the hostility; it was not safe to be open.

Some spouses decided that their partner behaved a certain way just to cause problems in the marriage. Within months of their baby's death, one husband who had managed to "return to normal" began to question the reason behind his wife's continued emotional outbursts. Instead of understanding her pain, he wondered if she was just trying to force him to meet her needs. In more than one marriage, one partner interpreted silence as an attempt to create distance in the marriage. One woman decided that her husband's silence and inability to listen to her pain meant that "he didn't care....I thought he didn't care how I felt." This kind of explanation increased marital stress and tension.

Some partners also used negative evaluations of themselves and each other as explanations. A few parents decided that their inability to handle their grief as well as their partner meant that they were "weak," while their partner was "strong." This attitude made them feel worse and increased the likelihood that they would begin to hide their pain. Others thought they were "stronger" than their partner because they could grieve without showing their pain or without needing outside help. Again, this attitude prevented honest communication about the naturalness of differences. Either approach contributed to the belief that there was a right and a wrong way to grieve. Some criticized their spouse for being too needy, "irrational," or "stupid." Instead of creating a sense of connection and caring in the relationship, negative evaluations caused conflict and distance in relationships. They did nothing to create a sense of loving partnership.

No matter what effect these destructive explanations had on relationships, at least they helped to restore a sense of order to the parents' lives. Those who were used to thinking negatively about themselves, their spouse, or their marriage usually found a negative explanation for confusing behavior. Making sense of behavior helped the parents to **carry on**. Eventually, they were ready to **learn how to let go**.

Chapter 5
Understanding the Parents' Experience: Learning to Let Go

Answering the Why Question

In the beginning weeks of this terrible nightmare, parents focused on the *search for a reason* or a medical explanation for their baby's death. Eventually most accepted SIDS as the cause of death. However, this diagnosis did not explain the circumstances of the death. In an attempt to make sense of what happened, parents looked for someone to blame. Even after assigning blame, parents continued to search for a logical explanation for their baby's death. I call this part of their search the *search for logic*. They wanted to find an "answer to the why question," to "find the logic" behind this apparently "senseless death." Many parents turned to religion. As one parent said, "If you believe in God or you believe in any religion, [there] has to be two reasons then why the person died": a medical reason and a spiritual reason. Until now, parents had treated the search for someone to blame and the search for the reason for the death separately. As the intensity of their grief subsided, parents could think clearly enough to think of the two questions simultaneously. This resulted in four possible explanations for their baby's death: punishment, faith, lesson, or fate. Once the four explanations had been generated, they had to decide which one to accept.

One parent described this process as "little games [we] play[ed] with [our] minds to make [our]selves feel better." These "mind games" were complex and the stakes were high. First, parents explored an explanation to see if it fit with their evidence: their decision about what had caused their baby's death and their perception of themselves and their God. The next step involved "chucking" any explanation that did not fit. Parents eliminated any explanations that caused "intellectual" or "emotional" discomfort. Finally, the parents selected the explanation or answer that made the most sense to them. Once they found an acceptable explanation, it affected their ability to **let go** of their grief and, to varying degrees, their baby.

Dimensions of the final reason

Accepting blame

Many medical experts had already told most parents that SIDS has no known cause. They also said that SIDS can neither be predicted nor prevented. Nonetheless, parents blamed themselves for their baby's death anyway. These parents held themselves directly responsible, believing they had been consciously or unconsciously "negligent." In their minds, somehow this death could have been prevented:

> I [was] just absolutely stone cold convinced…that I definitely killed her. It was a combination of factors, and in retrospect, certainly had I not done those things, she would have been alive today.…It [was my] negligence.

Other parents refused to blame themselves; instead, they held others responsible. But no matter whom they blamed, in the end, they felt indirectly responsible. Somehow they had "killed" their baby by believing doctors who said their baby was fine or by leaving their baby in the care of others.

Some parents believed that no one could be held responsible. Educating themselves about SIDS helped these parents to eventually come to the conclusion that "if you have a real SIDS baby, there is nothing you can do about it. They're going to go." Believing that SIDS cannot be prevented and that parents have no control over it helped one mother find peace: "When you know that it is SIDS, then you know there was nothing you could do. There was nothing you could do. There was nothing you could do to change it."

Others eventually found a way to explain what caused the death: they assigned the baby's death to "fate" or bad luck. Still others thought their baby died because of "God's will." In either case, parents wanted to believe they had no control over this death. It had been out of their hands all along. These explanations alone were not enough. Parents needed to add another piece to the puzzle before they could understand the whole picture.

Looking for spiritual meaning

Although they believed in God, some parents did not "relate to the religious attitude that there is meaning in [the baby's death]." They just accepted death as a part of life. Others did not look for any spiritual meaning because they did not believe in God. Still others looked for and found meaning in the baby's death: "When something like death happens to you, if you have a supernatural, a belief in a supernatural, that kind of answers that why question somehow."

Living with the final explanation

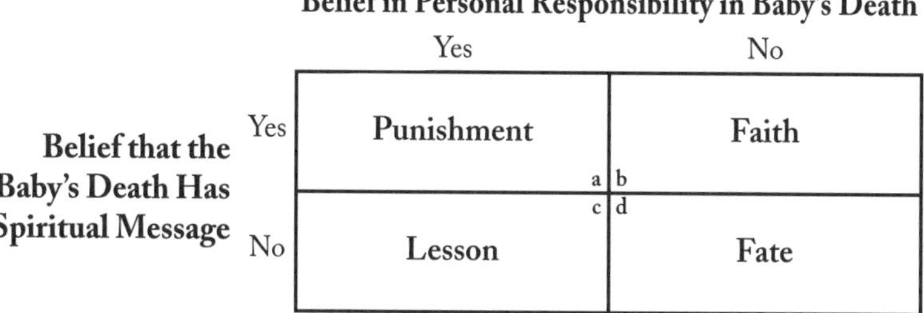

Figure 4 Typology of the parents' final explanations for their baby's death based on the belief in personal responsibility for the death and the belief that the death had a spiritual message

The punishment explanation

The parents who accepted the *punishment explanation* were just as likely to understand that SIDS had caused the baby's death as other parents. However, they also decided that God had taken their baby from them through SIDS to "punish [them] in a sense for something [they had] done bad" (cell a). Parents who accepted this explanation had reviewed every mistake they had ever made. They all found something "bad" enough to deserve some kind of punishment. The degree of perceived badness varied. Some felt guilty for breaking God's commandments at one time or another:

> I had done something very foolish…and when [my baby] died, my first thought was, "You are being punished for [this]." And I don't know maybe. Who knows? I really can't say. That might play something in it.

Others could not think of any specific behavior "bad" enough to bring on this much suffering. Consequently, they focused their search on how they could have been a "better" person. They wondered if God had taken their baby because He wanted them to change their behavior or attitude towards life. They remembered times when they had been an "unfeeling kind of person" or too "frivolous" or "materialistic." One woman worried that she had "loved [her baby] too much" and that God wanted her to know that this was wrong. Another speculated that "maybe if [she] had been a better Christian, maybe if [she] had been [going to church regularly], you know, maybe [the baby] wouldn't have been taken."

In each case, parents believed that they could have chosen to be different. Therefore, indirectly, they had caused their baby's death. Although these parents believed that they deserved to be punished, most had trouble accepting the severity of the punishment. Many initially felt "furious" and "angry at God" for taking their baby. Eventually, they accepted their "punishment," but life held little joy. They could not **let go** of their grief because they believed that they deserved to suffer. They had "chosen" this path, so they had to learn to live with it.

The faith explanation

The *faith explanation* (cell b) fit for parents who believed that the death had meaning and that they had no role in causing it to happen. After a thorough review of the evidence, these parents concluded that SIDS just happens to some babies. They also concluded that God had viewed them as "good parents" and good people: "He knows I'm a good parent.…God did not strike [the baby] dead because of my, uhm, I don't know, because of my past sins or something." Now they were confronted with a problem: "There has to be a reason why [God] wanted [the baby]," but "we do not want to blame God for, for bad things because he is a good God. He doesn't do bad things."

A punishing God was out of the question for these parents. As one put it, "When I thought about the character of God, it didn't seem…that punishing and all that kind of stuff fit in with the character of God as I know it. Okay? So yeah, so it didn't take very long to chuck that one out." Instead, this mother needed to believe in a loving God.

To eliminate the image of a vengeful God who had taken their baby, some parents decided that God had established natural laws when He created the world. When people were sick or "not perfect," death happened as a part of the "natural progression" of life. In some cases, people died slowly. SIDS took babies suddenly. Although these parents concluded that God had not taken their baby on purpose, they still believed that God played a role in their baby's death: "God was there to receive [our baby] when he was no longer going to be with us. He was there to receive [him] and look after him. [God] is there now with him, and He was also there to help us get through it."

Parents who reached this conclusion found comfort in prayer and in their faith. They felt God cried with them and understood their pain because He, too, is a bereaved father. The message behind the death had been a "faith message": "That is very joyful to know that, to know that hey, no matter where I go, He's there. He's with you. He walks with you."

Other parents also found a *faith explanation,* but their version was slightly different. Although they sincerely believed in a loving God, they found a way to explain why God had intentionally taken their baby's life. A pastoral visitor offered one mother the following explanation:

> God didn't want your baby to suffer. There is so much violence in this world, there is drugs and alcohol, there's war, there's everything.... God didn't want your daughter to suffer.... That's why He took her away. And He also wanted someone to look after you from up there and look down on you and to watch over you. That's why He took her.

The mother rejected this explanation at first. Then the more she thought about it, the more, "you know, it made sense." When she accepted this explanation, she stopped feeling angry with God. It also explained why her perfectly healthy baby had died and others had lived. God loved her baby so much that He took her to prevent further pain. Other parents found similar explanations that "help[ed] with the why." In each case, the parents saw God's decision to take the baby in a positive light. In each case, taking the baby reduced the possibility of future suffering:

> Maybe there was something awful that was going to happen [to the baby]. Maybe that's why God took him.

> Because maybe he was sick. Maybe he was going to be, something was going to happen to him or something was going to or he was going to be a handicapped person or something like that. There are certain things going through your mind, thinking, "Well, if he has apnea,

> could he grow out of it or not?" See? He may or he may not, and he may have a problem breathing, or he may have a heart problem.
>
> Like what's the reasoning? And I couldn't understand it....How I answered my question is I thought that maybe God felt that [our baby] maybe had, if he had his destiny was to be something, something [bad] was going to happen to him, and [God] felt I wouldn't be strong enough to cope with that and that is he just passed away in his sleep; it would be easier than to have something horrible, more horrible happen.

A few parents made halfhearted attempts to forgive God for taking their baby. They explained that God "needed somebody little up there with wings, and that's just, that's just my belief." When asked if he felt like God had stolen his baby, one father replied, "Yeah, but then, why him? Why us? And then we thought, what a more, you couldn't have a more perfect fellow to have if you needed another angel so." This explanation seemed tentative. Parents usually offered this type of explanation in combination with another one.

Others stopped trying to understand "the reason" and took a "leap of faith." Although they did not understand why God had taken their baby, they knew one thing for sure: they could "trust in Him" and "lean on their faith" to get them through this tragedy. For these parents, "prayer in a sense brought comfort." Having "blind faith" restored a sense of safety and order. Parents tried to accept that they might never understand God's reasoning and that they just had to learn to **carry on** anyway: "This is the Lord's way and there's no way I'm going to understand it....This is something I can't do anything about, and I'm going to accept that." Many who thought this way jokingly talked about what they intended to do once they finally met God; they intended to ask for an explanation.

The lesson explanation

Other parents used the *lesson explanation* (cell c). They did not think their baby's death had any divine meaning; instead, they believed that they had simply made a mistake in caring for their child: "I did still blame myself even though I know I shouldn't, logically I knew I shouldn't. But you still do. What if I had slept in her room that night? What if—you know all those things." In their minds, their baby died as a logical consequence of an unintentional error in parental judgement. To ensure that his next child would be safe from a repetition of the error, one father who felt responsible for the baby's death learned his lesson well. He developed a plan of action to prevent himself from making another lethal mistake with his next baby:

> Although I don't think I'll be questioning my every single move, I think I'm going to map them out before I go and then stay with the pattern and just say this is the way, and I'll have a set mind set of what's right and what's wrong, and I'll have them all mapped out, and I'll just do them.

Once these parents isolated their error, they just had to be sure they never repeated it. In some cases, this meant taking better care of themselves during pregnancy, changing doctors, becoming more vigilant about the next baby's health, or doing everything possible to avoid "the risk factors" connected with SIDS. They had learned their lesson. Parents who blamed themselves and could not isolate the specific and lethal act remained nervous and hyper-vigilant.

The fate explanation

Parents also used the *fate explanation* (cell d): They attributed their baby's death to "fate." Those who accepted this explanation refused to believe that they had caused the death; they also refused to "embrace religion" for an explanation. Instead, some chose a medical explanation, using all that they had learned about SIDS. Their baby's death "made sense" because, purely by chance and not by design, the circumstances had been just right for SIDS to strike: the time of the year and the baby's age combined with fact that the baby had a slight cold. Parents believed the death had nothing to do with them; they could be "absolved."

Other parents talked about chance and the "luck of the draw." In their minds, out of 500 healthy babies, 499 did not die of SIDS. By chance, they had given birth to the one destined to die. There was nothing personal about the baby's death: "Shit happens. It just happens, and there is nothing you can do about it."

Still others believed that the length of each person's life had been predetermined and, therefore, was beyond human control. Their baby just had less time on this earth than most: "Maybe that was on the calendar, type thing, that's the way it was set out to be":

> [People said to us], "Don't blame yourself. You couldn't do anything."...We really didn't believe that, you know, at the time. But we do now, I think. We do, we really couldn't do anything at that time. It

> was fate, I suppose. Fate, I suppose you could say. Fate takes people at the weirdest time. The oddest time, I should say. At any age, I suppose.

These parents found some comfort in believing that "a plan" existed. This did not stop them from wanting to understand the reason behind such a plan. Parents who said they were "not even searching" anymore for an explanation made comments such as "When the time comes for me to know, I'll know." At the moment, they knew as much as they needed to know to let go of their grief.

Playing mind games

Challenging and changing the explanation

Parents felt more comfortable having an explanation than not having one. As a consequence, when something or someone challenged the explanation that had made them feel better, some parents panicked. One mother derived great comfort from believing that her baby died of SIDS. To her this diagnosis meant she had no control over it. Because it absolved her of any responsibility, it gave her peace. As she said, "I have to believe it was SIDS or I would fall apart." Many years after her baby's death her carefully constructed explanation fell apart and then so did she. During a casual conversation, a doctor suggested that perhaps her baby had not died of SIDS. This suggestion "set [her] back for a loop":

> After that experience with [the doctor], I researched my little heart out.... I reread the autopsy report. I called the medical examiner. I did the whole research thing again. So now, I've accepted that [it was SIDS], but knowing that it's SIDS does relieve your mind because there's, you have no control.

This mother had to work hard to reconstruct and prove her original explanation; otherwise, she had to accept responsibility for her baby's death, something she just could not do.

Another parent eventually decided not to "blame anyone for it happening. It happened." In the beginning though, she blamed herself for being a smoker. To decide whether to assign blame to herself, she asked her doctor about this. When he told her that parental smoking had nothing to do with the incidence of SIDS, she felt better. She stopped blaming herself. That is, until years later

> [when she] found out that smoking, uh, contributes and so that I can say that I contributed to his death because I was a smoker and [her husband] as well at the time so that's the only blame. But I didn't know that at the time so, you know, now. And it really bothered me when I found that out, too.... You have enough guilt anyway.

Confronted with new information that challenged her long-held comfortable explanation, this mother worked hard to forgive herself for smoking. She told herself, "If I had known, I wouldn't have [smoked]. But I didn't and it's too bad but I can't change that." This example points to the dilemma with reporting each new theory about the cause of SIDS. As scientists uncover possible risk factors or trigger mechanisms, their discoveries challenge the explanations that parents work so very hard to construct. These challenges often cause the parents to reevaluate their role in the baby's death.

Other parents chose explanations that had nothing to do with SIDS specifically. They chose an explanation that made them uncomfortable but that made sense, given what they believed about God and themselves. One woman decided that God had taken her baby to punish her. This thought tortured her for years, preventing her from receiving comfort from prayer and from being able to **let go** of her grief or her baby. When both she and her husband rededicated themselves to their faith and to God, they found another explanation—one that made them both feel better. They decided that God had not been the villain; Satan had taken their baby. Satan had taken their baby to tempt them away from God's love:

> Satan is there to try to kill and to destroy, so he brings sickness and he brings, if he can he brings, you know, diseases and all that. He comes here to try and kill and to destroy, so if he takes the child away and the child dies and he can break up the family, then he has done an excellent part on his part because that's all he's there for.

Once this couple found a new and comforting explanation, they were able to **let go** of their grief. For the first time since the baby's death, they cried together and shared their pain. They also found a new place for the baby, a place that finally gave them peace for the first time in over 10 years.

Feeling lost without an explanation

Unfortunately, some parents could not find an explanation that offered them comfort. This troubled them deeply and added to their pain. They "yo yo[ed]" back and forth between an explanation that involved self-blame and one that "absolved" them of responsibility. Even after the autopsy and a thorough review of research about SIDS, one mother still felt confused: "The whole thing...it's not totally explained to me." She desperately wanted to believe that her baby died because of a problem in the "brain stem." However, the autopsy had not provided her with enough concrete evidence to accept a purely medical explanation. Within minutes of sharing her medical explanation in the interview, this mother blamed herself for "not checking [the baby] sooner." She also bounced back and forth between believing that this death held some spiritual message for her and then believing it did not. Although she wanted to derive comfort from her faith, she was "still at the point where [she was] questioning everything." She felt unsettled by both her questions and her answers. As long as comfortable or sensible answers eluded her, grief and pain overwhelmed her. As long as she could not settle on one explanation, she felt afraid and very vulnerable: "You start to think of all the terrible things that could happen" because "if this can happen, anything can happen."

Benefitting from the final explanation

Parents who ended their ***search for logic*** felt better than those who could not settle on one explanation. Each explanation restored the parents' sense of order.

Those who accepted the *punishment explanation* could now see a connection between their behavior and their baby's death. It all made sense now. God had acted logically, not randomly. People who were bad or not good enough got what they deserved. To prevent further problems, these parents just had to become better people. They also had to accept their punishment without complaint.

Those who accepted the *lesson explanation* could also see the connection between their behavior and their baby's death. They had made a specific mistake as a parent. Their baby's death had not happened randomly; in fact, it occurred because of their mistake (at least in their minds). As long as they could pinpoint that mistake and make sure never to repeat it, they could prevent further deaths. They just had to change the way they cared for their children in the future. Then they had to find a way to live with their mistake and to forgive themselves.

Parents who accepted the *faith explanation* felt loved and cared for by God, whether they chose to believe that God had personally intervened or not. In either case, they learned that God cared about them and their suffering, so they turned to God for strength and support. They had also learned that they were not alone and that their world had order. Even though these parents realized that some things in life were beyond their control, they took a "leap of faith"; they trusted that God knew best and that He would always be there to "lean on."

Parents who accepted the *fate explanation* felt better, too. They no longer felt like victims; they realized that no one had maliciously singled them out. They could stop taking the baby's death personally. They finally understood that everyone stood an equal chance of losing a baby to SIDS. Some parents derived comfort from the existence of "a plan" for everyone. It restored their sense of order.

Each type of explanation restored a sense of structure and order in the parents' lives. Their baby had either died for a purpose or for a logical reason. In either case, each explanation restored their sense of control. Parents felt less vulnerable and less afraid. Finding an answer to the why question freed them from their pain. As a result, they were able to begin to **let go** of their grief.

Letting Go of Grief

At first, grief overwhelmed the parents. Then, they slowly learned how to manage it well enough to **carry on** with their lives. Managing grief was not enough; parents wanted to stop grieving. To do that, they needed to find a way to let go of their pain. Once parents found an explanation for their baby's death that made sense to them, it became a bit easier to **let go** of their grief. They used many different strategies, some more effective and constructive than others.

Strategies for letting go of grief

Repressing grief

Parents tried to deal with their grief by putting it away, either consciously or unconsciously. Some parents consciously put their feelings away so they could go on with life. In the early stages of this experience, many fathers chose to block their own pain so that they could "be strong" for their wives. Mothers found it more difficult to set aside their grief. Sometimes they decided they had to—for the health of their new baby or for the health of their marriage. One mother felt she had to "put a lot of feelings up on the shelf" to cope with the "SIDS fear" and her frustrations with her marriage. She had to keep "say[ing to herself], 'You're not going to think about it.'" Then, she and her family got used to keeping the grief locked inside a "box."

After awhile, she seldom talked about her pain. Although others assumed she had dealt with her grief, she had really just put it away. After awhile, the very thought of taking down "Pandora's box" frightened her.

Others did not consciously choose to repress or "harbor" their grief. They just did not know what else to do with it. They followed a lifetime pattern of being a "rock," although they hated what it did to them: "Like I say, the man is, you don't cry, you don't show feelings, you don't. This is not, you know, this is not your role. But damn the role. Go out and do it." Some men spoke with considerable frustration about being locked into this "role." They also described numerous health problems that they attributed to their inability to do anything with their grief but "harbor" it.

A few parents did more than repress their grief: they also repressed their love. Fearing that another loss would destroy them, some parents consciously avoided deep involvements with their other children: "I was scared to really maybe try and get, uh, really involved at, you know, really maybe get attached. I don't know.... If [this next baby] was gonna, you know, gonna lose [it] again." Sometimes, parents stopped caring much about life in general. Although holding love at bay reduced the chances of getting hurt again, it also reduced the opportunity to live fully.

Replacing grief

Instead of trying to put away their grief, some parents tried to replace it with other thoughts and feelings. Some tried to change how they felt by "mak[ing] up your mind, too, that it is not the end of the world, that you have to, you have to go on, that you've got a lot still left. You might have lost something, but you still have a lot left." Instead of focusing on the missing baby, these parents remembered that "[God] didn't take everything away from me." They tried to replace their pain with increased appreciation for their other children. They also tried to replace their grief with the "joy" of having another baby. Having another baby "does put something back into your life that you can be, you can be happy about."

Some parents replaced their grief with action. They committed themselves to doing something about SIDS by jumping on the "SIDS bandwagon." While some devoted themselves to raising money for research, others became involved in public education or parent support.

Releasing grief

Releasing grief took many forms. Many years after the death of her baby, one mother decided to do a "forgiveness thing." She made a special effort to release the remnants of her grief by forgiving all "the players." She wanted to set aside her anger towards God for taking her baby and towards her husband for being a "jerk father" at the time. In addition, she tried to forgive herself and release the last vestiges of her guilt:

> If I had done anything wrong, and I'm not sure about that, in my mothering skills or if I hadn't taken her to the doctor or if [I had not] put her in the buggy without a hat, whatever those things were, that I forgave myself for that because I did the best that I could with what I knew.

After choosing to release her anger and guilt, this mother could just "feel the healing." For the first time in many years, the hurting stopped. Another mother did a similar exercise. Besides forgiving God, she thanked Him for giving her the baby, if only for a short time. For the first time in years, she, too, felt a sense of peace.

Other parents got angry with God. They released their anger by "direct[ing]" it or "channell[ing] it in the right place. When I got angry, if I was angry at God, I told him how angry I was with him." Although a few people tried to stop parents from showing their anger with God, parents believed that "God understood" and that He accepted their anger. Many parents also let people who had angered them know about their hurt. In addition, release was accomplished by: crying, talking, praying, writing in a journal, turning the whole problem over to God, and rigorous exercise and physical activities.

Parents also released some of their grief by attending a support group, talking to other grieving parents on the telephone, or talking with sympathetic friends and relatives. Those who needed to talk about their baby, their experience, and their grief got perspective and distance from their pain. Distancing helped them sort out their feelings. Some parents, usually fathers, attended support group meetings only until they had gathered "enough information" to stop all their internal questions and guilt. Once these parents had the information they needed, they released themselves from the "thousand guilts." Then they worked on releasing the rest of their grief in other ways, often privately in their cars and in their heads.

Although many people told the parents shortly after the baby's death that the passage of time would help them feel better, this kind of statement irritated the parents. Eventually, they learned on their own to "let grief run its course" and that, in fact, "time does heal." Once parents stopped trying to force their grief to go away and just accepted its presence in their lives, the intensity gradually subsided. Accepting grief helped to release it. One woman tried to force herself to "get better too fast." Fortunately, a public health nurse explained that she needed to "give [her]self a year" to grieve, to feel "all the changes that you're going through....You've got to go through the shock, disbelief, anger and acceptance." Receiving "permission" to take time to grieve immediately made this mother feel better.

Another form of releasing was to forget the pain. Some parents could remember the smallest details about events on the day their baby died and for days afterwards; these parents found it hard to forget. For others, the whole experience was just a "big fog." Although the inability to remember frustrated some parents during the interviews, others expressed relief that their memories had been erased: "I don't even recall....I don't know if that's the healing process or the process of trying to forget or whatever. Thank God it's probably there. And I really don't have much recollection."

The last form of releasing grief is what I call leaking. Rather than consciously and purposefully **letting go** of their grief, some parents slowly released it in other situations. While some cried more easily, other became angry quite quickly and over very little. Most felt very sensitive about comments anyone made about their parenting. Although these parents did not always realize it, they were slowly releasing their "stored feelings." Release came at funerals, when other people tried to discuss death or the need to write a will, when parents heard about the murder or abuse of children, or when they saw a baby that reminded them of their own child.

Reducing grief

Parents also tried hard to reduce the intensity and devastation of their loss. Several tried to "find a silver lining" in this awful experience; they looked for positives in their situation. Others looked "for things that could be worse"; this strategy involved finding the negatives in related experiences. While some parents just used one approach, others used both. Each strategy had the same effect though: it helped parents put their loss in perspective. It allowed them to **let go** of some of the pain.

Instead of continually focusing on the pain that the baby's death had caused, several parents found the "silver lining." They chose to celebrate and be thankful for the "months of happiness and joy" their baby had given them. As one mother said, "I think going on with life is acceptance and thinking back and being happy....It's not putting up a front that I feel that I was lucky. I was lucky to have [the baby]. We were lucky to have him." These parents talked about their baby freely, celebrating special moments and accomplishments. Over the years, others had encouraged or tolerated this kind of talk. The baby was physically gone but much loved and valued.

It took awhile, but some parents even managed to find a "silver lining" in losing a baby to SIDS: "If I had to lose a child, I'm glad that I lost a child this way. He went to sleep, and there was no pain, and he just fell asleep." Many parents talked about how glad they were that their baby had not suffered. This "silver lining" brought a great deal of comfort. Babies who died of SIDS usually died early in life: "If you can find a silver lining, [the baby] was only 16 weeks, and maybe if he was 16 months, I'm sure that that is much more vivid, and it probably would have added a touch more bitterness."

Gradually parents emerged from their own pain and began to look at the suffering of other parents. Then they began to realize that "it could have been worse." Those who attended a support group had the opportunity to compare experiences with other grieving parents. This helped some feel better. A mother who had lost one of her twins "went to a SIDS group, and I went away feeling so sorry for some people there." The arms of other parents truly were "empty"; at least she had a baby to cuddle and love. She realized then that her pain "could have been worse." Parents who still had other children wondered about the pain of those who had lost their only child. Some also began to realize that they had more support and resources than other people who came to a support group alone and isolated. A support group also gave parents the opportunity to hear about the circumstances of other parents' loss. They began to realize that perhaps, in a strange way, they had been fortunate:

> Like there was no doubt in my mind that there was no reviving him. Like he was cold and very stiff already. But then you hear stories of people that there was a, they found him and he'd maybe stopped breathing for, I don't know, 5 minutes, so they went through the process of trying to revive them just to no avail, like taking him to the hospital and then it was over. Like that's got to be really traumatic, going though all that. And that is one thing that we didn't have to do. There again, like if it were to happen, I think the way it happened with us. There wasn't a bunch of people involved, you know, because, that, if there was a chance to revive him, you would, I would blame the people who didn't do their job or whatever. No doubt and no hope, which was not great, the no hope. It's over and I'm saying this from going to the meetings like and knowing what other people went through.

Beyond comparing their experience with other parents who had lost babies to SIDS, parents also thought of worse ways their baby could have died. One mother talked with a friend whose severely handicapped child frequently came close to death and then recovered: SIDS "is considerably easier in a way to deal with because it is over and done with. It is not an ongoing thing." A father "looked around" and decided that watching "our child suffering something that was irreversible and watching the pain" would have been far worse than losing the baby suddenly to SIDS. Another parent found a situation that made her appreciate the suddenness, peacefulness, and lack of control in a SIDS death:

> A little 3 year old was murdered. Like abducted from an apartment, like she was going downstairs and her grandmother lived between or whatever floors, and she was kidnapped and she was sexually molested and then murdered at 3 years old. And I thought to have to live with that, you know. And I thought, how would you get over that because the main thing I find with grief and the understanding is you get over it as soon as you start finding out, I couldn't, I wasn't responsible. It happened and [there was] nothing I could have done.

Despite the power of these grief-reducing strategies, parents rejected other people's attempts to provide them with "silver linings" or "it could be worse" situations. They had to find their own:

> [Another couple at the group] had just lost their baby [and they said], "We are really happy because our baby is now with God. It is just a perfect place for people to be, and uh, we'll be just waiting to see him....Oh you should be happy [about your baby dying, too]!"...I said, "I don't want to wait 50 or 60 years! I want to hold him now! Who cares?" You know? I said, "I had plans for him and me. I don't want to do this 60 years from now. I want to do it now." I said, "Don't push this religion crap on me, you know. Forget it. Don't try to lecture me."
>
> It will always be with me. [A coworker] says, "Well, it's a good thing he wasn't 15 or 16 years old," and I thought, "you know, I would give anything to have my son until he was 15 or 16." And I won't forget that 'til the day I die. That was, uh, a hard one to swallow.

Reliving and remembering grief

Some parents refuse to **let go** of their grief because grieving keeps them connected to their baby. Others want to **let go** but they cannot. Some parents annually relive and remember their grief on the anniversary of their baby's death. On that day, they are again "in pain." Once that day is over, they go back to living life again. Other parents experience an annual resurgence of sadness on the baby's birthday or on other special occasions or holidays. One mother always misses her baby the most on Mother's Day: "In the back of [her] mind [she had] the sense that there should have been somebody else there on Mother's Day." Sometimes the resurgence of grief strikes without warning when parents realize what life events their baby is missing:

> I love Christmas concerts. And I was not even thinking of [our son] and the kindergartens walked in and 'Ah! My God, that's [our son's] kindergarten class! Like, he should be up there!' And I just started crying. . . . It just hit me. That's [our son's] kindergarten class. Like those are all the little boys that he'd be with, you know? And it just hit me, and then after they were gone, you know, I pulled myself together and it was all right.

Because this is so closely related to **letting go** of the baby, I will leave further comments about this until that section.

Remnants of grief

As time passed and as parents tried to **learn how to let go** of their grief, the intensity of the pain slowly began to subside. Life returned to some semblance of normal. Nonetheless, despite all their best efforts, many parents were left with remnants of grief: resentment, sadness, vulnerability, and guilt.

Resentment

No matter how much healing they had done or how much time had passed, most parents continued to resent other parents who had not lost a baby. They got angry when they heard about unwed mothers or when they saw

> babies that weren't being cared for. That's when I went through the anger again, every time. Because, and you read about it in the paper, the little babies that are beaten and the little babies that their parents can't even afford to have them, but they keep having them. Uhm, that angered me. People aborting babies. I was, I was never for abortion ever anyway, but I was very anti-it after I lost my [baby].

Some parents could not forgive family members, friends, or their spouse for not being helpful or supportive in the early stages of the experience. Some relationships never healed. The "insensitive" comments, the fights, the silence, some parents remembered it all, and they would not **let it go**: "[The family] just didn't talk about it. It was something they kept to themselves. So although I understood it, I still kind of resented it."

And some parents just remained angry at anything and everything. At the slightest hint of a problem, they seemed prepared for an argument. They looked at the negatives of every situation and every person they met instead of looking for anything positive. Few of these parents had found an acceptable explanation for their baby's death; they still felt "cheated" and "robbed."

Sadness

And like the simmering resentment, some parents remained generally saddened. They "went through the motions" in life with little sense of anticipation and happiness. Some previously joyous and "frivolous" parents now take life very "seriously."

Vulnerability

Although they tried to control their tendency to worry, some parents just could not **let go** of their fears, even years later: "And one of the things that I'm working through right now, and I'm sure this is a result of this whole thing, is just fear. I have a lot of fears." Parents feared specific things like storms, travelling, car accidents, the abduction and illness of their children, and looking after other people's children. Several women said they even feared becoming a grandmother. They did not want their own children to lose a baby to SIDS. Parents tried to devote extra time to their children. Often in the back of their minds, they had the fear that "maybe one day [the children] aren't going to be here." While some parents had learned to appreciate the transient nature of life, others continually worried about safety issues. They did everything they could to control the circumstances of their lives; they just could not **let it go**.

Guilt

As parents worked through the creation of their own explanation of the baby's death, the number of "what ifs" decreased. Once parents reached their own conclusion about why their baby had died, they relaxed a bit. As previously discussed, at the slightest hint of a challenge to their explanation, the parents' guilt could rise again and overwhelm them. As one mother described it, you always have "guilt hanging around like a bogey man." Parents continued to monitor the popular press for new research results that could either absolve them or point the final finger of blame. Many also read the obituaries every day to see if babies continued to die of SIDS.

One other important source of guilt came from the parents' commitment to volunteering for the CFSID. Some parents dealt with their grief by becoming involved as volunteers for the Foundation; it made them feel better to be doing something in the fight against SIDS. After many years of devotion to the "SIDS bandwagon," some parents felt guilty about needing to reduce their commitment or quitting altogether. Guilt came from two sources: first, the lack of new volunteers made it difficult to think about quitting; and second, quitting the group felt like abandoning their baby. Just thinking about it sometimes made parents feel guilty.

Benefitting from letting go of grief

Despite the presences of the remnants, most parents who **let go** of their grief began to "move on" with their lives. They had freed themselves from most of their pain. At least the pain had "softened around the edges." Although they would never be the same as before their baby's death, most parents tried to enjoy life again. Those who did not let go of their grief "move[d] on" with little joy. Instead of basing their lives on what they had, these parents focused on what was "missing." This became very apparent when it came time to think about **letting go** of the baby.

Finding a Place for the Baby

All the parents kept a special and often private place in their heart for their baby. Parents varied in their need to make the baby part of their everyday life. Variations in this need could be placed along a continuum, with parents who let go of their baby entirely at one end. In the minds of these parents, the baby was "absent, just absent." At the start of the interview, these parents often said they had not thought of their baby in years. At the opposite end of the continuum were parents who visited their baby in his or her place weekly, who thought of the baby every day no matter how many years had passed, and whose actions showed a continued connection to the baby. In the middle were parents who vacillated between the two extremes. Parents tried to hold onto their baby by keeping the memory alive and by keeping the baby in the family. Parents tried to let go by finding a safe place to put the baby and by devoting themselves to their other children.

Holding on

Keeping the memory alive

No parent wanted to forget this baby had ever been born, but some parents felt comfortable letting the memories fade over time. Other parents worked hard to keep their baby's memory alive; they just refused to let go. "Counting the baby," "marking time," and "doing for" the baby helped the parents keep their baby's memory alive.

Counting the baby

When asked how many children they had, most parents wanted to "count" this baby: "I want them to know that this is my third baby and the second baby's life did count and I'm not going to wipe it out." This problem bothered most parents; they felt guilty if they did not count their baby, and they knew it upset people when they did.

"Counting" took other forms as well. A few parents talked about their baby frequently, not about the death, but about the baby's short life. They did not want to forget the joy the baby had brought them. This also gave them the opportunity to use the baby's name. Although a few parents gave permission for others to use their baby's name, other parents guarded it. They did not want anyone else to use this name or even one that sounded similar. Some parents felt pleased, however, when their other children said they planned to name their own baby after their baby brother or sister.

Parents also "count[ed]" the baby by displaying his or her pictures with other family photographs, even if other family members objected. One sibling asked her mother to take the baby's picture down from a prominent place in the house because it "bother[ed]" her. The mother replied,

> He is my son. [His picture] belongs there, and I don't care how you cope with it or how you deal with it, but that is my picture....I don't care what you do. If you have to walk by it with closed eyes, then you'll have to do that.

A few parents also tried to make the baby's death count for something. They made sure that friends and family sent donations to the CFSID. One mother helped her friends to "raise funds for an infant incubator in [her baby's] memory." Being on the "SIDS bandwagon" also helped the parents "count" their baby.

Marking time

Many parents kept their baby's memory alive by "mark[ing]" time. This meant keeping track of the baby's birthday and deathday, how much time had past since the death, and how old the baby would be if he or she had lived. Parents also "mark[ed]" the baby's missed "milestones."

More women than men "mark[ed]" time. One mother even remembered when she found out she was pregnant with this baby and "when [she] started labor." Another became seriously ill every year during her baby's birth month; she interpreted this as her body "miss[ing] the baby." Mothers frequently set aside time for the baby on special days such as birthdays and the anniversary of the death. A few women avoided the annual resurgence of pain; they refused to "mark" time. For them, significant days went by and they "didn't bat an eye." Their baby was just "absent" from their lives and their minds. They preferred to concentrate on loving their living children.

Few fathers kept track of the passage of time. One father, however, "mark[ed]" his son's deathdate with a cross on his calendar. Then, on the anniversary of the baby's death, he made a special point of "remembering" him. Another father remembers finding his baby; this continues to be a painful day for him. Other fathers notice the date, but they keep their pain private. Still others try to avoid remembering, but changes in their wives' behavior always let them know what day it is. One husband reported that

> [his wife] turns into a different person for about 3 days and just does not care about anything....It usually takes me a day or so to realize what's going on, and then I think about it. It's coming up again....It's that time of the year again.

A few fathers completely "wiped out" any connection with special days. To them, it made no sense to keep hurting themselves with memories.

Another form of "marking time" was thinking of the baby fleetingly during the year. Seeing a baby the same age as their baby had been or seeing children who were the same as their baby "would have been" made many parents think about the baby they had lost. In most parents' minds their baby stayed a baby. Occasionally though, parents wondered about their baby's appearance or what accomplishments they would have made to the world had he or she lived. For example, watching his other children play hockey made one father wonder what kind of hockey player his deceased son would have been.

Besides wondering what their baby would have been like had she or he lived, parents also "mark[ed]" the passing of missed "milestone" events.

These other "would have been[s]" included: starting school, graduating, getting married, and having children. Parents who allowed themselves to "mark" time this way knew that "there's going to be these things that you have to deal with the rest of your life." To these parents, the pain of remembering was worth it. They did not want to forget their baby.

Doing for the baby

Besides "marking time" and "counting" the baby, a few parents found other ways to prove their love for their baby. They tried to continue to "do for" their baby. Some parents visited their baby's grave occasionally. One mother did more than that. She "place[d] flowers [at the grave] every week" and left holiday treats there as well. It was her "way of not letting him think I've forgotten, which might sound really corny but, but it's my way of saying, '[Baby], I haven't forgotten about you." Several months after their baby's death, one couple moved their baby from a civic cemetery to a more beautiful private cemetery. Thinking of their baby and wanting to do something nice for him, they chose a lovely spot under a shady tree.

When parents continued to "do for" the baby despite the passage of many years, relatives and friends often expressed concern. They wondered if the parents were "dwelling on something that is no longer there and you're not letting it go." Few parents listened to these concerns. They just accepted that "maybe part of me will never let it go."

Getting on the "SIDS bandwagon" provided another way for some parents to "do for" their baby:

> This is the one thing that I can do for my [child] that's not here. And that's the way I look at it, and I think most of the other SIDS people that work with the group look at it that way, too. That there's so much we can do for our other children but this is the one thing I can do for the one I don't have any more.

Being on the "bandwagon" meant doing any of four types of activities: public awareness, fund-raising, parent support, and administration of the local chapter or the national office of CFSID. Some parents were involved in all four areas, devoting hours and hours of their time as volunteers.

Parents often carried out their own public awareness campaigns by telling everyone they could about SIDS and about their experience. They gave away brochures to people who did not understand SIDS. One woman tried to organize a public forum in her community so that more health professionals could learn about SIDS. A few parents shared their personal experiences with the media, particularly during SIDS Awareness Month. Parents also shared their experiences with professionals and other volunteer programs whose work brought them into contact with new SIDS parents.

Parents also worked hard to raise money for the Foundation. Some couples asked that people send In Memorium donations to the Foundation. In addition, parents also donated money themselves and organized large fund-raising events such as a giant garage sale or by selling crafts on a small scale. One couple became "crazed" with the idea of raising money. They were determined that people were "going to donate as much money as they can to this cause. We've got to find out a reason." Others gave their time regularly to the local group's fund-raising activities. Raising money for SIDS helped the parents feel like they were doing something about this dreaded syndrome. They wanted more people to know about SIDS, more money to be devoted to SIDS research, and more services for newly bereaved families.

Some parents, mostly mothers, dedicated themselves, their time, and their energy to helping newly bereaved parents. In one urban centre, after dealing with their own pain first, parents could volunteer to be part of the parent support team. They could answer calls on the SIDS Line, lead the monthly support group, or make home visits to newly bereaved parents. This intense involvement usually stirred up painful memories of their own experience. Parents who answered the SIDS line could be on the telephone for hours at a time, taking time away from family obligations, relationships, and sometimes sleep since the line operates 24 hours a day. Parents who led the support group sometimes had to deal with as many as 20 parents at a time, each with their own needs and issues. The needs of newly bereaved parents sometimes conflicted with the needs of parents dealing with concerns about a subsequent pregnancy or the anniversary of their baby's death. Some parents needed more help than these volunteers could give. Home visits sometimes required the intervention of professionals. In some communities, parents who volunteered to help with the support program received little or no training or supervision. They had to learn by experience.

Parents also became involved in the administration of the Foundation, either at the local or national level. Locally, parents served on committees and took on executive positions. Nationally, parents could serve on the Foundation's board. Again, this kind of commitment took time away from family activities and from the personal lives of the parents. These activities were not without frustration. Some local chapters felt dissatisfied with the services and support they received from the national office. Members felt equally frustrated by the lack of community support. There were never enough volunteers to do all that the parents wanted to do. Because they would not compromise their need to continue the fight against SIDS, involved parents often took on more than one job.

When parents volunteered in all four areas, there was the possibility of burnout. The fact that these parents could not stop giving their time to the "SIDS bandwagon" without feeling guilty made it worse. For some parents, withdrawing as a volunteer for CFSID felt like abandoning their baby. Working on the "SIDS bandwagon" had created a strong but indirect connection to their baby. So even when they were obviously exhausted, even when their spouse, children, or family asked them to quit the group, some parents continued to be involved. Being involved with CFSID was a substitute for "do[ing] for" their baby. For some parents, this meant they could never stop. They just could not **let go**.

Keeping the baby in the family

The need to keep a place for the baby in the family lessened over time for some parents. It did not bother them to **let go** of the baby. Other parents could not **let go**; instead, they developed a variety of strategies to ensure that their baby continued to be a special member of the family. Besides keeping the baby's memory alive, parents kept their baby in the family. They did this by giving the baby a special job, including the baby in family celebrations, and encouraging the siblings to have a relationship with the baby.

Giving the baby a special job

Some parents who used religion to help them deal with the death of their baby transformed the baby into "the family's guardian angel." The baby either "watched over [the] family" or became the siblings' "guardian angel now." Some parents found "that a little reassuring that [the baby is] there to protect [everyone] from anything." A few parents recounted many "close calls" that could have resulted in tragedy. Because tragedy had been averted, these parents felt confident that their "guardian angel" had intervened. Turning the baby into a "guardian angel" also gave the baby a home and a pleasing physical appearance. More mothers than fathers talked about their baby as an angel.

Involving the baby in family celebrations

To keep the baby in the family, some parents involved their baby in all family celebrations throughout the year. This involvement came in two forms: mental and physical.

By keeping their baby in mind on certain days, parents made sure the baby attended special functions. Some thought about their "missing" child on holidays and special occasions such as Mother's Day:

> You know the big things that are made of Mother's Day in schools and stuff. I think that I was very attuned to the children's needs, and I did not make it horrid for them, like I didn't cry and all those kinds of things. But in the back of my mind the sense that there should have been somebody else there on Mother's Day.

While some parents kept such thoughts to themselves, others talked about them. A few parents casually mentioned to their other children that they missed the baby on special days. Other parents went even further. They expected the whole family to visit the cemetery on special days throughout the year, no matter how many years had passed. They also appreciated it when other family members sent flowers to the cemetery; it showed they still thought of the baby as a part of the family, too. When families visited the grave, they left flowers, gifts, drawings, messages, Christmas trees, and Easter eggs.

Instead of focusing on who was missing from the family, a few parents tried to use the baby's birthday or deathday as a reason to celebrate who was in the family. Every year on the anniversary of her baby's death, one mother took the day off work and took her children out of school. They spent the day having fun together. Another family goes out for a special meal together on their baby's birthday: "You have to celebrate whatever you can.... We don't say we are celebrating a birthday, but it is our special day, our family day."

Encouraging a sibling relationship

Some parents tried to keep the baby in the family by encouraging their children to have a relationship with their baby brother or sister. The intensity of this relationship usually mirrored the parents' relationship with the baby. To foster interest in the baby, parents encouraged their children to commemorate and remember the baby through conversations, mementoes and pictures, and grieving. As a consequence of different parental behaviors, sibling connections to the baby varied. When put on a continuum, the intensity of the relationship ranged from total silence about what happened to a comfortable awareness of the baby's existence and death to a consuming, passionate, and troubled connection.

Some parents never talked about the baby's death at all with their other children, but parental grieving continued for a long time. This led siblings to feel ambivalent and confused about the whole situation. One older sibling just "blanked out" the years surrounding the baby's death until years later when her parents got some help. Although the parents can now talk openly about their grief and the baby's death, their daughter still finds it very difficult to talk about this whole experience.

In some families, the baby's birth and death became part of the family history, although the baby continued to hold a special place in everyone's heart. Those children who hardly ever mentioned the baby anymore and who expressed only a passing but comfortable interest in the baby had parents who seldom mentioned the baby themselves. These parents seldom encouraged the children to commemorate the baby's birthday or deathday. These parents either displayed the baby's photographs discretely or kept them in family albums. Having **let go** of their own grief, these parents gave their children permission to do the same. They knew it is in their children's best interests to **let go,** too:

> About a year after [the baby] died, maybe a year and a half, just out of the blue, we were driving down the road and [my daughter] says, "You know what mom? I don't even think about [the baby] anymore. I don't even care that he was here any more. I don't even think about him. It doesn't make me sad any more." And inside I was just, "Oh, I didn't want to hear that!" But on the outside, I said, "You know what? I'm glad. I'm glad that you don't hurt anymore, and I'm glad that you don't think about him anymore," I said, "That's nice," because I wanted her to know it was okay, but inside I didn't think it was.

In other families, "[the baby] is talked about an awful lot," no matter how many years have passed. Children follow the lead of their parents. Pictures are prominently displayed so that the children cannot avoid looking at them. Parents may commemorate and visit the baby's grave regularly, often with their children. Every special holiday involves a visit to the cemetery. Instead of subtly encouraging their children to **let go** of their grief and to focus on the present, some parents expressed a certain pride in their children's preoccupation with the baby. One mother is amazed at how long and how often her older son remembers his baby brother:

> This is just the year before last. They had to make poppies, and there were big pictures and on the back, they had to put what they would like, who they would like to remember on Remembrance Day, and it's

> always his brother. It's always his brother, and there are times I worry about that, but then I think, "Well, it's better than keeping it in."

In these families, even children born after the baby's death grieve and try to talk about the baby they never met. One mother said that "out of the blue" her child born after the baby's death said, "I never got to know [the baby] and that makes me mad." As parents continued to grieve themselves, they often confused their children's curiosity about the baby's death with an abiding connection to the baby. Parents who had no adults with whom they could share their grief sometimes chose to share their pain with their children. This made it more difficult for the children to **let go**.

A few of these children even questioned whether their parents really valued and loved them for themselves. They wanted to know if they had been born only because their parents desperately wanted to "replace" the lost baby. Once they learned about the existence and death of a sibling they could never know, it made sense for the children to wonder or even to ask, "If [the baby] didn't die, would you still have me?" One mother told her adopted teenage son who was beginning to get into trouble, "You probably thought you were a replacement for [the baby] and you probably were, except that now we accept you for yourself." She had never discussed this with him before. She worried that all his life he had not fit into the family because "he felt he was a replacement" who could never compete with their much loved natural born baby who had died.

Perhaps because they felt overprotected, and therefore constricted by an event that had nothing to do with them, some children challenged their parents' frequent assertions of love, saying, "Oh, you don't love me." A few parents had to struggle to make their next born children "understand the fact that, yeah, we really did want [them] and we do really love [them], no matter what. I think it's really hard to make [them] understand that as a kid." Since these children thought of themselves only in relationship to their deceased sibling, it is no wonder that they questioned their value. They could see that their parents had not yet **let go** of the baby.

Letting go of the baby

Putting the baby away

While parents held onto their baby in their minds and their hearts and their families, they still had to deal with the baby as a physical being. For their own peace of mind, most parents needed to find a place to put their baby's body. Many put their baby's care "in God's hands." They believed that "[the baby] went to heaven...where he's got it made." Parents felt reassured that their baby would get the best of care. Because God was "going to change [the baby's] diapers in heaven," the parents no longer had to worry. Heaven was a wonderful and beautiful place. One mother who had been bothered by thoughts of her son in his grave found a great sense of peace after "seeing" him in heaven. She stopped worrying about him. Like other parents who turned their baby's care over to God, she knew he would be safe now.

One mother felt confused about the location of her baby, and her uncertainty made it very difficult to think about **letting go**:

> I do think that she's in heaven, but I'm not sure what she, like I don't know what form she is in, whether she is a baby or whether she can communicate. That kind of bothers me, and sometimes I think she's kind of around the house a bit, too....That kind of scares me a bit sometimes when I think she's around or when she might or her soul or spirit might kind of be watching over [our family].

Other parents wondered whether their baby's spirit resided in one of their subsequent children. Sometimes when children looked alike, parents felt comforted by the resemblance.

Some parents needed to maintain a physical connection to their baby. They could not let go completely, so they kept their baby's ashes in a special place or they visited the cemetery or spot where they had scattered the ashes: "Whenever [they were] in the area, [some parents] would stop by...and just stand there for a few minutes." While some parents "visited" frequently at first, most stopped visiting after a while. Others visited only on special occasions. Many years after her baby's death, one mother continued to visit the grave "every week." Despite suggestions from her family that she stop, and although intellectually she knew her visits made no sense, this mother could not stop visiting the cemetery: she could not **let go**:

> In the winter, well, in the winter, maybe every couple of weeks, but in the summer, I'm there every week....There are days that I go and I'm there for 10 seconds. I don't stand and mope, and it doesn't upset me anymore. On occasions, it upsets me. Birthdays, deathdays, all of those anniversary sorts of things, but now I can go and I can smile and I just say a quick little prayer and then I leave. I don't dwell on it.

Sharing the love

Some parents **let go** of their deceased baby by trying to love their other children even more or by having another baby. Previously uninvolved fathers started "clutching" and appreciating their other children: "I don't know if your awareness heightens of your children, maybe with the death of one. But I can remember a lot about that specific year [after the baby's death]." Even very involved parents became more dedicated to their children. Some parents set aside everything else to listen to and be with their other children: "Mess[ing] around with [their other children]" served as a "key stress reducer in the whole scheme of things." Many parents eventually had another baby. Again, some fathers who had shown little interest in their baby previously now devoted themselves to spending hours and hours after work "doing the bottles and doing the diapers." Something had definitely happened: not only had these parents lost a baby, they had been **changed** by the experience.

Chapter 6
Understanding the Parents' Experience: Being Changed

Rebuilding the Foundations

When the baby died of SIDS, it destroyed the foundation upon which the parents had built their lives. External changes were obvious. The most important change was that the baby was missing. Some parents became temporarily childless; others suddenly had one less child. Siblings lost a baby brother or sister; grandparents lost a precious grandchild. Family compositions changed, too, because, as one mother pointed out, if the baby had not died, "we would have had another kind of family." Children born or adopted after the baby's death wondered if they would have been wanted at all if the baby had not died. To cope with the stress, a few families moved. But these changes were obvious.

Less obvious changes occurred as well. Within an instant, parents just felt differently about life. The baby's death had not only changed their family, it had destroyed or damaged the foundation upon which they had built their lives. Parents used metaphors to describe the abruptness of this life-altering experience:

> I remember every time I turned a light out, it bothered me because I thought, "Ah, this is how quick it happens!" You know, to me that light

> switch was very significant. Yeah. Like that's how one day you're here and the next second you're gone, you know. And just, just like turning on and off a light switch. Your whole life can change that quickly.
>
> You just think you know what you're up to and all of a sudden, boom. You know and the roof just caved right in.
>
> It's unbelievable. It's like the rug's pulled out from under you.
>
> It was sort of like a real punch in the stomach, wake up.
>
> It changed our whole life....Somehow things take a turn. Nature gives things taking a turn. Like a hurricane does, an earthquake does, and death does. It turns your life around.
>
> I remember thinking that as if to that point my past and all of the things I had done and everything was like this train going along this track, and then all of a sudden, we had this huge derailment and that track was not available to us anymore or to me anymore. We had to start a whole new track from then on. Like all the past and all that stuff began, began, we began a new life almost after [the baby] died, and we started with a new history and with new expectations and new all of that kind of stuff and maybe that stuff that I took was just, after sitting in the rubble in this train wreck, so you pick up your foot and you walk over and you begin a new life. I don't know, but that's the way I've thought of it in retrospect.

The existence of a "new history" and "new expectations" for the future meant that parents had to build a new foundation for their lives: "The rest of my life has been kind of built on [the baby's death] because it was such a big trauma, a big part of my life, and so the rest of my life has been built there." Because of the new foundation and because they felt differently about themselves, their partner, their children, their faith, and about life in general, parents needed to find a new "purpose for life and a purpose for your being here and going through life and, you know, some of the hardships and stuff."

Searching for a Purpose

Once parents found an explanation for their baby's death, they began ***searching for the meaning*** behind their baby's death. They needed a reason to go on, so they looked for a new purpose in life. In the parents' minds, "there had to be a reason" for this death "because otherwise, you know, you'd just keep thinking it's such a senseless death." The purpose parents chose reflected their inner changes. It also reflected their final explanation for their baby's death. In turn, their new purpose then affected their relationships and attitudes about the future.

Some tried to "make the best of what's given," both as individuals and within their relationships. They did their best to focus on the positives and on what they could learn and gain from their loss. Others felt so "undermined" by the experience that they could see only negatives in the experience, themselves, their relationships, and life in general.

Feeling undermined

In the beginning, losing a baby to SIDS "undermined" and shook the parents' "confidence in everything." Although most parents worked through their pain and found ways to move forward with a "new life" despite their suffering, a few parents could not recover from their loss: "I don't know that I feel any less sad today than I felt…years ago, so I don't think the process heals itself." Besides losing their baby, these parents had also lost their "youth and innocence." They continued to feel devastated "by all this shit" and suffering for years.

Some parents could find no positive purpose for their baby's death; they just could not make "something good come out it." Although they appeared to function as parents, partners in marriage, and as members of their community, something inside had been destroyed. Some no longer planned for their future because they believed they had little control over their future: "You take things as they come, I suppose. Day after day. You shouldn't even think about down in the future, a year or two because things will always change." Some no longer loved without fearing loss. SIDS had not only taken their baby's life, it had taken their zest for living.

Some parents felt very alone and isolated. Relationships with other people seemed distant and troubled. These parents were "not really that sympathetic towards other people's problems," particularly when the problems seemed so "minor" when compared to losing a baby to SIDS. In addition, their grief experience had taught them that "you really can't depend on other people." Some people had even lost their faith in God, making them feel even lonelier. A few who had previously found comfort in their faith or in the existence of God felt "turned off of religion." Others felt only "animosity." Religion had either made them feel worse or had offered little comfort. These parents seemed disappointed in the way they had handled the whole experience. Some chastised themselves for being "weak" or for not offering enough support to their spouse. They had neither forgiven themselves nor let go of their grief.

A few parents did manage to find a purpose for their baby's death, but it was negative. Those who believed that "the only way you learn is through suffering" continued to suffer. This was their new purpose: to keep doing penance. They could let little joy into their lives. They prevented themselves from **letting go** of their grief by continually focusing on what was missing from their lives. But whether they found a negative purpose or no purpose at all, parents who felt personally undermined usually experienced problems in their marriage and in their relationship with their children.

Undermined marriages

While the sense of isolation grew in some marriages, other marriages became more and more conflicted (see Figure 3 [page 149] to review marital typology).

Isolated marriages

Before the baby's death, some parents felt happy, close, and passionate about their marriage. After the baby died, all that changed. Other marriages had always been distant. The baby's death did not cause the isolation, it just intensified the problem.

In the beginning, some partners had turned inward because they "could barely get through [their] own grief without dealing with [their spouse's]." Even after the intense grieving had subsided, however, these people remained emotionally unavailable to each another. Some couples created distance by fighting and then withdrawing emotional energy from the relationship. Others just never recovered from the shock of their baby's death; they remained almost unaware of each other. Each person continued to grieve "our own way, by ourselves." Instead of leaning on each other for support, these partners turned away from the relationship. They could neither identify nor resolve their differences. Negative explanations for their differences increased the sense of distance and dissatisfaction with the relationship.

Over the years, some spouses turned to work, to community and recreational activities, and to relationships outside the marriage for their fulfillment. A few turned to their children: "We live for [our child]." Some spouses became "totally disinterested" in their marriages. They "could care less [about marriage]....Like I have my [children]. Who needs a [spouse] now?" Even their sexual relationship deteriorated.

Although each partner seemed dissatisfied with the relationship, neither spouse made any serious attempts to end it. Rather than being committed to the relationship and to each other, these couples stayed together for other reasons: apathy, fear of another loss, need to stay together for the children, community embarrassment, too much time invested in the marriage to give it up, and being "used to each other." Despite the sense of isolation, some couples still believed there was some quiet love left in their relationship. Nonetheless, living in an *isolated marriage* made couples feel distant and "very lonely":

> [The baby's death] had to have a big impact on our relationship. And uhm, oh wow, there's so many things that come into my mind when I think about this whole thing. It's, it's like a crevasse or a slice that is not replaced, like something's missing, like uhm, like a gouge in the life span with this not healed. And I don't know how much of that is my perception that if you don't talk about things, that they don't get healed, and I have this real thing about communication and unfinished business, and I think that [the baby's] death between us is unfinished business.

Conflicted marriages

Instead of living in a distant and passionless relationship, other couples fought over everything. They could not step back from one another because they were emotionally interdependent; one spouse's pain directly affected the other. When one partner could not step back to comfort the other, the relationship suffered. Instead of reaching out to each other, these couples found new reasons to be angry. They could not resolve their problems because they argued over everything: how to grieve, how to give or receive comfort, how long to grieve, when to have another baby, whether there was any meaning to the baby's death, and how to look after the other children. They also judged each other's mourning strategies negatively and complained if they thought their spouse was too dependent or too distant, too "rational" or "too emotional." Instead of understanding that grief caused his wife to behave in certain ways, one husband took her behavior personally. He wondered if she was just trying to "manipulate" him with her emotional outbursts. Some partners even misinterpreted silence or the inability to talk about grief negatively. To them, it could only mean their spouse no longer cared.

Unable to resolve their conflicts, these relationships never recovered from the damaging words, the accusations, and the fact that at some point the word "divorce" had been mentioned. During my interviews, a few marriages teetered on the brink of dissolution. One or both members of the couple had started questioning why they had ever married in the first place. A few marriages had already ended. Of those that were still together, sometimes the children provided the only "glue" holding the relationship together. In some cases, it seemed as if a child had replaced the spouse. Again, while some couples had described their marriage as satisfying before the baby's death, this devastating event damaged some marriages beyond repair. The foundation was permanently destroyed. For other couples, the baby's death was just one more crisis in an already unsatisfying and conflict-ridden relationship.

Undermined relationships with children

Some parents never regained their sense of confidence, not just in themselves as a mother or father, but also in their environment. They no longer believed that bad things only happened to other people; their baby's death had taught them that bad things can happen to anybody. Convinced that their baby had died because of their own error or because God wanted to punish them, these parents became obsessed with their other children. This contributed to overprotectiveness and concern for their children's welfare and safety. These parents could seldom relax and enjoy their children; instead, they worried about everything they did. They dreaded their children's independence and actively discouraged it by pointing out all that could go wrong in any activity:

> It totally changed the way I treated [my older son]. I'm still bad with him. Uhm, I was very, very protective. Overly so and I think that that is probably a normal, and I'm still that way. I mean, they went skiing on Monday. I was a wreck all day, like, "Oh God, I hope he doesn't break his leg and drive into a tree." You know, those things still go through my mind, and I will probably always be that way.

Making the best of it

Fortunately, most parents found a way to "make the best of what [was] given" to them. Although they did not suffer any less hardship than those who found either no purpose or a negative purpose, these parents seemed determined to find "the good things that we can make come out this." One mother described the importance of a positive attitude:

> Try to look at all the good things. Don't just be negative. Don't just sit down and say, "Life is horrible." It's mean, sometimes, but sometimes it isn't all that mean. There is always somewhere along the line something good. Like this might not be anything good, but the happiness that you had was good. If you wouldn't have had this baby, you would not have had this happiness.

While a couple of parents decided that God was responsible for making something good happen after the baby's death, most parents constructed their own sense of purpose. First, they decided what they had learned from their baby's death, and then they acted on it. The most frequently mentioned lesson was "not to take life for granted." Through the death of their baby, parents learned to value and appreciate their life and relationships:

> The biggest change was the fact that you realize that you are not infallible and your family is not safe from disaster. And so you, I think, treat, I treat things differently than I may have. I don't take a lot for granted. And that could be one of the biggest things because I don't take an awful lot for granted.

> [Before our baby died, I just took everything] for granted. You have children, they grow up, they live, you'll die before they do, you know. And it didn't happen that way.

Because they had learned "not to take life for granted" anymore, parents also tried to change their priorities:

> Once the baby's gone and you just realize you know that, you know, things you've been doing on a day-to-day basis and rushing and hurrying, all of a sudden, they're not important anymore. Your family is important.

> It definitely changed my whole life. Like I, you get busy in your life and you don't put priorities first and all of sudden, it's bang! You realize just what is important in your life and what isn't any more.

As the parents' priorities changed, so did their perspective on suffering. No matter how difficult other problems in life seemed, nothing could compare with what the parents had already survived:

> It gives you a different perspective on life. Uhm, and we remind ourselves of that, too, once in a while. You, uh, no matter how tough things get, you know, the job's going tough or everything you're doing doesn't seem to work the way you think it should or your finances are tight or whatever, no matter how bleak it gets, it's still compared to [losing your baby], it's nothing. You gotta put it into perspective.

Parents also changed their attitude towards death: "The thought of death before horrified me. Terrified me." Parents who once thought of death "as an end" stopped thinking this way. For their own peace of mind, they needed to think of their baby continuing to exist somewhere else: "I don't allow myself to think of it as [my baby's] end, so…how could it be mine?"

With a new perspective on both life and death, parents were ready to "make something good come out of" their experience. Some worked hard to "change society." A few became involved in the anti-abortion movement. One woman eventually became very involved in bereavement education and support services for her community. Others devoted themselves to the "SIDS bandwagon":

> In my eyes and my eyes of what I see something good coming out of it is that we could possibly get closer to even finding a cure or even preventing it. That they could do some ways of finding which babies are the ones, you know, which ones are the more susceptible. To help other parents cope could be another positive thing, you know. There's a lot of people out there that wouldn't have the support that we had, and I know we had a lot of support, and I don't know how they do it without the support.

Besides trying to improve society, most parents also made positive personal changes. One mother described this experience as "characterbuilding." Others said they felt "more empathetic," "supportive," "open with feelings," "strengthened," "mature," and "mellowed." A number felt an even deeper commitment to their faith. They felt God had supported them during their suffering, and they appreciated it. The positiveness with which they approached their experience showed itself in their relationships, too. Some parents just quietly appreciated their families and friends more than they had previously. One mother went one step further. She "let people know how I cared about them [by] saying it in words and not just assuming that they knew it or understood it." Making the best of a bad situation at a personal level affected the parents' marriage and their relationship with their children.

Building better marriages

While some marriages remained virtually unchanged in the eyes of the partners, others became stronger and closer.

Parallel marriages

Partners in parallel marriages were pragmatic people. They did not see the death of the baby "as a big strain on [their] marriage." Both strongly committed to their careers as well as to their family life before the baby's death, these partners dealt with the experience by talking about common problems. Although they dealt with their grief separately, they were not isolated from each another. Since they had built the foundation for their relationship on their ability to tolerate and accept their differences, the marriage remained solid. They continued to respect each other; they expressed a certain pride in having survived this ordeal together.

Connected marriages

Very few troubled marriages improved after the baby died, but this crisis did give some couples an opportunity to learn how to accept and trust each another more than they ever had before. It also taught them how to become comfortably connected. Almost all of the connected marriages had been strong and healthy before the baby died. These couples had a history of trust, flexibility, satisfaction, and acceptance. One mother commented on the deepening of her marriage after their baby died:

> If any one would have said to me I could have had a closer marriage, I would have said, "How? We're good friends. You know, we're doing well together. We're close!" But uh, after we lost [our baby], you do, we did get much closer, and yet, before that I wouldn't [have] thought it was possible. I thought we were as close as a couple could get.

When confronted with the loss of their baby, these couples worked together towards healing for both of them. This experience drew them closer. These couples shared several characteristics. Partners in connected marriages could:

- acknowledge and cope with their own grief,
- acknowledge and accept their partner's grief,
- share their grief with their partner,

- recognize and accept different mourning strategies,
- support and be supported by their partner,
- trust their partner to provide support,
- recognize their own and their partner's limitations, and
- commit themselves to each other and to the relationship.

Becoming a better parent

Some parents felt that "the death really changed [them]. I think it made me a better mother. I know that I wasn't the perfect mother, but I think it made me a better mother." Being a better parent meant being more involved and more appreciative of their children. By rediscovering his faith and finding a new purpose in life, one previously distant father learned what it meant to be a good father:

> Love [my son]. Care for him. Take care of him. Go out with him. Do things with him. Uh, you know, be a father for him. Be strict, too. I mean, you know, you can't all have it one way. There has to be discipline, too.

While these parents still seemed somewhat cautious and protective of their children's safety, they seemed able to relax and enjoy their children far more than parents who always worried about their children. As more than one parent said, "You know the grieving process is getting over when you look at one of your subsequent kids and you say, 'I want to kill you!'" When parents felt relaxed enough to even think this thought, they knew they had healed.

Chapter 7
Learning from the Parents' Experience: How People Cope with Traumatic Events

How Parents Coped with the Death of their Baby to SIDS

Searching for reason

The underlying cognitive process that helped the parents to eventually "accept the unacceptable" (Parkes & Weiss, 1983, p. 74) death of their baby is their **search for reason**. In technical terms, this process is called the central theme (Hutchinson, 1986) or the core category (Morse & Johnson, 1991; Strauss & Corbin, 1990). The **search for reason** is at the "heart" (Stern, 1985, p. 156) of both the grief experience and this study. It involves three steps: ***searching for a reason***, ***searching for logic***, and ***searching for meaning***.

Searching for a reason

The first step in the process involves the parents' need to explain why any baby could die so suddenly and without warning. Because the parents need an explanation for the physical cause of their baby's death, they examine any and every past circumstance that might have contributed to it. This is very much like a police investigation of an actual crime. The police ask questions and gather and study the evidence; they look for someone or something to blame for the death. Then, eventually, they may charge someone with the crime. The parents carry out a similar investigation. They ask questions of themselves, each other, and the experts; they review the evidence contained in the autopsy report, in their own behavior and thoughts, and in the reactions of significant people. Eventually, they, too, assign blame for the baby's death. Finding someone to blame helps the parents regain a sense of control over their lives.

Searching for logic

The next step in the process involves a different kind of investigation. To follow the police analogy further, this phase is similar to the trial that examines the circumstances and events leading to a death. The cause of death is no longer the central issue. Like the lawyers, the parents' goal is to make sense of everything that has happened. They want to know if there is any connection between their past behavior and what happened to their baby. Parents also want to make sense of their own mourning behavior and that of others. Unlike the legal investigation, however, parents play mind games. They try to make their evidence fit their preconceived conclusions because they want to hold onto their beliefs about how the world works and how people behave. Uncovering the logical framework or reasoning underlying this event helps parents predict future events and people's behavior. It also helps them regain a sense of order, comprehensibility, and manageability in their lives.

Searching for meaning

The last step involves the need to find the existential or philosophical reason for their baby's death and for the parents' suffering. This search focuses on the future consequences of the event for the survivors. At this point, parents need to find a new purpose for their lives. This part of the investigation can be likened to an inquiry in which the circumstances of a death are carefully studied to see if something can be learned from it that might benefit others in the future. Once parents uncover the purpose of their baby's death, their lives regain a sense of meaning and direction.

Searching for reason while grieving the baby's death

Loving a new baby

The grief experience began with the parents' commitment to **loving a new baby**. Over the course of the pregnancy, parents had time to make room for the baby in their hearts, their minds, their families, and their lives. After the baby was born, new mothers and fathers sometimes struggled to manage all the responsibilities of parenthood. Because they loved this baby and because they wanted to be good parents, they accepted the responsibility and did the best they could. They nurtured and cared for their baby; they did everything they could to ensure the baby's safety and well-being. When life was going well, parents did not question their good fortune: they assumed their world was safe and predictable. They expected to have a happy future with their growing baby and family.

Being devastated

The sudden and unexpected death of their baby seriously challenged the parents' assumptions about their world. For a time, this traumatic event devastated the parents to their very core. As they entered the nightmare, the passage of time seemed warped and nothing made sense at all. Parents fought to maintain their sanity, often by shutting down their emotions and functioning like robots.

Despite all the confusion and commotion that surrounded them, parents started ***searching for a reason*** for their baby's death almost immediately. They needed to understand what had caused their baby to die so suddenly and unexpectedly. Besides asking questions of the medical experts, parents also began to ask themselves questions about their part in the death. They quickly reviewed the evidence by examining every parental act, decision, and thought they had ever had. Some parents immediately assigned blame to themselves; others could not function well enough to decide who to blame. They stopped searching until later.

Besides, the parents' attention had returned to the baby again. The time had come to begin the long and painful process of saying goodbye to the baby. As parents released their baby to the officials, as they planned and attended the funeral, and as they decided what to do with all the reminders of the baby, they kept returning to the same questions: Why? How could this happen? At first parents could not find any comforting answers. Nothing could take away the pain. When the numbness finally began to subside, parents felt like they were waking up to devastation. Everything in their lives seemed damaged and destroyed, particularly their feelings of safety and sanity. Everything about life seemed different now. The unthinkable had happened; nothing else mattered.

Trying to carry on while struggling for control

And yet something inside these parents pushed them to find a way to survive this traumatic loss. External forces pushed them to **try to carry on** by fulfilling their roles as workers, parents, spouses, and members of the community. In the beginning, internal forces often made playing these roles difficult. When parents lost the **struggle for control**, they fell apart. Thoughts and feelings associated with grief made them feel overwhelmed. Until they learned how to manage their grief and how to prevent it from overwhelming them, the parents bounced back and forth. Sometimes they could **carry on**, and sometimes they **struggled for control**.

Eventually parents learned to manage their grief by adopting mourning strategies. Other people's reactions to the parents' strategies either provided comfort or caused more pain. This was particularly evident in the parents' marriages. Because the mourning strategies employed different approaches to handling grief, their use had the potential to create marital problems. Parents who were in previously satisfying relationships in which differences were accepted had few problems. They could manage their grief within the context of their relationship. In fact, parents who shared their grief increased their sense of connection. Those in unsatisfying marriages had difficulties tolerating differences. Preexisting marital problems, such as conflict and isolation, increased.

To cope with all the changes and confusion in their lives, parents tried to make sense of it all. Although they were still ***searching for a reason*** for their baby's death, the parents began a new kind of search: ***searching for logic***. They wanted to understand the logic behind everything. If they could not find the logic, then the world seemed to have no order or predictability.

At this point, parents were still trying to understand the reason for their baby's death. When they received the autopsy report that provided the official explanation of the death, they tried to make sense of it. They began asking questions and reviewing the evidence again. Often, the official explanation made no sense to them. Accepting it meant believing that healthy babies could die with no warning and for no apparent reason. Few parents could tolerate this explanation. Instead, most parents tried to assign blame for the baby's death. Finding someone to blame, even if they blamed themselves, felt better than accepting this death as a random and uncontrollable event. Finding someone to blame also restored their sense of control. Each time they reexamined their tentative explanation and doubted their reasoning, they fell apart; grief overwhelmed them again.

Besides trying to make sense of the death, parents also tried to explain their own and their spouse's mourning behavior. By asking questions of each other, reading books about grief, or attending a support group, parents tried to understand their differences and their pain. Initially, they treated their differences as evidence of a problem. Then they reviewed this evidence carefully. Those with a negative attitude assumed the worst of themselves and their spouse. Those with a positive attitude assumed everyone was doing their best to cope with this difficult situation. Once parents made sense of their differences, their marriages were either strengthened or strained.

Learning to let go

Over time and with practice, parents learned to **carry on** for longer and longer periods of time without having to **struggle for control**. By answering the why question, parents slowly **learned to let go** of their grief and, to a lesser degree, to let go of their baby. To construct their final explanation for their baby's death, they began playing mind games. In this, the final phase of *searching for logic*, parents tried to find an explanation that fit their definition of themselves and the way the world worked. If they believed in a punishing God, then they found a reason why God would take their baby to punish them. If they believed in a loving God, then they worked hard to find an explanation for the baby's death that reflected that image. Parents who believed the baby's death had been their fault decided to learn from their mistake; they tried to become better parents. Other parents managed to see a certain logic behind their baby's death. Although the parents vacillated between two explanations for a while, eventually most settled on just one. Some parents had to work very hard to make their explanation fit. Sometimes definitions of self or the way the world worked had to change to accommodate the most reasonable explanation. No matter which explanation parents finally selected, they felt better just because they now understood their baby's death. Finally it all made sense.

Finding an explanation for the baby's death also affected the degree to which parents could **let go** of their grief and their baby. While some explanations encouraged the parents to **let go** and get on with their lives, others prevented it. For instance, some parents had to continue grieving because they believed they deserved to be in pain. Parents who chose explanations that involved a divine explanation often believed that God had assumed responsibility for their baby. Although this relieved their worry about their baby's well-being, many parents continued to find ways to remain connected. Few parents **let go** of their baby entirely. They all, however, found a place for the baby that helped them feel comfortable.

Being changed

Having uncovered the logic behind the baby's death, parents began to focus their energies on rebuilding the foundation of their lives. This experience **changed** parents and families in obvious and not so obvious ways. Besides changing the constellation of the family and the way in which family members related to each another, this experience changed the way parents thought about themselves, their marriage, their children, their life, and the way their world worked. These changes caused the parents to begin ***searching for meaning***. This led them to find a new purpose for their lives. Some parents took a positive approach and made the best of what they had been through. They found ways to put their suffering to good use, either personally or for the benefit of others. Other parents could not see anything positive in their lives at all. The baby's death had undermined the very foundation of their lives, causing them to have trouble enjoying and appreciating themselves, their marriage, their children, or life in general. Like any life-changing experience, there is no end to this process. The death of their baby and the way in which they grieved continues to affect the parents' lives no matter how many years go by.

Implications of the Findings

Grieving is a very emotional process. The raw and wrenching pain caused by the death of a baby should neither be denied nor minimized. It is real; it is devastating. Those who work with these families need to realize, however, that besides trying to deal with the absence of their baby parents are also dealing with something else: a challenge to their beliefs about their world and themselves. To cope with this challenge, parents undergo a rigorous examination of their fundamental beliefs. Among other things, the death of a baby to SIDS challenges the parents' beliefs about cause and effect, how much control they have in their lives, their ability to withstand trauma, and their belief in God and religion. This study shows that grief involves more than emotional pain, it also involves intellectual and spiritual pain. Since the ability to cope with this challenge to one's beliefs directly affects the outcome of the emotional part of grieving, it is important that those who work with grieving families understand how the bereaved deal with both parts of the experience.

To that end, I have combined the results of this study with theoretical work about how people cope with other challenges to the assumptive world. Figure 5 depicts the process that I describe below.

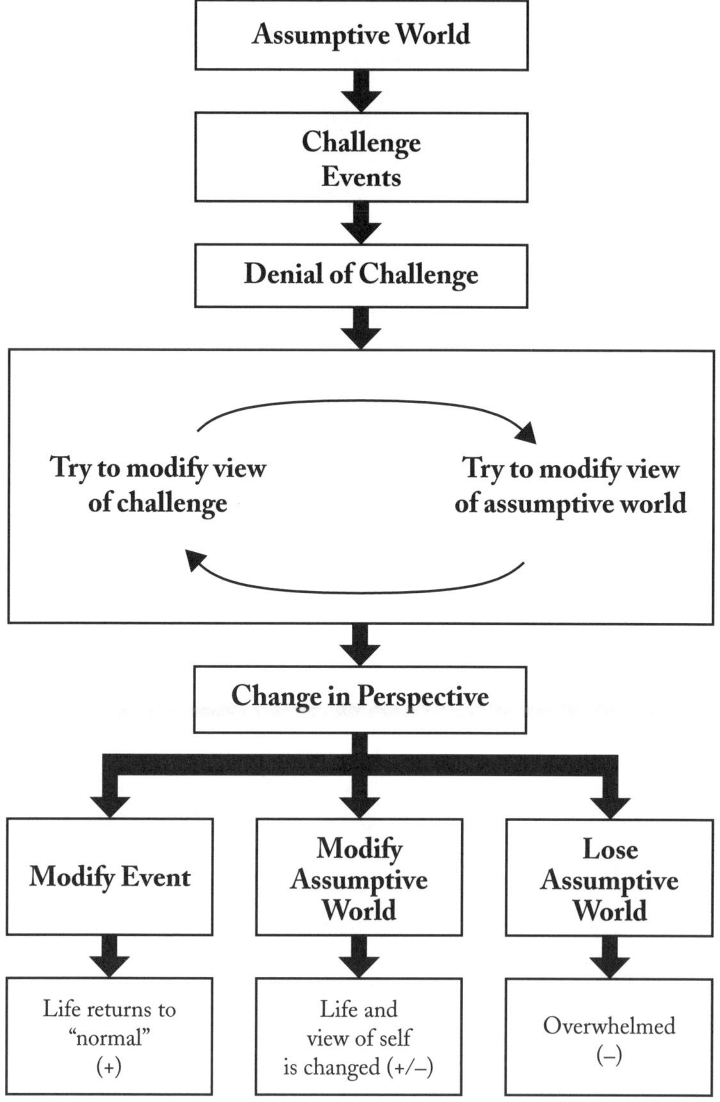

Figure 5 Theoretical model of how people deal with traumatic events by changing their perspective

Building a Theory about How People Cope with Traumatic Events

The assumptive world

People have certain beliefs about how the world works, beliefs that they learn by "experienc[ing] the world in fundamentally practical terms" (Attig, 1996, p. 106). These beliefs coalesce to form an "internal assumptive world" (Parkes & Weiss, 1983, p. 71) or "worldview, that [provides] the philosophical or religious underpinnings" for people's lives (Klass, 1992–1993, p. 255). This assumptive world or worldview begins to develop during infancy when children learn, through repeated experiences, whether they can trust themselves, their caretakers, and the world in general to meet their needs (Janoff-Bulman, 1992). As they grow older, this model helps people to "orient [themselves], recognize what is happening, and plan [their] behavior accordingly" (Parkes, 1988, p. 56). It serves as a "map of both visible and invisible reality on which individuals locate external and internal events, from which individuals discover or choose religious, political, or ideological affiliations, and upon which individuals base moral judgments and actions" (Klass, 1992–1993, p. 258). They use their beliefs about how the world works to help them explain and give meaning to whatever happens to them (Attig, 1996; Kruglanski, Baldwin, & Towson, 1983). People assume that their views of the world and the people in it reflect the truth.

People with a positive worldview believe that they are "good people who live in a benevolent, meaningful world" (Janoff-Bulman, 1992, p. 12). Those with a negative worldview try to see themselves as good, but they think of the world as less than safe and sometimes confusing. Because most people hold a positive worldview, I will explain its three basic components.

First, people want to believe that they are good, capable, and moral (Janoff-Bulman, 1992, p. 11). They want to believe that they will do what is right and that they will exercise control over their actions to ensure good outcomes. They also want to believe that they are competent. Second, people want to believe in a benevolent world. They want to believe that rather than living in a "hostile and malevolent world" they live in a safe world (Janoff-Bulman, 1992, p. 7). Because people want to believe that mostly good things will happen to them and to those they love, most people carry with them a certain sense of invulnerability. Third, people also want to believe in a meaningful world. If bad things do happen, then people assume there must be a reasonable explanation. There are two types of explanations: one is related to justice and the other to control. The justice explanation says that if something bad happens, then the person must have deserved it. The control explanation says that if something bad happens, then the person must have done something to cause it. By accepting either or both explanations, people can maintain a belief in a "meaningful, orderly world" (Janoff-Bulman, 1992, p. 8). Such an explanation implies that randomness is impossible. When a person's internal world has order and structure, it makes sense, it is comprehensible, and it feels safe.

A positive assumptive world is very similar to Antonovsky's (1979, 1987) Sense of Coherence (SOC). Antonovksy (1979) defines the SOC as: "a global orientation that expresses the extent to which one has a pervasive, enduring though dynamic feeling of confidence that one's internal and external environment are predictable and there is a high probability that things will work out as well as can be expected" (p. 184).

Prior to their baby's death, most of the parents in this study had a high Sense of Coherence (SOC). When people have a high SOC, their world seems comprehensible, manageable, and meaningful. A comprehensible world is an orderly world in which events do not happen randomly. People believe that every event has an explanation and that if they try hard enough they can explain it. A manageable world does not demand more resources of people than they have; people believe they will be competent enough to meet any of life's challenges. Finally, a meaningful world is one in which things make sense emotionally. No matter how unwelcome an event may be, people believe they will eventually find its purpose or meaning.

Challenges to the assumptive world

As the parents in this study learned when their baby died, the positive assumptive world and, therefore, people's sense of coherence are really only illusions (Janoff-Bulman, 1992; Taylor, 1983). People do not have as much control over their lives as they think they do (Langer, 1975). The world is not always safe, predictable, and meaningful. Sometimes bad things do happen to good people (Kushner, 1983), that is, sometimes things happen to people that defy their understanding and ability to cope. Events like the sudden and unexpected death of a baby "damage" people's "interpretations of life" (Craig, 1977, p. 45) and, therefore, their beliefs about their world and themselves (Attig, 1996; Lepore, Silver, Wortman, & Wayment, 1996). Such a sudden, life-altering, and negative event "require[s] people to undertake a major revision in their assumptions about the world" (Parkes, 1988, p. 55). Without warning, there is a "massive gap between the world that is and the world that should be" (Parkes & Weiss, 1983, p. 73). The death of a baby to SIDS severely challenged the parents' assumptive world. Besides dealing with their grief, parents had to learn to deal with the challenge to their assumptive world.

Dealing with the challenge

When people's assumptive world is challenged, they have four choices. They can

- try to deny the challenge;
- modify the challenge so it fits into their existing model;
- modify their assumptive world to accommodate the challenge; or
- lose their assumptive world and let the challenge overwhelm them.

Trying to deny the challenge

At first, most people try to deny or ignore an event that challenges their worldview. They also try to ignore all the feelings caused by such a challenge (Janoff-Bulman, 1992; Parkes & Weiss, 1983). They deny the event by going into shock. This means they have a "diminished capacity to feel" (Lifton, 1982, p. 197). In this study, the death of the baby devastated the parents' ability to think and feel for some time. No matter what we call this reaction, the goal is still the same: avoid the harsh and upsetting reality (Wolfelt, 1993). To maintain the illusion that nothing has changed, people withdraw from others and from situations that make the new reality hard to ignore. For a short while, they try to block out what has happened. While this may work temporarily, reality cannot be denied forever.

Eventually, awareness of the event begins to intrude into people's protective shell; it confronts and chips away at the illusion of a comprehensive, manageable, and meaningful world. Janoff-Bulman (1992) calls this "intrusive re-experiencing" (p. 103). While asleep and awake, people keep replaying the offending event, repeatedly reexperiencing the emotions and thoughts that go with it. While some see this as evidence of the development of Posttraumatic Stress Disorder (l'Hoir & Wolters, 1993; Raphael & Misso, 1993), Lepore et al. (1996) assert that these troubling thoughts and feelings serve a purpose: they force the bereaved to begin processing the new and difficult reality. Faced with the reality that their child has died, parents have three choices: They can change the way they view their baby's death; they can change their assumptive world to accommodate this harsh reality; or they can stop trying to make any sense of it at all and give up.

After a period of shock and numbness, parents in this study began to confront the fact that their baby really had died. Every time they walked past their baby's room, every time they thought of their baby, every time they looked at their baby's pictures, parents had to accept these horrible challenges to their assumptive world: babies do die. They can die for no reason at all. Even worse, their baby died.

Modifying the challenge by changing perspective

Once people can no longer deny the challenge to their assumptive world, they must decide what to do with it. Because the thought of giving up the long-held worldview triggers such anxiety (Parkes & Weiss, 1983), most people try to fit the challenging event into their existing model. People can change their perspective of the event by comparing their experience with others, by reinterpreting the challenging event, and by looking for the hidden meaning in it (Janoff-Bulman, 1992; McIntosh, Silver, & Wortman, 1993; Moos & Schaefer, 1986; Taylor, 1983).

Comparing self with others

Rather than comparing themselves to people who are better off, people who want to think of themselves as competent and their world as benevolent and meaningful compare themselves with real or hypothetical people who are less fortunate than themselves (Janoff-Bulman, 1992; Taylor, 1983). Downward comparisons give people a new perspective on their situation. They realize things could have been worse: they could feel worse than they do, or they could have had more problems handling the situation. With either interpretation, the positive worldview and the view of the self are restored. People conclude that they are competent enough, considering the situation.

As parents began to let go of their grief, they compared their loss to the experiences of other parents who had also lost a baby to SIDS. This strategy was available only to those parents who attended a support group. Some found SIDS-related situations that seemed worse than their own: having to go to the hospital or not having a supportive family. Others compared their situation to parents who lost children in other ways, or they compared their child's death to other more horrible ways to die. These comparisons allowed the parents to modify their definition of their tragedy. They found ways to believe that as awful as their loss had been it could have worse.

Reinterpreting the challenge

This process parallels the parents' ***searching for logic***, which allows them see their baby's death in a new way over time. Beyond using comparisons to make the event fit, people try to reinterpret the event itself (Klass, 1992–1993). They begin this process by asking why-type questions that reflect assumptions about a controllable, predictable, and meaningful world (Wong & Weiner, 1981; Zagdanski, 1995). One body of theoretical literature that deals with people's attempts to answer why-type questions describes the attribution theory or the "psychological study of causality" (Hewstone, 1983, p. 2). Attribution theory is based on the assumption that people want to make sense of what they experience and witness (Downey, Silver, & Wortman, 1990; Spilka, Shaver, & Kirkpatrick, 1985). Attributions serve an important purpose: they help people understand and have "control over the physical and social world" (Hewstone, 1983, p. 17). Attributions also help people understand their own internal experiences (Proudfoot & Shaver, 1975) and what happens to them as well as protecting their self-esteem (Spilka et al., 1985).

When confronted with an unexpected event or experience, people ask a variety of questions (Lalljee & Abelson, 1983). First, they may concern themselves with who or what caused the event in question: Was the event caused by a person or by a situation? Second, they may concern themselves with whether the event or behavior could be controlled: Was it intentional or accidental? Third, they may concern themselves with whether the event was stable: Is it likely to happen again? Once people find the answers to these questions, they believe they understand the past, present, and potential future circumstances of such an event (Hamilton, 1980). Understanding an event helps people fit it into their assumptive world. While some people use religious attributions, others do not.

Religion provides people with an organized framework of attributions with which they can interpret or "make sense of their experiences" (Proudfoot & Shaver, 1975, p. 318). As well, religion can reduce people's anxiety when they are confronted with "experiences and events that bring them face to face with the limits of their worlds, e. g., birth, death, inexplicable suffering" (p. 318). When people "submit to [the] ready made system" provided by religion, they can give up their search for the meaning of such events (p. 327). Using the tenets of their religion as a "cognitive schema" (McIntosh, Silver, & Wortman, 1993, p. 813), people can explain difficult events such as the death of their child to SIDS by assigning responsibility to their higher power, a being external to themselves. Their interpretation of God's personality and motives is then reflected in what they assign to God's doing. People are more likely to use religious attributions when they have a history of religious involvement, when the event and the context of the event lend themselves to such an attribution, and when circumstances encourage this kind of attribution.

Other people prefer to use nonreligious explanations. They appeal to their own common sense for explanation, a common sense that is often based on a belief in scientific explanations. Common sense investigators do not follow the rules of the scientific method. Instead of developing hypotheses and then gathering and evaluating evidence dispassionately, common sense investigators follow a different procedure (Jaspars, 1983). When trying to understand an unusual event, people usually ignore evidence that contradicts their assumptions; instead, they emphasize evidence that supports their assumptions. Once people achieve "closure" (Kruglanski et al., 1983, p. 83) on an explanation, they are no longer willing to test it against contradictory evidence. Once a belief is "frozen" (p. 83), it is accepted as fact or knowledge, and it becomes increasingly resistant to change.

The speed with which a person freezes a belief is related to the "capacity and motivation to generate alternate hypotheses on a given topic" (Kruglanski et al., 1983, p. 84). Capacity refers to knowledge of a subject, availability of ideas about it, and recent experiences with it. The greater the capacity to generate alternate hypotheses, the greater the likelihood that they will be generated. As a consequence, people with little information will stop looking for alternate explanations sooner than those who know more about the subject. This suggests that the less parents know about SIDS, the less likely they will be to accept it as a reasonable explanation for their baby's death. Instead, they will assume they must have caused their baby's death. On the surface, this explanation makes the most sense.

People must also be motivated to generate a variety of hypotheses. Kruglanski et al. (1983) identify three possible sources of motivation. The first source of motivation is the need for structure. People vary in their ability to tolerate ambiguity. The greater the need for clarity and structure, the sooner people will freeze their beliefs about an event. A second motivating source is the need for a conclusion. The lack of a decision makes some people anxious; others can tolerate uncertainty. Those who are anxious for closure are likely to freeze their belief about the event sooner than those who can handle uncertainty. A third motivating source is the need for validity. People have trouble maintaining a belief when they know it is inconsistent with their other beliefs. Therefore, unless they can make their beliefs fit into their assumptive world, they will keep generating new hypotheses until they find one that fits.

By redefining the event and using "cognitive adaptation" (Taylor, 1983, p. 1161), people change the way they see the challenge, thus eliminating its threat to their assumptive world. If people want to believe that an event was controllable and predictable, then they may find a way to blame themselves for its occurrence. For example, parents in this study often blamed themselves for their baby's death, although there was no evidence that they had, in fact, done anything to cause the death. Janoff-Bulman (1992) suggests that when confronted with a traumatic event people choose to blame either their character or their behavior. If people blame their character, then they allow an attack on their self-worth to maintain their worldview; they treat their character as stable and unchangeable. Some parents in this study believed that God had taken their baby to punish them for not being good-enough people. Other parents blamed their behavior as parents. They believed that they had made an error in judgement concerning the baby's care. Therefore, they could choose to be different in the future. This belief restored a sense of predictability and control in their world.

Finding meaning

People use one last way to fit the challenge into their assumptive world: they try to find meaning in it (Attig, 1996; Braun & Berg, 1994; Klass, 1992–1993). Parents who lose a baby to SIDS struggle to find meaning in the death and in their suffering (McIntosh, Silver, & Wortman, 1993). As Cassel (1982) suggests, "Suffering is reduced when it can be located within a coherent set of meanings" (p. 644). The meaning may be either positive or negative. At first, an event such as the death of a baby to SIDS appears meaningless. Then parents may decide that despite their suffering or maybe because they have suffered they have learned a valuable lesson about life and themselves. Klass (1992-1993) found that grieving parents seldom believe that their child died so something good could happen, but the parents do accept that good things can happen from such a tragedy. Some parents decide that their child died because they had done something to deserve punishment. No matter what explanation the parents choose, order has been restored to their world; the event now has meaning. Once the event has meaning, it no longer disturbs the parents' assumptive world. They feel safe again; they can proceed with life, changed by the event but not permanently destroyed by it.

Modifying the assumptive world by changing perspective

Some people cannot modify the event. It continues to be a devastating event that cannot be any worse, cannot be reinterpreted, and cannot be given any acceptable meaning. Therefore, their assumptive world must change. Letting go of the assumptive world frightens most people. The old ways no longer work, and until a new view is adopted, people feel vulnerable and confused (Janoff-Bulman, 1992), perhaps because the world seems malevolent and meaningless. Consequently, the bereaved feel helpless and less than worthy. Janoff-Bulman (1992) suggests that people use both their emotions and their thinking to get them through this dilemma. They alternate between handling the new realities and wanting to retreat from them. Like the parents in this study, people alternate between being able to carry on and struggling for control. While they are in transition, they need to feel supported and safe; they also need information and assistance to help them deal with the modified assumptive world (Parkes, 1988).

In most cases, people's new worldview is not drastically different from their old one. It is modified only slightly. The naive belief in invulnerability is gone, replaced by the awareness that, to a certain degree, everyone is vulnerable to tragedy. A few parents in the study fit this description. They could be described as sadder but wiser. Janoff-Bulman (1992) describes the modified perspective:

> The world is benevolent, but not absolutely; events that happen make sense, but not always; the self can be counted on to be decent and competent, but helplessness is at times a reality. Survivors are often guardedly optimistic, but the rosy absolutism of earlier days is gone. (p. 174)

Parents in this study who modified their assumptions about their world were often very cautious and protective parents. They knew that no matter how good they were their children were not totally safe from harm. They also knew that absolute control over the future was impossible.

Losing the assumptive world and changing perspective

Some people can neither regain nor modify their original assumptive world after the challenging event; instead, they lose their assumptive world. They begin to believe that their actions have nothing to do with what happens to them. Utter despair sets in, and soon they develop a feeling of powerlessness and helplessness (Bugen, 1977). In addition, these people can find no meaning for the event despite the passage of many years. They are stuck between worlds: they cannot make the challenging event fit into their assumptive world, and they cannot accept a modified world. One mother in this study temporarily lost her assumptive world. She was still struggling with this during her interview. Another mother lost her assumptive world for many years, that is, until she gained a new assumptive world by rededicating her life to God. My assumption is that parents who permanently lose their assumptive world would be unlikely to volunteer for a study like this one. Since they can make no sense of their experience themselves, they would likely see little value in a study of this kind. These parents are truly the hidden, silent, and living victims of SIDS.

These are the people who are severely and perhaps permanently damaged by their experience. Weiss (1988) says some people cannot recover from a traumatic experience, partly because they cannot develop a "satisfactory account" of the event for themselves (p. 48). After reviewing many victimization studies, Wortman and Silver (1986) share Weiss's conclusion. Instead of moving on and integrating their experiences, these people "continually re-experience the [event] for the rest of their lives" (p. 213).

For example, Silver, Boon, and Stones (1983) found that some female incest survivors just could not make sense of their experience even 40 years later. Their continued search for meaning years later was associated with signs of significant distress and poor social functioning. These are the people who never recover. They can neither live in a meaningless and malevolent world nor can they return to their naive belief in a benevolent and meaningful world. They are stuck between worlds, living in despair and fear.

Weiss (1988) suggests that those who cannot recover may try to compartmentalize their pain and suffering by walling it off so they cannot pay attention to it. They may go so far as to prevent themselves from loving again to avoid further pain. Others suffer chronic grief reactions. They get stuck somewhere in the process, either in denial or in the struggle for control over the pain. They can neither detach from the deceased nor admit the reality of their loss. As a result, they cannot enjoy life. While some might say that these people suffer from Posttraumatic Stress Disorder (l"Hoir & Wolters, 1993; Raphael & Misso, 1993), others call it pathological grief (Horowitz, Bonanno, & Holen, 1993).

CONCLUSION AND IMPLICATIONS

The "heart" of the experience of parents who have lost their baby to SIDS is ***searching for reason***. As I tracked the parents' journey through their grief process, I noted their attempts to deal with challenges to their assumptive world. The baby's sudden and unexplainable death initially challenged their belief that what happens to them in life can be explained. The apparently senseless death challenged their belief in a rational and predictable universe. It also threatened their belief in fairness. Before their baby's death, they believed that people who lived a good life could avoid suffering. On a more practical level, their baby's death made them question their own sanity and strength. It made them wonder if they could manage this crisis. They also questioned the strength and foundations of their marriage. Finally, this tragedy made them wonder whether their lives would ever have a purpose again. For a time, life felt meaningless.

As parents created or constructed some logic for their baby's death, they changed their definitions of the event. Therefore, ***searching for reason*** is equivalent to the "change in perspective." When parents could find explanations that helped them fit their baby's death into their previously held worldview, they could "return to normal." When parents had to accept a new worldview, they were significantly changed: some changed for the better and some for the worse. When parents could not make any sense at all out of their baby's death, they lost their assumptive world. This experience overwhelmed them and made it almost impossible for them to function. The interesting thing is that the facts of this experience did not change over time, only the parents' perspective on the facts changed. And the nature of those changes made the difference between eventual healing or continual hell.

When we try to comfort someone who has survived a traumatic event, we usually focus on their emotional pain. We may not realize that they are also dealing with what may be called "cognitive pain," that is, a challenge to their assumptive world. Such a challenge triggers more pain: emotional, intellectual, and spiritual. And as Lepore et al. (1996) found, most people who are struggling with something as traumatic as the death of an child need to talk about it. Talking helps people to deal with intrusive thoughts and to gain some perspective on their situation. With this in mind, if we want to help survivors of traumatic events, then we need to understand, accept, and support them as they work through the process of ***searching for reason***. One of the best ways to do this is to offer "a sympathetic ear, assistance, or words of comfort" (Lepore et al., 1996, p. 273).

Chapter 8
Making Connections to Other Research

Searching for Reason

Support for steps in searching for reason

Searching for a reason

Numerous studies and press clippings about ordinary life show that parents whose child dies suddenly want to know and understand the cause of death. Their need for an explanation triggers their ***search for a reason***. Like the parents in this study, other parents want to understand what events or circumstances might have caused: a pregnancy loss due to spontaneous abortion, fetal or neonatal death, and ectopic pregnancies (Dunn, Goldbach, Lasker, & Toedter, 1991); miscarriage (DeFrain, 1991); stillbirth (DeFrain, Martens, Stork, & Stork, 1990); drowning (Bradey, 1989; Daly, 1992; Lord, 1992; Staples, 1991); murder (Knapp, 1986; Rosof, 1994); accidental killing (Bunting, 1992); suicide (Miles & Demi, 1992); or a car accident (Davis, Lehman, Thompson, Silver, & Wortman, 1991; Miles & Demi, 1992; Rosof, 1994). It is not just the death of a child that triggers this search. When parents give birth to a child with problems, they also look for the cause. Parents who give birth to a child who is deaf (Gregory, 1976) or who has Down's syndrome (Ballard, 1979) wonder whether they did something wrong during the pregnancy to cause the problem. When children become ill, their parents also begin ***searching for a reason***. For example, parents who know their child is dying of cancer (Chodoff, Friedman, & Hamburg, 1964) or parents whose child has a chronic illness (Miles & Demi, 1992) want to understand the cause of the illness.

Although it is a fictional account of how a whole family deals with the drowning of the oldest son, Judith Guest's *Ordinary People* (1976) clearly describes some of the issues that relate to the survivors' need to find the cause of a tragic event. Guest describes how the father tortures himself with his thinking: "He does not believe himself to be innocent. It has to be his fault, because fault equals responsibility equals control equals eventual understanding." This quotation helps to illustrate the purpose of this search. The goal is to make the situation manageable, to try to reestablish a sense of control: "Finding a cause is seen as a way of protecting against trauma in the future and gaining some control to negate the powerlessness that is otherwise felt" (Raphael, 1983, p. 256). Finding the cause and assigning responsibility or blame reduces the anxiety that comes from thinking that the event might have been random and, therefore, uncontrollable in the future.

Searching for the logic

Even when experts provide parents with comprehensive and medical explanations for a death, after several months have passed, parents seem to question or reject this explanation. Why? Because they need more than a medical explanation to make themselves feel better. They need to make sense of the loss. Dunn et al. (1991) found that shortly after a pregnancy loss parents accepted their doctor's medical and physical explanations. Within 1 to 2 years, however, these same parents had modified their explanations. Many blamed fate or God instead of problems with the baby. The parents had shifted from searching for a specific cause to ***searching for the logic*** in the loss of their baby.

But it is not so easy to find this logic, as Finkbeiner (1996), a bereaved mother and science journalist, found out:

> A child's death is disorienting. The human mind is wired to find patterns and attach meanings, to associate things that are alike, to generalize from one example to another, in short, to make sense of things. Your mind could no more consciously stop doing this than your heart could consciously stop beating. [Because children's deaths seems so

> senseless], "parents fight their wiring, change their perspectives, and adjust to a reality that makes little sense." (p. xiii)

The following quotation from the autobiographical account of a father's grief further illustrates a parent's need to confront the irrationality of their child's death: "But six? It wasn't fair. It was completely irrational that my young son should be touched by this killer disease. What random malevolent force out there picks on little children and kills them when they are only six years old" (Oosterveen, 1988, p. 33)?

When a child dies, parents want to know why the death occurred at all (DeFrain, 1991), partly because it is so out of the natural order. They may ruminate about this to the point of obsession (Finkbeiner, 1996; Kaplan, 1995; Rosof, 1994; Sanders, 1988; Zagdanski, 1995), often in the form of "why questions." Why questions are connected to the ***search for logic***, the need to fit the death into some kind of logical and orderly framework. This search takes parents on a journey that may involve an exploration of the "nature of God and life" (DeFrain, 1991, p. 217):

> When I learned my son would die, what I knew intellectually about God gave way to what I had always felt about him in the secret recesses of my soul. All my old, angry feelings about God surfaced.... Questions without number spawned in my mind. What kind of vicious God is this anyway?" (Oosterveen, 1988, pp. 50–51)

Parents struggle to "work through" and find answers to these questions (Lehman, Wortman, & Williams, 1987, p. 229). They try to make sense by finding and applying a "schema or system of thought" that helps to put the loss into perspective (Storr, 1988, p. 74). Those who cannot make sense of the event may continue to struggle with it for years, often showing signs of depression and despair (Lehman et al., 1987). Fortunately, most parents manage to find or create a framework that helps them deal with their loss.

Many parents in this study and others use a religious framework. Seventy percent of the bereaved parents in Knapp's study (1986) turned to religion to help them deal with their child's death. This makes sense since one function of religion is to make sense of suffering. Geertz (1973, cited in Wuthnow, Christiano, & Kuzlowski, 1980) writes about the functions of religion:

> The problem of suffering is, paradoxically, not how to avoid suffering but how to suffer, how to make of physical pain, personal loss, worldly

> defect, or the helpless contemplation of others' agony something bearable, supportable, something, as we say, sufferable. (p. 409)

Religion helps some grieving parents find an acceptable explanation for their child's death. Cook and Wimberly (1983) discovered five explanations that parents used to help them cope with their child's death due to cancer or blood disorders. The three most commonly used explanations were: "an uncaring and unmerciful supreme being" had taken the child's life; the child's death was meant to punish the parents; and the child's death was meant to serve some kind of purpose (Cook & Wimberly, 1983, p. 227). A few parents used nonreligious explanations: there had been little suffering according to the parents' definition of the situation, and the death had no meaning. These parents attributed the death to fate, not a supreme being.

Religious explanations also gave parents somewhere for their child to be: heaven. Such explanations also provided parents with a goal: to be reunited with their child. When viewed from within a religious framework, even the death of a child can make sense. Parents' believe that God's or nature's reasoning can be uncovered if they just work at it.

Some parents did not have to work hard at all. They had a preexisting view of the world that easily incorporated tragedy. Some already believed that bad things can happen to good people (Kushner, 1983); others accepted a general lack of control over some life events. These are the parents who did not need to ask "Why" or "Why me?" The death of their child, as awful as it made them feel, did not upset their sense of justice or their sense of orderliness in the universe. Now they had to decide what the loss meant and how it would affect them in the future.

Searching for meaning

Searching for meaning is common after many types of losses: after a miscarriage (DeFrain, 1991; Thomas, Striegel, Dudley, Gibson, & Wilkins, 1992); stillbirth (DeFrain, 1991); car accident (Lehman, Wortman, & Williams, 1987); and death in a war (Florian, 1989). When the child has cancer, parents may begin searching for meaning even before their child dies (Chodoff et al., 1964). Writing generally about parental grief, Braun and Berg (1994), Craig (1977), and Miles and Crandall (1983) all assert that parents have a great need to find meaning after their child dies.

Although the usual focus of the *search for meaning* is on the survivors' need to find a purpose for their own lives, Doka (1988) suggests that parents may also need to find meaning for their child's short existence. He calls this the "search for significance" (p. 35). In some cases, parents carry out a child's dream or they focus on what medicine could learn from studying their child's illness. Finding a purpose helps parents believe that their child's life and illness were not wasted or completely meaningless. Even suffering achieves value.

Miles and Crandall (1983) also found that many parents put their suffering to work: they become more empathetic to the pain and needs of other people. Because of the positive changes, their child's death and their own grief begin to make sense. Both become meaningful. The ability to find a positive meaning in the child's death or a purpose for life helps to reduce the negative impact of grief. It also helps people heal from their experience (Ulmer, Range, & Smith, 1991). Perhaps "to have a reason to get up in the morning, it is necessary to possess a guiding principle. A belief of some kind" (Guest, 1976, p. 1).

A few parents in my study never found any positive meaning in their baby's death. Some gave up the search and, in a sense, gave up on life. Others continued to struggle with the questions. Other researchers have made similar observations (Florian, 1989; Lehman et al., 1987). These people seemed to be in poor physical health; they showed signs of unresolved grief; their marriages were shells.

Searching for reason

The ability to fit this devastating experience into some kind of metaphysical framework or to find a general reason for their baby's death helps parents deal with the whole experience. Over the past 10 years, researchers have begun to examine the connection between the process of ***searching for reason*** and people's overall ability to cope with loss or traumatic experiences. Originally, counselors believed that the more one "worked through" a traumatic experience, the sooner the problem would be resolved (Wortman & Silver, 1986). Within the context of studying parents who had lost a baby to SIDS, Wortman and Silver (1986) define working through as: "active attempts by the parents to make sense of and process the death, including searching for an answer for why the baby had died, thinking of ways the death could have been avoided, and being preoccupied with thoughts about the loss" (p. 207).

Parkes and Weiss (1983) found that widows and widowers who had trouble "working through" their experience soon after their spouse's death continued to have trouble when interviewed 1 year later. Incest victims who could not make sense of their experience years later were still asking questions about why it happened to them (Silver, Boon, & Stones, 1983). These women showed more psychological distress, greater impairment in social functioning, and lower self-esteem than those who had found an explanation. The inability to make sense of the experience leaves people in limbo. Despite their need to find an explanation, many people who had lost either a child or a spouse in a car accident years earlier could not make sense of their loss (Lehman et al., 1987). Wortman and Silver (1987, cited in Wortman & Silver, 1989) report that newly bereaved parents who had not made sense of the death of their baby to SIDS at 3 weeks were likely to be struggling with the same questions at 18 months.

These studies suggest that there is a group of people who cannot stop *searching for reason*. No matter how hard they try and no matter how much time passes, these people cannot decide what caused the event, why it happened to them and their baby, and what purpose it served. The issue is not that they are still asking the questions, it is that they cannot find any acceptable answers. Some parents in this study either had no framework into which they could integrate their experience or the one they had was so severely challenged that they lost it entirely. This left them with no baby and no way to make sense of their world. Like some of the bereaved in the Lehman et al. (1987) study, these parents could no longer trust their world; it felt hostile and unsafe. These parents needed special assistance.

At the other end of the scale are those victims of trauma who say they have never tried to make sense of their experience. Downey, Silver, and Wortman (1990) found that of the parents in their study who had lost a baby to SIDS close to one third said they had never asked, "Why me?" (p. 934). These parents also said they had no need to find any meaning in their experience. Silver et al. (1983) also found that a minority of incest victims had never pursued these questions. Why might this be? Silver et al. (1983) have a point when they wonder whether their respondents might have offered a different picture if researchers had asked them how they made sense of their experience. This question can uncover the person's view of the way the world works. Asking people if they have ever wondered why a traumatic event happened to them leads to different issues, such as whether they think of themselves as victims. Perhaps these people really had no need to ask questions because they already knew the answers. Perhaps their experience already made sense to them. This needs further exploration.

Parents in this study who had no trouble making sense of their loss had quite rapidly accepted the doctor's thorough explanation for their baby's death. These parents also had no need to assign any kind of spiritual meaning to the death. They just moved on. The phrase "shit happens," as used by one father, describes their approach to life in general. As Wortman and Silver (1989) suggest, "Some people may have something in place beforehand—a religious or philosophical orientation or outlook on life that enables them to cope with their experiences almost immediately" (p. 354).

And then there are those who struggle with ***searching for reason***. Eventually they find some kind of logic to their experience. For the parents in this study though, the explanation always seems provisional. It is as if they are saying, "Given the evidence I have on hand, this is my explanation, at least for now." Having one explanation does not prevent these parents from continuing to gather information from the popular press or from forums about SIDS research. Incest survivors studied by Silver et al. (1983) did the same thing. Eighty percent of those who said they had already made some sense of their experience were still searching "for some reason, meaning, or way to make sense of the incest at least sometimes" (p. 92).

To illustrate how important this reasoning process is, I draw from a book about how people manage to carry on relatively normal lives while living in war-torn Beirut (Friedman, 1989). People there developed "logical explanations for why each person died, which, if noted, would save them from a similar fate. Without such rationalizations no one would have left home" (p. 37). People's explanations and mind games helped them "impose order on chaos" (p. 36). This situation suggests that people struggle to understand troublesome community events as well as more personal events. Finding the underlying logic helps people cope with most situations. It may also prevent them from tackling the problem if they decide that they deserve to suffer or they believe their problem is just a matter of fate. This suggests that if we want to solve a community problem, then perhaps we need to begin with people's perceptions of the logic behind the problem.

Implications

Now that we understand that a major part of the parents' healing involves *searching for reason*, we can look for ways to help them in their search.

First, the parents' need to understand the cause of death. As Rosof (1994) put it, "The combination of loss and mystification [associated with why SIDS strikes] makes a fertile breeding ground for self-blame" (p. 162). It is not enough to tell the parents that SIDS took their baby's life. Parents quickly discover that this diagnosis really means the cause is a mystery. They then launch their own investigation. Although we can never fully stop the parents from *searching for a reason*, doctors can at least start parents on the right foot. Although doctors and pathologists may have the best of intentions when they tell parents how perfectly healthy their baby was, this only adds to the parents' confusion. Perfectly healthy babies should not die, and if they do, there must be a reason. ***Searching for a reason*** for their baby's death helps parents make sense of it.

Parents might find it more helpful if doctors and pathologists explained that current research suggests that babies who die of SIDS have a silent and undetectable medical problem that causes their death. This might take away some of the mystery. By providing parents with up-to-date information about SIDS research within hours or days of the baby's death, medical authorities could reduce some of the confusion.

After the parents begin their ***search for a reason*** for their baby's death, they also begin ***searching for the logic*** behind the death and ***searching for meaning***. They do not benefit from hearing other people's theories about why the baby died; parents need to find their own. They do not need our view of the meaning or purpose for their baby's death; they need to find their own. Besides providing information about SIDS, grief, and the existence of support groups, people need to learn how to be nonjudgemental listeners. Parents need someone who can listen to them while they create and test various theories about why their baby died. As Lepore et al. (1996) found, just talking about the baby's death and why they think it may have happened seems to reduce the parents intrusive thoughts and depressive symptoms. If parents feel constrained when they need to talk, they stop talking, and their grief goes underground. They also need someone to help them find meaning in their suffering

Grieving the Death of a Baby to SIDS

Portraying the image of grief

Wortman and Silver (1986) suggest that grief is "a series of overlapping clusters of reactions or phases [that occur] over time" (p. 194). Futterman and Hoffman (1983) describe a similar image: "a series of interwoven and interdependent processes" (p. 368). Not only do the actual phases overlap, but the tasks of each phase also overlap. My image of the overall grief process is similar to these descriptions (see Figure 1). Although this model looks linear on paper, if it is extended into the birth of the next baby and followed through, it loses some of this linearity. It is similar in process to the Pathways through Grief Model, which is in the shape of a figure eight, with meaning at its centre point (see Martin & Elder, 1993, p. 78).

Portraying the phases of the grief process

I found five interconnected phases: **loving a new baby; being devastated; trying to carry on while struggling for control; learning to let go**; and **being changed**. I deal with them one at a time, focusing on the general issues rather than the specific experiences that make up each phase.

Loving someone

The process of grief begins with attachment. Almost all the previously reviewed empirical studies and literature reviews link the nature of the parent-child attachment to the nature of parental grief. Since I have thoroughly covered this in my literature review, I will not repeat these references here. In self-help books written for and about grieving parents, other authors begin with or include this topic (Davis, 1991; Finkbeiner, 1996; Kaplan, 1995; Rosof, 1994). Looking at the nature of the attachment before looking at the nature of grief is very useful. It can help explain and, to some degree, predict differences in the depth and intensity of grief and the issues that might arise during the grieving process.

Being devastated

And then a child dies, or to make this more general, a traumatic event occurs that ends a valued relationship. At first, people may try to withdraw from the truth or deny reality (Parkes, 1988; Parkes & Weiss, 1983; Weiss, 1988). After a period of disorientation, numbness, and shock (Johansen, 1988; Rosof, 1994) in which people often feel nothing, the devastating nature of the event begins to hit them. A grieving mother whose son died in a skiing accident described her pain this way: "The physical and emotional pain was so great, it was as though someone had blown a hole through my heart with a shotgun" (Beattie & Stesin, 1991, p. 28). People who are bereaved do not just feel devastated, they are devastated. For a time nothing matters and nothing makes sense. They become "engulfed with suffering" (Hogan, Morse, & Tasón, 1996, p. 53). Connections to life and purpose seem meaningless:

> How hard it is to leave a graveyard when you must leave behind a coffin containing the body of someone so precious. It is like the final tearing of the tissues of one's heart, an unravelling of all those strands that have been intertwined over so many years. Now suddenly there was nothing more for us to do. (Oosterveen, 1988, p. 145)

There is something to do, however. As reality forces survivors to acknowledge that a loss has occurred (Futterman & Hoffman, 1983), the real work of mourning begins. Or as Rosof (1994) describes it, the 'long haul" begins (p. 75).

Trying to carry on while struggling for control

According to crisis theory, once survivors confront the reality of their loss, they enter a period of "disequilibrium" (Moos & Schaefer, 1986, p. 9). For a time they seem to oscillate between two points on a continuum, all the while feeling out of balance. Futterman and Hoffman (1983) suggest that grieving involves "work[ing] out balances between apparently polar conflicting, adaptive tasks" (p. 368). Survivors struggle to find a balance between

- acknowledging the ultimate loss of the child and maintaining hope, tending to immediate needs and planning for the future, cherishing the child and allowing separations to occur, maintaining day-to-day functioning and expressing disturbing feelings (Futtereman & Hoffman, 1983, p. 368);

- carrying on normally and permanent mourning, between denial of the child's existence and constant preoccupation, between assimilating and avoiding the memory, and between forgetting and remembering (Rubin, 1985, p. 348); and

- protesting the loss and accepting it enough to try to learn about it, despairing over the loss and finding signs of hope for the future, and detaching oneself from life and new attachments and investing in life and new relationships (Martin & Elder, 1993).

This suggests that grief work might look like a swinging pendulum, moving between an "encounter and a retreat," from the event and from all that it means to the survivor (Wortman & Silver, 1986, p. 193). Using my informants' words, I called these two phases **trying to carry on** and **struggling for control**.

Each end of the continuum generates some kind of emotional or intellectual pain. Part of the work of grieving is learning to "regulate" that pain (Futterman & Hoffman, 1983, p. 372). Survivors must work towards actively dealing with the reality of the loss while trying to avoid being overwhelmed by it. As survivors switch from gaining and losing control over their pain, they slowly learn how to handle and accept their loss intellectually and emotionally (Weiss, 1988). Gradually, they work out what Brice (1991) calls the "paradoxes" (p. 1).

Learning to let go

Eventually, survivors stop vacillating. They begin to move toward a goal or end point. On their way to this end point, survivors need to find a new way to relate to the deceased (Futterman & Hoffman, 1983; McClowry, Davies, May, Kulenkamp, & Martinson, 1987; Rubin, 1981, 1985). Contrary to what researchers and clinicians have been saying for years, the goal of grieving is not to detach from or let go of the deceased; instead, the goal of grieving is to forge a new kind of relationship with the deceased (Attig, 1996; Brice, 1991; Finkbeiner, 1996; Kaplan, 1996; Klass, Silverman, & Nickman, 1996; Rubin, 1996). In the second edition of his book on grief counselling, Worden (1991) acknowledges this shift in thinking. Whereas before his fourth task of mourning was "withdrawing emotional energy from the deceased and reinvesting it in another relationship," Worden now says it is "to emotionally relocate the deceased and move on with life" (p. 16). As Vaillant (1985) says, "Grief work is remembering, not forgetting" (p. 63). Since survivors must also deal with a change in their own identity (Weiss, 1988) and the way they feel about their world (Attig, 1996; Futterman & Hoffman, 1983; Wortman & Silver, 1986, 1989), they must also let go of their old identities and their old world. These tasks relate to the **learning to let go** phase described by the parents in this study.

Being changed

Many authors use terms like recovery or resolution to describe grief's apparent goal (Florian, 1989; Lehman et al., 1987; Parkes & Weiss, 1983; Stevens, Pfost, & Wessel, 1987; Stroebe, Stroebe, & Domittner, 1988; Ulmer et al., 1991; Weiss, 1988; Wortman & Silver, 1986, 1989). Hogan, Morse, and Tasón (1996) go so far as to use the phrase: "experiencing personal growth" as the last phase of the grief process (p. 58). The problem with these terms is that they imply an ideal goal, not a realistic one.

In fact, after a thorough review of a variety of studies of trauma victims, Wortman and Silver (1986, 1989) challenge the myth that people ever completely recover from a traumatic event. Weiss (1988) identifies the characteristics of people who cannot recover at all: they cannot make any sense of the event; they feel ambivalent towards the deceased; they feel hopeless; and they cannot return to previous levels of functioning. However, sometimes the opposite seems to happen. Miles and Crandall (1983) describe the tremendous growth that some parents undergo after the death of their child. They may become more compassionate and more open with their affections; their faith may be strengthened. It seems that survivors can do more than recover; they can even improve.

Since some people improve and some people never function well again, I propose that we stop using the word "recovery" to describe the goal of the grief process. We need to start talking about how traumatic experiences can change survivors. My study clearly shows that the death of a child changed the parents, some negatively and some positively.

Knapp (1986) also found that many parents in his study felt differently about their lives. The death of their child had "shake[n their] attachments to traditional values and goals of success and personal achievement and brought into play new commitments to more intangible values" (p. 37). Because "life itself now seemed so fragile" (p. 38), parents tried to use their time differently. Knapp also found that some parents seemed negatively affected. He described them as people who could no longer respond to life. "Emotional dullness" (p. 41) may be characteristic of parents who are changed negatively. They carry a "shadow grief" (p. 41) with them for years.

Using the word change instead of recovery reminds us that when people confront one loss experience it affects how they handle the next one. One event affects the interpretation of the next. Therefore, there really is no end to the grief process (Martin & Elder, 1993). This is certainly the language used by the parents in my study, which is why the last phase of their grief process is called **being changed**.

Implications

These findings can assist those who are grieving the loss of any important relationship. Knowing what the grief process looks like gives the bereaved a sense of direction and a sense of control over their grief. It also gives them hope. Professionals and self-help groups can use the picture of the process to educate the newly bereaved about what lies ahead. Others who are in the middle of the experience might also find the identification of the phases helpful. Learning about the phases helps people understand that their experience is normal, that others have survived it, and that there is some order in what appears to be chaos. Finally, both the picture of the process and the identification of the phases can be used to educate professionals about the parents' experiences, which will enable them to help the parents understand the process.

Mourning Strategies

To cope with their grief, parents in this study found ways to manage the display and internal experiences of their grief. They used what I call mourning strategies.

Definition of terms

Grief refers to a person's private and internal reactions to loss (Worden, 1982). These reactions appear to be universal (Rosenblatt, 1988). *Mourning* refers to how a person displays and handles their grief (Worden, 1982; see Hochschild, 1983 for a discussion of the management and display of emotions). Rosenblatt (1988) suggests that people's mourning is partially determined by culturally defined rules. These rules govern the timing, intensity, and appropriate location for mourning (Hochschild, 1983). Besides learning how to deal with their grief, those experiencing their first loss must learn the rules of acceptable mourning behavior (Rosenblatt, 1988). The bereaved learn these rules over time and through their interactions with others.

At the same time, the bereaved also want to learn how to make themselves feel better. Highly stressful situations like the death of a loved one disrupt people's sense of equilibrium and identity. This disruption causes them to look for ways to restore their balance (Albas & Albas, 1988). Trial and error helps people find the most effective methods to reduce their anxiety. The parents in this study described many approaches to dealing with their grief. At first, most worked hard just to prevent grief from overwhelming them. Then they gradually learned how to manage their grief so that it was less disruptive to themselves and to those around them. I called their attempts to manage their grief mourning strategies.

Other authors use the term *strategy* as well. Gauthier and Marshall (1977) use this word just once in their article to describe behavior designed to intentionally avoid "intrusive thoughts" about the deceased or about sadness (p. 41). Cook (1988) also used this term to refer to the ways people "dealt with their grief" (p. 294). Other authors, however, use terms like *grieving style* (Stinson et al., 1992, p. 218), *coping skills* (Moos & Schaefer, 1986, p. 13), and *grief response patterns* (Wolfelt, 1993. pp. 1, 16) to describe some of the same behaviors.

Dimensions of grief

As parents tried to handle their grief, their thoughts and feelings affected their behavior. While some parents felt comfortable displaying or sharing their emotions, others did not. While some benefitted from thinking about their loss, others did not. Other authors have observed similar approaches to grief.

Stinson et al. (1992) focus on the feeling side of grieving. They call it the "female dimension of grief" (p. 222). Women commonly manifest or express their grief through sadness, crying, and continued preoccupation with the loss experience. These authors suggest that perhaps for too long we have assumed that the stereotypical women's way of grieving "is grief" (p. 222). They suggest that further research is needed to uncover the "male grieving process" (p. 222).

Stinson et al. (1992) reviewed the literature about men's inexpressiveness. They concluded that men are socialized to be "in control." Men are more comfortable "making decisions rationally, devoid of personal involvement and feelings" (p. 219). Although they do not say so specifically, these authors imply that the male "dimension of grief" involves the use of the mind rather than the use of affect to deal with grief. Chartier (1987) agrees. He suggests that "men are socialized to restrict and control emotional and affectionate expression" (p. 12). Instead of expressing their grief, Chartier says men work hard to suppress it. Cook's (1988) ethnographic study suggests that instead of suppressing their grief men have their own way of controlling it and working it out privately. Grieving fathers keep much of their grief locked inside instead of sharing it with others. They primarily use thought control or deflection to deal with their grief.

Since the literature seems to suggest that all women express their grief and that all men control or suppress it, this implies that gender determines mourning strategies. However, I interviewed a few very expressive men; I also interviewed a few women who used thought control and deflection very effectively. My findings do not coincide with what the literature appears to suggest. This presented a problem until I looked closer.

After rereading Cook (1988), I noticed her brief cautionary note: "There were some men, although they were rare, who said they dealt with their upsetting feelings by freely expressing them and discussing them (p. 301). Cook's findings compared to mine. Perhaps gender is not the only thing that determines mourning strategies.

The work of Moos and Schaefer (1986) provides more useful information. Instead of focusing on gender, they look at coping skills. They divide these skills into three domains: appraisal-focused coping, emotion-focused coping, and problem-focused coping. People seldom use only one skill at a time. The main instrument of appraisal-focused coping is the mind; it is used to redefine, analyze, avoid troubling situations, and suppress or deny feelings. The main instrument of emotion-focused coping is the affect; it is regulated and discharged. The explanations and examples given by Moos and Schaefer (1986) matched what my informants told me about how they had coped with grief. Some used their minds much more than their affect; others were the opposite. Some parents used combinations of both; others avoided using either their mind or their affect to deal with their grief. Since problem-focused coping used both the mind and the affect, I integrated it into all four mourning strategies.

Mourning strategies

I used the two dimensions of emotion-focused coping and appraisal-focused coping to produce four different mourning strategies: *frozen*, *dependent*, *expressive*, and *controlled*. The name of each of these strategies comes from the words of the parents.

Frozen strategy

Those who adopted the *frozen mourning strategy* were unable to either think about or feel their grief. Reiterating Lifton's studies of death camp survivors, Dershimer (1990) suggests that some people have both a "diminished capacity to feel" and a "radical disassociation of the mind" (p. 34). This is similar to being in shock, which, in most cases, is temporary. The extreme version of this is severe denial or "conscious suppression" of all memories or feelings (Moos & Schaefer, p. 16). Worden (1982) calls this "inhibited or suppressed grief" (p. 59), as does Raphael (1983). It seems to originate in earlier unresolved losses.

Dependent strategy

Those who adopted the *dependent mourning strategy* were unable to do anything with their grief but let the feelings overwhelm them. They could not think straight, so they turned to others to help them feel safe. While this strategy is used temporarily by most grievers within the first few weeks, some people could not stop depending on others. They did not know how to handle their grief any other way. These grievers experienced "intense yearning…feelings of helplessness, and indecisiveness shortly after the death" (Parkes & Weiss, 1983, cited in Wortman & Silver, 1986, p. 217). When this strategy is taken to the extreme, some people could not regulate or control their grief at all except by "act[ing] out" (Moos & Schaefer, 1986, p. 18): drinking, taking drugs, becoming promiscuous, and generally losing control of their emotions. Others did the opposite; they became exceptionally withdrawn, angry, or depressed. Lindemann (1944, cited in Dershimer, 1990) identifies some behaviors indicative of "an exaggerated grief reaction" (Worden, 1982, p. 60): "overactivity without a sense of loss, engagement in activities detrimental to one's own social and economic existence, and alterations in relationships with friends and relatives" (Dershimer, 1990, p. 35). Worden (1982) suggests that people who adopt this strategy cannot do any "reality testing" (p. 60). Because they cannot confront their grief or distance themselves from it, they cannot manage it. It continuously overwhelms them.

Expressive strategy

Those who adopted the *expressive mourning strategy* could release or express both their thoughts and their emotions. While some needed to have people to talk to, others expressed their grief by crying, writing in journals, or praying. They needed to release their grief. This is likely the idealized grief to which many authors refer. Books about bereavement counselling suggest that people should always be encouraged to express their grief (Dershimer, 1990; Worden, 1982). Lepore et al. (1996) found that those who could talk to encouraging and sympathetic others did better than those who felt unable to talk. Taken to the extreme, however, the release of any and all thoughts and feelings, no matter how negative and no matter how others respond, has the potential to produce problems in intimate relationships.

Controlled strategy

Those who adopted the *controlled mourning strategy* used their minds to control the display of their emotions and to talk themselves out of their grief. For the most part, these parents did their grieving privately. Cook (1988) details the specific activities that grieving fathers employed; I found evidence of all these activities in parents of both sexes who adopted the controlled strategy: thinking about something else, reason/reflection, doing something else, and solitary expressiveness. Cook (1988) says that the strategies are "essentially individualistic" and "fairly inexpressive" (p. 301). This strategy "emphasized control over engulfment by affective distress" (p. 302). In extreme cases, people who use this strategy appear to be totally cut off from their feelings. This "emotional numbing" (Chartier, 1987, p. 6) may cause problems with intimate relationships (Cook, 1988).

Implications

Now that we know that these four different strategies exist, of what use are they? First of all, they help the bereaved understand their own behavior. This helps them make sense of previously confusing actions, thoughts, and feelings. Because sometimes grieving makes people feel like they are "going crazy," learning about the mourning strategies gives them a measure of control. It helps them feel normal again.

Second, knowing about mourning strategies helps people make sense of other's reactions, particularly their spouse's reactions. This reduces the ambiguity and confusion that comes from not understanding the reasons behind a person's behavior. Knowing about these strategies also reduces the likelihood that people will use negative attributions to explain their spouse's behavior; they will understand them better.

Third, counselors can use these strategies to help the bereaved learn how to manage their grief more effectively. If those who are grieving know only one strategy and it is not effective, then they could benefit from learning about other strategies. Counselors can also use these strategies to help them predict what kinds of help people might need. For instance, after noticing that a client continually uses phrases like "looking for the logic" or "I need to understand," a counselor might suggest books to read rather than trying to make the client talk about feelings.

Marital Types

Other researchers support my findings about marital types in two major areas: the identification of two factors, that is, the degree of emotional interdependence and the parents' perceptions of the events, that explain how marriages are affected by grief and the resulting four marital types.

Factors that affect marital outcome

Lehman et al. (1989) found that the death of a child can create long-term strain in marital relationships. Some couples rise to the challenge, and their marriage becomes more satisfying; some couples cannot meet the challenge, and their marriage becomes unsatisfying. Few marriages remain unchanged by the death of a child. These authors provide no specific explanations for why this happens. I have uncovered two significant and interacting factors that help to explain it.

Emotional interdependence

The first factor is the degree of emotional interdependence in the relationship. Fitzpatrick (1988), who also used this factor to create a typology of marriages, defines *interdependence* as "the connectedness of relational partners physically, temporally, and psychologically" (p. 99). Day and Hooks (1987) use a similar term, cohesion, to describe the "level of emotional bonding" between partners (p. 308). The amount of cohesion in a relationship moves along a continuum, ranging from complete independence to complete dependence. Couples continually negotiate how much dependence they can tolerate, always trying to find a mutually satisfying spot along the continuum. While some reach a compromise, others continually struggle with this issue. Those who cannot compromise are already in trouble when their child dies.

When their child dies, parents must not only work through their grief as individuals, they must also work on their grief within their relationship (Rosenblatt et al., 1991). Each partner's capacity to care about the other and the relationship may be drastically affected. Their need for privacy, comfort, and dependence may also change, causing the relationship to lose its equilibrium. To further complicate matters, grieving parents simultaneously feel two conflicting emotions: a sense of terrible isolation because they believe no one understands their pain and, at the same time, intense intimacy with their partner because they have shared such a devastating experience (Smart, 1992). This false sense of intimacy may increase expectations about closeness and mutual support in the relationship.

Rosenblatt et al. (1991) found that when two people in a relationship are both grieving problems are likely to develop. The most problematic relationship involves mothers and fathers grieving the death of their child. Even before the child's death, the relationship itself may have a history of unresolved difficulties. Grief may exaggerate or highlight these problems, making them harder to ignore. In addition, grief usually makes people turn inward. They find it difficult to pay attention to other people's needs. Just meeting their own needs takes priority. At the same time, people usually feel irritable and easily frustrated when they grieve. Their tolerance levels are low. This sets the stage for arguments and fights, often over unmet needs. On top of all this, people who are close to one another can trigger each other's grief. The situation is ripe for conflict and dissatisfaction. Nonetheless, spouses may still turn to one another for support. They may expect that since they share the same loss they can count on one another for support. When the relationship is one of interdependence, partners seem to expect more of each other. If these expectations are not met, one of the long-term consequences could be a new awareness of "how much a spouse could or could not be relied on at a time of loss. What was grieved was not [just] the loss of [a child] but the loss of a dream, expectation, or hope of full spouse support in times of need" (Rosenblatt & Burns, 1986, p. 248).

Assigning positive attributions

The other factor that explains how grief affects marriages concerns the parents' perception of events. When confronted with a confusing or ambiguous situation, people need to "define what has happened. Without definitional clarity, it is difficult to know what to feel, what to do, and what to ask for" (Rosenblatt & Burns, 1986, p. 246). The death of a child and the grief reactions that follow provide many confusing and ambiguous moments. Because of their different experiences with life, with the child, and with grief, it is very difficult for couples to reach some kind of "shared definition" (Rosenblatt & Burns, 1986, p. 249) or worldview (Attig, 1996), particularly if they cannot discuss what they are feeling and thinking. Disparities can seriously strain relationships if couples do not understand their source (Gage & Holcomb, 1991).

Couples who successfully meet the challenge of coping with the death of a child are adaptable and flexible (Day & Hooks, 1987; Gilbert, 1989). They "redefine the situation" (Day & Hooks, 1987, p. 308) or reframe it (Gilbert, 1989) positively. Reframing involves changing one's perception of an event or person so that the meaning is changed without changing the facts. Satisfied couples try their best to perceive their spouse and their marriage in a positive light. Because they assume positive intent, they try to come up with positive explanations for behavior they do not understand.

In any marriage, attributions or explanations that spouses create about one another's behavior and intentions play a "mediating role in the level of marital satisfaction" (Fincham, Beach, & Nelson, 1987, p. 83). Distressed couples often consider their partner's behavior to be the source of marital difficulties and to be selfishly motivated and intentional (Fincham et al., 1987; Fincham & Grych, 1991). Gilbert (1989) found that couples who experience high levels of conflict after the death of their baby frequently argued about "their interpretation of each other's behavior" (p. 613). For example, a husband may want his wife to know she can rely on him. He tries to appear strong by suppressing his own grief. His wife, however, may misinterpret his silence as meaning that he has no feelings for either her or her pain. Instead of leaning on him, she may withdraw in anger.

Each negative attribution has the potential to weaken the marriage. Soon there is reciprocal interaction: negative attributions increase marital dissatisfaction, which in turn increases the number and frequency of negative attributions. Fincham et al. (1987) suggest that couples who continually make negative attributions risk the gradual deterioration of their relationship. As long as partners continue to perceive each other's behavior and intentions negatively, there is little hope for mutual understanding and satisfaction in their relationship (Guthrie & Noller, 1988).

Four different marital types

When I combined these two factors, emotional interdependence in the relationship and the ability to find positive explanations for ambiguous situations, four different marital types emerged: *connected*, *parallel*, *conflicted*, and *isolated*.

Connected marriages

Connected couples feel satisfied with emotional interdependence in their relationship. In this way, they are similar to what Fitzpatrick (1988) calls traditional couples. When their baby died, some *connected couples* took turns comforting each another. Smart (1992) identifies a similar pattern of helping after a child dies; she calls it the "mutual husband-wife helping" pattern (p. 88). Both husband and wife gave and received support from each other. Smart also found another type of helping relationship: "husband primary helper" (p. 90). Though this is one-sided helping, since the arrangement satisfies the needs of both partners, it will lead to a *connected marriage*. Like the low-conflict couples in Gilbert's (1989) study, connected couples shared their grief to a mutually satisfying level. They were flexible and aware of one another's needs, and they worked hard to develop a positive point of view. When confronted with confusing behavior, connected couples tried to find positive explanations for their spouse's behavior and intentions. They wanted to think the best of each other. Beyond being committed to one another, they were also deeply committed to the health and future of their relationship. This trait also parallels Fitzpatrick's traditionals. Knapp (1986) found a similar pattern in marriage. He calls the couples "integrated" (p. 118).

Parallel marriage

Couples in a *parallel marriage* are highly independent and in that regard are like Fitzpatrick's (1988) separates. These partners "are not very companionable and [they] share very little with their spouses" (Fitzpatrick, 1988, p. 101). The important thing is that this arrangement satisfies both partners. Smart (1992) also found a pattern of helping she calls "separates" (p. 92). In her study, these couples may have helped each another shortly after the baby's death, but helping quickly decreased to almost nothing. While some might construe lack of communication and direct helping as potentially destructive, *parallel couples* in this study had come to expect minimal emotional support from each another. Therefore, they were not disappointed. Like Smart's and Fitzpatrick's separates, parallel couples looked for support outside of their marriage. Because they respected each another, they assumed positive intent when confronted with their spouse's confusing grieving behavior. Their commitment to each other and to the marriage remained strong.

Isolated marriage

Couples in *isolated marriages* are at the far end of the continuum of independence. Some of their behavior also corresponds with Smart's (1992) separates. The major difference between them is that *isolated couples* do not seek help outside the marriage. The length of time they offer one another any support is also very short. Soon after their baby's death they withdraw from each other and from outside help: their grief severely isolates them. This communication pattern does not fit with any of Fitzpatrick's types, but it does correspond with Knapp's (1986) "isolates" (p. 118). These couples did not treat the death as a couple event, and therefore, they did not share their grief. In many cases, the child's death devastated one or both partners.

Some of Gilbert's (1989) high-conflict couples are similar to the *isolated couples*. These partners frequently misinterpret one another's behavior and intentions, causing them to have difficulty creating a shared definition of the experience. In fact, they do not even try. Smart (1992) found that couples who did not help one another but who remained married did so because of their "commitment to the institution of marriage" (p. 94). She does not address the role of children as marital "glue"—one of the reasons the *isolated couples* in this study stayed together.

Conflicted marriage

In the *conflicted marriage*, one or both spouses feel unhappy about the level of interdependence in the relationship. Smart (1992) found that in the "husband primary help" pattern some men felt "overburdened" by the demands of having to be the strong one (p. 90). Some women became frustrated by their husband's inability to express feelings. The perception of excessive dependency or excessive silence caused many fights in *conflicted marriages*. Gilbert (1989) identifies other subjects that caused high conflict: incongruent grieving as well as differences in perceptions of the meaning of the child, the individual experience, and the view of themselves as a couple. Disparate perceptions and consistently negative explanations fueled the fire of conflict in these marriages, leading some to dissolve eventually. Others stayed together for the sake of the children or to avoid another loss.

Implications

Of what use are these four marital types? Dealing with marriages that are troubled by conflicts about dependency is the domain of marriage counselors. Other professionals, however, can reduce the development of marital problems by educating the bereaved about the different mourning strategies. They can help them understand that differences in mourning strategies can lead to confusion and the misinterpretation of behavior and intentions. If couples understood more about mourning strategies and about the grief process in general, chances are they might be less negative about how they define their differences. By educating people about this, we might help to reduce the ambiguities of the situation. We can make the grief experience more understandable and predictable.

Chapter 9
Recommendations

The Need for Further Research

The parents' experience

Sense of coherence and grieving

The parents' ***search for reason*** proved to be a major finding in this study. Parents who had difficulty managing their grief, making sense of it, and finding any positive meaning in their baby's death had the most troubled grief experience. Unfortunately, these people seldom came to the attention of professionals. If public health nurses visited all newly bereaved parents (both mothers and fathers), then perhaps some of these people could be identified and referred for help. If during their visit the nurses had the parents complete a questionnaire that could predict who might have difficulties dealing with their grief, then extra support could be promptly organized for those who need it.

Antonovsky's Sense of Coherence (SOC) Questionnaire (1987) might prove quite useful for this task. Using a Likert-scale format, this 29-item questionnaire measures the degree to which people find their lives manageable, meaningful, and comprehensible. The higher the score, the higher the Sense of Coherence (SOC); the lower the score, the more help the person might need. To see if this instrument can detect and predict problematic grief, researchers could test the following hypotheses:

- Hypothesis One: Newly bereaved parents will achieve a lower score on the SOC Questionnaire than nonbereaved parents;

- Hypothesis Two: Newly bereaved parents who feel unable to manage their grief will achieve a lower score on the SOC Questionnaire than other bereaved parents who feel satisfied with their mourning strategies;

- Hypothesis Three: Parents who have been bereaved for one year or less will achieve a lower score on the SOC Questionnaire than parents who have been bereaved for one year or more; and

- Hypothesis Four: If bereaved parents complete the SOC Questionnaire every 3 months for 3 years, then those whose scores do not decrease significantly after the first 6 months will likely need outside help.

Benefits of attending a support group

Some couples in this study attended a local support group together; in many situations, just the woman attended. Further research could investigate what effect couple or single attendance at a group has on marital health and marital satisfaction in the short- and long-term and to see what effect attendance at a support group has on each parent:

- Hypothesis Five: Bereaved parents who attend a support group together for more than 3 months will achieve a higher score on tests that measure marital satisfaction and marital interaction (like the Abbreviated Barrett Lennard Relationship Inventory reviewed in Friedman & Sherman [1987]) than those who never attend together or who attend less than twice; and

- Hypothesis Six: The scores on the SOC Questionnaire for bereaved parents who attend a support group at least 6 times will vary significantly from the scores of those parents who never attend or who attend less than 6 times.

The siblings' experience

Although this study focused on the parents' experiences, I learned about the children's reactions from the parents' comments about the ways in which their parenting styles changed after their baby died and their comments about their children's behavior, conversations, and concerns. I propose the following hypotheses for further study:

- Hypothesis Seven: Older siblings will achieve a higher score on instruments that measure the presence of anger and guilt than nonbereaved children their own age;
- Hypothesis Eight: Subsequent siblings will score lower on self-esteem measures than nonbereaved children their own age;
- Hypothesis Nine: Children whose parents encourage an active relationship with the deceased sibling will have more psychological, school, and behavioral problems within 5 years of the baby's death than children whose parents do not actively encourage this kind of relationship;
- Hypothesis Ten: When bereaved siblings are under the age of 12, they will score lower on instruments that measure trust in the environment than nonbereaved children their own age;
- Hypothesis Eleven: When bereaved siblings are over the age of 12, they will achieve higher scores on instruments that measure trouble achieving autonomy and independence than nonbereaved adolescents; and
- Hypothesis Twelve: When bereaved siblings have their own children, their level of anxiety about SIDS will be significantly higher than their cohorts who are also having children.

The Need for Community Education

The lack of knowledge about SIDS and about grief increased parental stress. There is an obvious need to educate both the lay public and professionals.

Public awareness of SIDS

Parents who had at least heard of SIDS before their baby's death seemed to cope with it better. They also accepted it as the diagnosis sooner than those who had never heard of it. Parents who had relatives and friends who had heard of SIDS also did better than those who did not:

- Recommendation One: The Canadian Foundation for the Study of Infant Deaths (CFSID) might consider developing an annual national public awareness campaign during an annual SIDS Awareness Month to educate the public about SIDS. This campaign could involve the use of the electronic media, billboards, newspaper advertising, and brochures and posters that could be adapted for use across the country. This effort might be combined with a fund-raising campaign.

Professional awareness of SIDS

Parents who dealt with knowledgeable medical professionals who did a good job of explaining SIDS did better than parents who received vague or incorrect information about SIDS. This finding suggests that time and effort spent educating medical professionals about the latest SIDS-related research and about how to explain SIDS to parents is important:

- Recommendation Two: The CFSID might consider making sure that medical and nursing schools across the country receive up-to-date information about SIDS research. Additionally, instead of waiting to be asked, members of the local CFSID chapters might consider volunteering on a regular basis to speak about their experiences at conferences and schools of nursing and medicine.

Public awareness about grief

Parents who had the support of people who understood the nature of the grief process did far better than those who had no one who understood their pain:

- Recommendation Three: The local chapters of the CFSID could work closely with other bereavement support groups, various social service organizations, ministers, and funeral homes to lobby for or to help organize information sessions about such topics as supporting the grieving parent, understanding the parental grief process, and explaining death to children. Counselling agencies that work with families are likely to be particularly helpful; and

- Recommendation Four: Information from this study about mourning strategies, the grief process, and the potential impact on marriages could easily be transformed into useful brochures or booklets that could form a part of the CFSID mail-out package.

Professional awareness about grief

There are a number of recommendations that flow from the parents' positive and negative experiences with first responders, doctors, nurses, funeral directors, and ministers:

- Recommendation Five: First responders and staff at hospitals need to understand that many parents benefit from seeing, holding, and spending private time with their baby once all resuscitation efforts have stopped. Although some parents will refuse this offer, making it gives them permission to do something they may not have thought of doing. Parents who wish to spend time with their baby need privacy and should be given as much time as they need. Time spent with the baby at this point facilitates the transformation of the baby to another form in the parents' minds;

- Recommendation Six: The sooner parents hear that someone in authority suspects or confirms SIDS as the cause of death the better. Although parents will still find reasons to blame themselves initially, knowing that SIDS is the cause of death eventually helps to reduce their need to blame themselves;

- Recommendation Seven: Funeral directors, public health nurses, hospital chaplains, ministers, and family doctors are in a good position to provide parents with information about the grief process, different mourning strategies, and the potential for marital problems after the baby's death. This normalizes the parents' experience and prepares them for what lies ahead. These professionals need to be exposed to the findings of this study;

- Recommendation Eight: Parents who took charge of planning their baby's funeral felt better about themselves and had fewer regrets about the funeral later. Funeral directors need to encourage parents to make decisions that reflect their own needs and wants instead of letting others take over the planning. This information needs to be shared with funeral directors; and

- Recommendation Nine: Parents often needed someone to listen to their fear that they had caused their baby's death. Professionals who can listen and encourage parents to explore their guilt can facilitate healing. This information needs to be shared with professionals so they can assist parents in their ***search for a reason***, ***search for logic***, and ***search for meaning***.

The Need to Consider Some Issues Within the CFSID and Agencies that Serve Grieving Parents

Volunteers

The amount of time and energy some parents dedicate to the work of organizations like the Canadian Foundation for the Study of Infant Deaths (CFSID) at the local level is impressive. Unfortunately, only a minority of parents who come to the group for support eventually become volunteers themselves. Consequently, a few volunteers provide many services normally offered by professionals and agencies that have far more resources. The volunteers receive little training or supervision, but they expect great things of themselves. There are too few volunteers for all the projects, but because of their dedication, the projects are seldom shelved. Volunteers quickly become overtaxed by excessive demands on their time and energy. If they consider withdrawing their services, then they feel guilty, knowing there is still so much to be done. Some stay involved for years, even though they may want to get on with other things in their lives. I wonder whether the inability to leave without feeling guilty is related to the parents' grief and their connection to their baby. I also wonder whether there is something about the organization of services for these parents that increases the problem. My concern is that this situation is not good for the well-being of either the parents, their families, or the CFSID. This leads me to pose some questions that local chapters and the board of the CFSID might like to consider. I have no answers; I only have questions:

- Issue One: Would mandatory training and supervision of group leaders help to prevent volunteer burn-out? Would this encourage more uninvolved parents to consider becoming involved? Would mandatory time-limited commitments to specific volunteer jobs allow more graceful exits and encourage the active recruitment of new volunteers?

- Issue Two: Why do some parents volunteer their time and others do not? Why are there so few male volunteers at the local level? Is there anything the organization can do to encourage more volunteers in general?

- Issue Three: Would the involvement of various professionals as unpaid consultants to chapters help reduce the stress of the small number of involved volunteers? I am thinking specifically about professionals in public relations, public education, fund-raising, and counselling. Also, is there a way to involve nonbereaved parents at the chapter level so that the work load could be more evenly distributed? Would nonbereaved volunteers feel welcome, or would they feel like "outsiders?"

- Issue Four: Is there something about the current organization of the CFSID that contributes to local chapters and individual parents feeling pressured to accomplish so much on their own? Can something be done organizationally to reduce frustration and burn-out at the local level?

Services

In view of the above concerns I hesitate to suggest the need for another service. However, I see a need to provide services to parents and families who deal with their grief by gathering information. The support group meets the needs of parents who want to share and express their grief. It also provides support for those who need to lean on others until they feel strong enough to cope on their own. This group does not meet the needs of those who want information about SIDS and grief presented in a nonemotional, structured setting. Help for grieving siblings is also lacking:

- Issue Five: Could local chapters offer regular information sessions about SIDS research and about the grief process for the benefit of those who just want information?

- Issue Six: Could local chapters work with social service organizations or counselling professionals to ensure that the needs of grieving siblings are being met?

CFSID and future research projects

It is my understanding that this study is the first nonmedical study ever funded by the CFSID. I hope it will not be the last. I uncovered several topics that future research could address:

- Topic One: Some jurisdictions require all suspected SIDS babies to be transported to the hospital; others leave this decision up to the discretion of the paramedics. Which situation is better for the parents as they grieve over time? In this study, hospital experiences seemed to create more stress than home situations. Is this always the case?

- Topic Two: There are a variety of professionals who play a significant role in parents' healing. Future studies could look at the role of paramedics, firefighters, medical examiner's investigators, police officers, RCMP, funeral directors, ministers, public health nurses, and doctors and nurses in emergency departments.

- Topic Three: The connection between the parent's changing image of the baby over time and the parent's ability to heal and go on with life has not been explored as a possible early indicator of future difficulties. Specifically, if parents do not see the transformation from baby to body before the funeral, does this suggest that they will have difficulties in the future?

- Topic Four: This study provides enough information about the parental grief experience to generate a grief inventory specific to the SIDS-loss experience. Would such an instrument assist professionals to identify parents who might be in need of extra help?

Chapter 10
Conclusion

EVALUATING THE STUDY

Strengths and weaknesses of the research instrument

As is often the case, people's strengths can also be their weaknesses. The trick is to find a happy and productive balance. Throughout the course of this study, I learned something about both my strengths and my weaknesses.

One of my strengths is my ability to connect with people in pain. This strength caused three problems. First of all, as I have already described, I very quickly moved from the position of interested researcher to what Lifton (1982) calls a "survivor by proxy" (p. 226). The extreme of this is what Field and Morse (1985) refer to as "going native" (p. 93). I became too close to the informants. Field and Morse suggest that this can alter the view of the data and make the researcher less effective. I concur with their comments, but fortunately, I had time to wait until the detachment came naturally. Because I eventually regained my objectivity, I am convinced that my journey into the parents' experience did not hurt the quality of my findings. In fact, I think it enriched the study immeasurably. When I look at my own research journal, I see how much I learned about the parents' pain by going through my own. It did mean, however, that the study took much longer to complete than I had predicted.

My ability to connect well with people in pain led to another problem. Fortunately, I became aware of it during the first couple of interviews. I have worked as a psychiatric nurse and counselor in the past. Although this experience helped me feel at ease during the interviews, it also caused some problems. I had to constantly fight against my tendency to counsel the informants through the kind of questions I asked or through the responses I made to their stories. Sometimes this fight got in the way of hearing what the informants said; sometimes it meant that I avoided asking certain questions that would make me feel like a counselor again. Once I became aware of the problem, I learned how to deal with it by tapping into the informant's experience and shutting out my own inner dialogue. Soon I no longer felt inhibited during interviews. I have no doubt, however, that I missed some valuable information in the beginning.

The ability to connect with people in pain caused me another problem. Because I learned so much from each participant, I wanted each story to be heard. Since this was impossible, I felt frustrated. I also resisted the need to elevate my findings from the parental experience to the theoretical level. I felt like I had used the parents' pain for my own personal gain somehow. I resolved this conflict by sharing some of my preliminary theoretical work with bereaved parents I had not interviewed. They said that the models I was developing gave them insight into their grief. This helped me feel more comfortable operating at the theoretical level.

My second relevant strength is my curiosity. I enjoy learning and tracking down information. Again, this has proven to be both a strength and a weakness for the completion of this study. I examined each developing concept very carefully, making sure that it was grounded in the data and not just in my imagination. I noticed tiny details about the experience and explored them until I understood their connection to other details. Although this is what a good grounded theorist should do, I had trouble knowing when to stop. The saturation point is still a confusing issue for me. When is enough enough? I had the same problem when I worked on the literature review and the theoretical and empirical connections. Finally, as my time ran out, I knew I had to stop digging for more information. I had to complete the study despite my awareness that I still have more to learn.

My third relevant strength is that I am an independent worker. I like to organize and control my work within my own schedule. I also like to work in the privacy of my home rather than on campus. This works well when I am comfortable with the task at hand. It proved to be a problem with this study because I learned the method by doing it. My independent spirit became a weakness when I needed help but could not ask for it. When I worked in Dr. Morse's research suite, I felt comfortable asking for help either from Dr. Morse or other students. They understood my questions because they dealt with similar issues every day. When Dr. Morse left the university and that environment was no longer available to me, I did not make the effort to replace it. At that point I was lost in the parents' experience. Consequently, I chose to isolate myself and deal with my research problems privately by reading and checking with my committee members infrequently. With hindsight, I realize I made a mistake. A grounded theory study, particularly when it is on such an emotional topic, should not be completed in isolation. I will never know how much my isolation affected the quality of the final results or how much better the study would have been had I found another collaborative work environment.

Evaluating the grounded theory method

One way to evaluate a study is to see how well the method matches the research topic. In this case, I think I had a good match between my subject matter and the grounded theory method. First of all, the theoretical perspective for grounded theory is symbolic interactionism. This social psychological theory focuses on how and when people change the definitions they assign to events, interactions, and other people. Since the parents in this study were continually trying to define and explain what was happening to them, having this theoretical perspective in the background helped me make sense of their behavior.

The second feature of this method flows directly from its theoretical perspective. Grounded theory allows the use of a flexible and unstructured interview process. Because the interview had no set structure, parents had the freedom to talk about their experience in the order that made the most sense to them. Mothers often started their interview by telling me something about themselves, their families, or their babies. Only after they had put the baby in some kind of context did the women begin to describe the death and the many events that followed. Most women shared their grief and tears with little hesitation. Only one women held back, and she had seldom talked about her experience with anyone. Generally though, most women were used to sharing the story of their grief and their baby. In contrast, many men began their interviews by talking almost immediately about the circumstances of the baby's death or about the way the death had affected the whole family. Most men only talked about themselves and their grief with encouragement and gentle prodding from me. Some men avoided highly emotional topics all together. They just did not want to share them with me. A few admitted that they had never before spoken about their grief at such a deep level. Armed with a structured interview schedule, I would have missed the opportunity to make these observations.

The third feature of this method is that it allows the researcher to use what is learned from one informant to influence the next interview. As I transcribed each interview, I asked questions of it. Then I used those answers to help me pose more specific questions to subsequent informants. When the next informant began talking about a topic of growing interest to me, I asked direct and specific questions. Once I understood the issues, I backed off to let the informant decide what topic to address next. By using a combination of focused and unfocused interviewing techniques, I continued to learn about the experience right up to the end of my last interview.

The fourth positive feature of grounded theory is that the researcher must follow the rigorous method of constant comparison. By constantly comparing features of people's experiences, I identified similarities and differences. Then I tried to explain the source of the differences by systematically analyzing the connections between contexts and conditions to see how the consequences differed. This process allowed me to compare a variety of unique and complex aspects of the grief process. Because of the precision of this method, this study's findings can be considered reliable.

Finally, grounded theory is the appropriate method when the goal of a study is to uncover new information about a process that occurs over time. Since this was the goal of this study, the method and the study's purpose fit well. The results generated several testable hypotheses and recommendations for other studies.

Evaluating the sample

Unlike some of the studies I reviewed, this study had a pure parent sample: all 21 parents had lost a baby to SIDS. This prevented contamination of the issues and allowed me to focus on the unique circumstances of this situation. Because I had a mixed sample in terms of gender (9 men and 12 women), I could compare the experiences of both mothers and fathers. Interviewing both the husband and the wife in nine couples allowed me to see how couples manage grief within their relationship. The sample was mixed in other ways: rural and urban, birth order of the baby, access to support groups and no access, and time since the baby's death. The inclusion of more parents who had lost their baby within the past 2 years would have enriched the study. Other parents who had lost a baby to SIDS but who had not participated in the study also became an informal but important part of my sample. As I talked with these parents individually or presented to parent groups at various CFSID functions, I received supportive feedback on my findings. The parents said I had captured the essence of their experience. This feedback not only increased my confidence in my findings, it proved the validity of the results.

Conclusion

As I look back on it now, I realize that I was unduly harsh to researchers who choose to take a detached position when studying parental grief. I understand now that anyone who does qualitative research has to be prepared to expend a great deal of emotional energy and time. Fortunately, I was in the position to afford both. This luxury is not available to everyone, nor is everyone temperamentally suited to this kind of work. Progress in our understanding of any human experience benefits from both the objectivity provided by quantitative work and the personal approach provided by qualitative work.

Concluding the Study

This study has dealt with certain inescapable facts. Fact One is that 12 families lost 12 beloved babies to SIDS. Some babies died within a year of my interview with the parents; some babies died over 25 years ago. Fact Two is that when each of these babies died, the parents thought they might never survive. Fact Three is that the parents did survive. The goal of this study has been to find out how.

Now that the study is complete we know how: parents who lose their baby to SIDS survive this traumatic experience by changing their perspective on their loss. The facts of the parents' tragic situation do not change over time. What changes is the parents' perception of these facts. This finding takes us back to one of the central tenets of symbolic interactionism: people act according to the definitions they assign to events, people, and interactions (Charon, 1979). These definitions are fluid and everchanging. This study provides empirical support for this abstract concept. To illustrate the power of these definitions, I elaborate on a few of the important shifts in the parents' perspectives.

The parents' changing definition of their baby

When parents looked into the eyes of their new and growing baby, they saw life. They also saw love and hope and dreams and the future. When their baby died, he/she changed from the keeper of dreams to the stuff of nightmares.

Despite the fact that most babies looked alike in death, what the parents saw differed considerably. In the minds of some, the baby had been replaced by a gruesome creature that bore no resemblance to the baby they loved. These parents could not bring themselves to hold or touch their baby. Some were repulsed by what they saw. This was not their baby, and they wanted nothing to do with it. Other parents noticed a transformation and seemed comforted by it: they watched as the baby's body changed into an empty lifeless shell. The essence or soul of the baby had gone. These parents hurt when their baby died, but they did not focus on their baby's suffering. Other parents could not or would not see the change. Their baby remained alive in their minds, despite the fact that it was mottled, cold, and stiff. These parents wanted to continue loving their baby for as long as possible. For as long as they could, they treated the baby as if he/she was alive.

The parents' definition of the baby continued to affect their behavior. Parents who were repulsed by the baby's appearance in the beginning seemed almost unconcerned about funeral details. They just wanted it to be over. Parents who had witnessed the transformation were also not very concerned about funeral details. They believed their baby had already gone; the funeral was only a formality. Parents who still thought their baby needed them could not stop loving and caring. Every detail of the funeral had to be perfect. Decisions were made on the basis of what the baby would have wanted. The burial or cremation proved to be very painful for these parents. They did not want to be separated from their baby. To other parents, the separation had already occurred. They were only disposing of the shell.

Most parents wanted to believe their baby had gone to be with God. Those with no faith in God or belief in heaven tried to be pragmatic; their baby was just gone. Parents who could neither accept nor reject the idea of heaven worried that their baby was lost. Even parents with very little faith in God preferred to believe in the existence of heaven. It gave them a sense of comfort to think of their baby there. Parents who needed to believe that their baby existed elsewhere usually decided that the baby had been transformed into a guardian angel. This helped them to imagine their baby more easily.

The differences in the parents' definition of the baby continued to affect their behavior for years. Some parents still work very hard to keep the memory of their baby alive despite pressure from others to let the baby go. In their hearts, their baby still needs them. As good parents, they must respond with love and attention. One or two parents seldom if ever think of their baby anymore. Most try to remember their baby fondly on special days, but some days the pain is remembered more than the baby.

The story of the parents' changing definition of the baby is poignant and powerful. More important though, it can also be predictive. Parents who had the most turbulent grief were those who could not see the baby's transformation. They could not stop responding to the baby as if it still needed them. The reasons why some parents see the transformation and others do not is unclear to me. What is clear, however, is that the parent's definition of their baby affects whether they ever heal from their loss. Those parents who still think of their baby as needing them do not allow themselves to heal. They keep the wound open by continually confronting the separation from their baby. They can never stop grieving.

The parents' changing definition of their grief experience

Parents began to grieve within seconds of realizing that their baby was dead. At that time and for months to come, they defined this event as the most devastating experience of their life. They felt overcome with guilt, impotence, sadness, fear, anger, and guilt. Their grief seemed unmanageable, their baby's death incomprehensible, and their life meaningless. They were not sure they would ever function again. And yet within weeks, parents were back at work and looking after their other children. Some were planning another pregnancy. Within 2 to 3 years, most parents had another baby to love. Over time, their grief had become manageable, their baby's death had become understandable, and their lives had meaning again. Once more, the painful facts had not changed. It was the parents' perceptions of their experience that had been transformed.

Through the process of ***searching for reason*** parents gradually found a way to explain their baby's death. They needed an explanation that made earthly and divine sense. They also needed an explanation that reduced their anxieties about the randomness, unfairness, and unpredictability of tragic events. Once they found an overall explanation that fit their needs, the pain of their grief diminished to manageable proportions. While some continued to feel responsible for their baby's death, most found explanations that absolved them of any blame. Those who accepted responsibility had to learn to live with what they believed they had done wrong.

With some temporal distance from their baby's death, parents gained a new perspective on their experience. They realized that they had managed to cope with the unmanageable. Most felt strengthened by this knowledge. Parents who had the ability to stand back from their experience began to realize that as bad as it had been the death of their baby could have been worse. This awareness reduced the intensity of their pain. Those who never reached this conclusion continued to feel undermined by their loss. Some parents went one step further: they put their anguish to work. Their suffering became meaningful and purposeful. Several parents could not find anything positive about their ordeal; they continued to suffer and to look at the world through a negative lens.

Once more the fact that the parents grieved the loss of their baby did not change. What changed over the years was their perception of themselves and their grieving. Parents with positive perceptions of themselves and others healed more constructively than those whose perceptions were negative. Those with positive perceptions of the experience could let go of their pain. Those who continued to see only the negatives held on to the pain.

Conclusion

The human mind is a wondrous thing. I realize that now more than ever. Before I started this study, I viewed grieving as an emotional process. Completing this study has changed my perception. Now I understand the power of the human mind to cope with the most tragic of all life events: the death of a child. I also appreciate the power of the human spirit in the face of such a devastating experience.

Appendix A
Methodology

Choosing the Theoretical Perspective

The theoretical perspective chosen for this study is symbolic interactionism. This social psychological theory focuses on the changing and interacting nature of the individual, society, mind, self, and truth (Charon, 1979; Prus, 1996). According to this theory, people are always in process rather than being a finished product. Symbolic interactionists believe that the self and society are so embedded in one another that neither can stand alone.

Theoretically, the self is composed of two abstract parts: the *I* and the *Me*. The *I* is the "immediate, spontaneous, and impulsive aspect of conduct" (Hewitt, 1984, p. 72). It is the doing part of the self, the part that acts on the spur of the moment. It feels emotions intensely, spontaneously, and is subjective in nature. The *Me* is the more objective and socialized part of the self. It observes and assesses *I*'s actions and compares them to internalized standards and beliefs. This part of the self manages the expression of emotions. The *Me* also allows a person to take the role of the other, that is, to see oneself as others might. This is the way in which society is embedded in the individual's consciousness. The *I* and *Me* continually interact so that the self is always in process.

When people are feeling at ease with themselves and their interactions with the world, the two parts of the self feel "fused" (Scheff, 1985, p. 258).

The self is in balance. This balance, and therefore one's sense of self, is precarious. The balanced self may be temporarily lost in times of crisis when previously held perceptions or definitions of reality, self, or others no longer fit the situation.

According to symbolic interactionists, people's "realities are [their] definitions of situations" (Charon, 1979, p. 136), and they act according to their definitions (Prus, 1996). Through their interactions, people continually define and redefine the meanings of objects, ideas, and other people. They even define, reflect upon, and evaluate their own thoughts, feelings, and actions (Blumer, 1969). These definitions are fluid and subjective. In social encounters, people continually observe themselves and others so that they can define the situation. Then they organize their behavior according to their definitions (Goffman, 1959). As long as the definitions are shared, interactions run smoothly; the social world gives off the appearance of structure and order. People think their world is safe, predictable, and, to some degree, controlled by logical forces.

When this apparent structure is disturbed somehow, interactions cannot run smoothly because people feel lost and confused. They do not know how to act, what to expect from others, or even what to expect from themselves. One disturbing experience that is likely to cause severe confusion is the death of a loved one. Rosenblatt (1988) asserts that "a significant loss is, among other things, a loss of reality. [Symbolic interactionism] helps us understand how important others are in defining a loss, feeling the loss, and coming to terms with it" (pp. 67–68). When confronted with a loss, the bereaved look "for structure, and where [they] do not find it, [they try to] create it" (Hewitt, 1984, p. 79). Until that sense of order and meaning is restored, people feel uncomfortable and alone. They may question their most basic assumptions about life, goals, and relationships. Because symbolic interactionism recognizes people's continuous efforts to define meanings when they are in crisis, it is appropriate as the theoretical base for this study.

Choosing the Research Method

According to Blumer (1969), if we wish to understand a group of people, then we must "lift the veils that obscure or hide what is going on" within that group (p. 39). This can be accomplished by being with and observing the people we want to understand so that we can gradually begin to see their world through their eyes. Blumer calls this stage exploration or "the direct examination of the actual empirical social world" (p. 48). To go beyond mere description to a deeper, more theoretical level of understanding, Blumer says we must move to the next level: inspection. The goal of inspection is to pose the research problem in theoretical terms, uncover common categories of experience, define relevant concepts, and to put forth theoretical propositions. Inspection then is similar to grounded theory. According to Strauss and Corbin (1994), "grounded theory is a general methodology for developing theory that is grounded in data systematically gathered and analyzed" (p. 273). Its purpose is to "generate a theory that accounts for a pattern of behavior which is relevant and problematic for those involved" (Glaser, 1978, p. 93).

I chose the grounded theory method because it is so closely aligned with symbolic interactionism. It is based on the assumption that people continually define and redefine the meaning of their experiences to achieve some sense of order and structure in their lives (Hutchinson, 1986). To build theory using this method, there must be a continuous "interaction between the researcher and the phenomenon under study" (Field & Morse, 1985, p. 111). Unlike purely deductive research methods that develop theories in the abstract, grounded theory begins with the experiences of the people. Then, using a systematic set of procedures to understand people's stories and the researcher's observations, the researcher inductively develops a theory about how people deal with the situation under study.

Doing the Research

Gathering data

Taking care of the research instrument

Unlike quantitative studies that use questionnaires, surveys, or objective research instruments, in grounded theory, the researcher is the instrument. Field and Morse (1985) use the term "researcher-as-an-instrument"; they suggest that the quality of the study is "dependent upon the ability of the researcher" (p. 115). I think it goes much further than interviewing and observational skills and the ability to put informants at ease. The actual mental and physical health of the researcher can become relevant, particularly when the phenomenon of interest is of a highly emotional nature. Therefore, I have chosen to comment on the emotional process I experienced as I completed this study.

Reading Field and Morse (1985) and grounded theory studies in Morse and Johnson (1991) and elsewhere convinced me that I would have to prepare myself emotionally and physically before embarking on my research. This passage from Swanson-Kauffman's (1986) study of women who had miscarried alerted me to what lay ahead:

> In many ways, I vicariously lived my informants' loss. Embracing their reality proved to be an emotional as well as an intellectual challenge. My reflections on miscarriage became my constant companion: I lived, walked, talked, and slept my study. (p. 65)

I knew that once I started my study I, too, would quickly become consumed by reflections on the painful experiences of bereaved parents. Like Reinhartz (1987), who also studied women's miscarriage experiences, I knew I would "interpret a [bereaved parent's] experience as if it were my own" (p. 230). I concluded that I would have to be strong, both physically and emotionally, to withstand the stress of doing the study. I made a conscious effort to prepare myself for what lay ahead.

First, I tried to make sure that I was physically healthy so that I could withstand the strain of doing the study. I began an exercise program to help reduce stress, and I set up a regular work schedule. Hoping to finish the study in about 10 months, I tried to clear my calendar of extraneous professional commitments. I wanted to be able to focus all my energy on the study. I also prepared my family and friends by telling them about the research, how it might affect me, and what I would need from them. I prepared myself intellectually by setting aside all that I had ever read or learned about the grief process. I stopped reading academic literature on grief and instead began to read autobiographical and fictional accounts of people who were dealing with major losses. Once I had completed all these tasks, I felt ready to begin the study by recruiting informants.

After I recruited informants and scheduled their interviews, I continued to consciously look after myself mentally and emotionally. As I entered the world of bereaved parents through the interviews, I began to live an as-if existence. I felt as if I, too, had lost a baby to SIDS. Reinhartz (1987) calls this "sympathetic introspection" (p. 230); Lifton (1982) calls it becoming a "survivor by proxy" (p. 226). As the interviews progressed, the problems of each bereaved parent became mine, too. At the conclusion of each interview, I often felt too exhausted to work. I had to start planning recuperation time between interviews. When I transcribed the interviews, their emotional content often overwhelmed me, so much so that transcription took almost twice as long as I predicted it might.

When I estimated that it would take me 10 months to complete the study, I had not allowed for this. I had assumed I could maintain a professional distance and discovered I could not. At times the collective pain of all the parents would overwhelm and immobilize me. Sometimes I could not tolerate the sound or sight of ambulances or the presence of new babies. It was just too painful. Soon I began to feel guilty when I was unable to work, but often I felt too overwhelmed by emotions to be productive. On those occasions, I could do little else but walk, sleep, stare out at the ocean, and talk for hours to my husband, a close friend, and anyone who expressed the slightest interest in what I was doing. Some people began to avoid me. I also wrote about how I was feeling. At the time, it seemed as if I was doing these things for self-preservation, not for the study at all.

Gradually I recovered my balance and objectivity. Perhaps as Lifton (1982) says, I achieved "selective professional numbing" (p. 198), a stance necessary for me to finish this study. I knew I achieved this position when I started to feel like an outsider when I was with bereaved parents. I realized that my experience of feeling overwhelmed by grief had paralleled that of the parents. I had been inside their experience, and I had been learning all along. The insights I gathered slowly started to make sense as I reread my personal research journal. Over time, I had become another informant. At least I had a choice: I could eventually step back from the world of bereaved parents. I could not return to the way I looked at life before I began the study. Like the parents, dealing with grief changed me.

Interviewing parents

Desired characteristics

Informants in a study of this nature should not be chosen randomly (Field & Morse, 1985). Usually grounded theorists look for articulate informants who can provide an eloquent and knowledgeable picture of the phenomena under study. Although I originally set out with this plan, I had to alter it to suit both reality and the goals of the study. The reality was that although some parents were very eloquent others had difficulty expressing themselves well. I realized within the first couple of interviews that the non-expressive parents communicated just as much by their struggle to communicate as those who were articulate. Because I wanted to understand the communication problems bereaved parents might have, I learned through experience that both articulate and reticent parents had much to teach me.

To facilitate the study of how parents managed their grief within their marriage over time, I needed to interview still-married mothers and fathers. In addition, I hoped to interview parents who had a range of experiences and demographic characteristics. However, I did not purposefully select parents on this basis. I wanted to interview parents who came from both the lower and middle classes, blue-collar workers as well as professionals. To compare their experiences and exposure to a support group, I wanted to interview parents who had lived in a large urban area, small city or town, rural area, or perhaps even outside the study area when the baby died. I also wanted parents who had been to a support group as well as those who had not. To examine the long-term grief process, I needed to interview parents who had lost their child well over 7 years ago as well as recently. The babies also needed to have a mix of characteristics: boys and girls; a variety of ages at the time of death; only children, oldest, middle and youngest children; and healthy and unhealthy before death. Although I did not select my sample at all on the basis of these characteristics, I did interview parents who fit into each of these categories. This broadened the base of the study considerably.

Recruitment

According to Morse (1989), there are four types of samples used in qualitative research. I used three to recruit parents: volunteer, snowball, and nominated. First, I solicited volunteers by contacting a chapter of a SIDS support group at the end of November 1990. The group's executive agreed to put a notice about the study in their next newsletter and let parents volunteer on their own. I prepared the notice in the form a Special Invitation (see Appendix B); it became part of the group's January 1991 newsletter. They had 135 families on their mailing list. The invitation in the newsletter and contact with the support group eventually generated 14 volunteers. I interviewed 12 of the 14. I did not interview 2 of the mothers who volunteered: one because she had been a single parent when her baby died and the other because she eventually decided not to participate.

While I waited for volunteers to call me, I used a modified snowball technique to find parents who were not connected to the support group. I discussed my research with bereavement counselors and community workers who might have had contact with SIDS parents. This generated one more couple. I also informed university classmates about my study, and I learned about another couple this way. A classmate hand-delivered a letter of invitation to a couple she knew (see Appendix C).

To facilitate the inclusion of parents who had a different kind of support program than the one in my area, I contacted the chapter leader for a SIDS support group in another area in March 1991. She thought of all the parents she knew through the support program and called some to see if they would consider being interviewed. The list she gave me consisted of those parents who agreed to be involved. This list provided a nominated sample. I interviewed a total of five parents from this particular list.

In all, I interviewed 21 parents: 9 couples and 3 women. The length of time since these babies had died ranged from less than 1 year to over 25 years.

Booking interviews

Overall, the women seemed more interested in participating than the men. Women called to volunteer themselves and their husbands. To ensure that their husbands really wanted to be involved, I tried to book my appointments with them directly. When I began their interviews, I asked the men why they decided to become involved. Some admitted that they were doing it for their wives, but most said they wanted to help other parents by participating.

I began by booking interviews with parents who lived in my area and who had lost their babies over 7 years ago. I wanted to learn about the long-term grief process first. Then I interviewed those who had lost a baby less than 7 years ago. Later, I completed out of town interviews based on the parents' availability instead of how long ago the baby had died. I purposefully scheduled the interviews so that the last couple I met was the one who had lost their baby most recently. I wanted to be sure I could handle their raw pain and understand all the issues that complicate this experience.

Originally, I assumed that I would have to interview each person twice. During the first interview, I expected that the informants would want to learn more about me and get comfortable with me, and then, during the second interview, they would tell me about their experience. This was not the case at all. Parents asked questions about the study and me on the telephone before we scheduled their first interview. Then minutes into the interview, most parents, particularly the women, opened up and told me their whole story. Two parents each said they had been waiting for over 20 years for someone to express an interest in their experience. I interviewed the first five informants twice. When I realized that parents repeated themselves during the second interview, I stopped scheduling second interviews. Although I was prepared to schedule more interviews if people wanted them and if I felt they were necessary, this was not needed. I interviewed the other 16 informants only once.

Scheduling interviews

I had to work around the parents' busy lives, considering their jobs, family demands, and community commitments. The women's interviews were the easiest to schedule, either because they did not work outside the home or they had more flexible work hours. Of the 15 interviews I did with 12 mothers, I completed all but three during the usual work day. I interviewed two women during the evening and one on a Saturday afternoon. I found it more difficult to schedule interviews with fathers because of their inflexible work hours. I completed 11 interviews with 9 fathers: two before the men started work, eight after their work day was over, and one during the work day.

Interview locations

When possible, I tried to interview people in their homes. This provided the opportunity to see photographs and mementoes of the baby. I interviewed all but two women in their homes. The others were interviewed in a hotel room and in an empty office on a weekend. I interviewed all the fathers but one in their homes; I interviewed one man in his office during his work day. Generally, it seemed harder to schedule it so the men could be home alone.

Interviewing

Before beginning each interview, I asked the parents to read the consent form (see Appendix D) and ask any questions that might arise from it. I then asked them not to sign the form until the interview was complete and they were comfortable with what they had told me. If they wanted to withdraw from the study at that point, they had that option, and I promised to erase their tape before I left. No one refused to sign the form.

I began each interview by asking each informant to tell me what losing a baby to SIDS had been like and how it had affected him or her as a person, as a parent, and as a partner in marriage. Using an unstructured format, I tried to let the parents tell me their story in the way that made the most sense to them. I asked clarifying questions and redirected the conversation only if they went off-topic or left out important information. All the interviews were tape-recorded. They varied in length from 40 minutes to 2.5 hours. When possible, I encouraged parents to decide when they wanted to end the interview instead of setting a time limit. I tried to keep my schedule free of commitments after interviews so that I could be flexible enough to respond to someone who wanted to talk for hours.

Between January and the end of August 1991, I completed a total of 26 interviews with 21 parents. I interviewed both the husband and the wife in nine couples. Although I intended to interview only couples, I also interviewed three women whose husbands did not want to be involved. One husband specifically said he did not want to be in the study. Another had said he would be involved, but he was working out of town, and somehow we could never arrange to meet. The third husband was no longer living with his wife. Although she had not asked him if he wanted to be interviewed, she was sure he would say no. Unfortunately, I had no way of finding him on my own and asking him myself. Because these women were so articulate about their experiences, I used their experiences to help me understand the grief process. I did not, however, include the data from these three interviews in my attempt to understand marital communication.

As I completed interviews, I sent thank you cards to each informant. Then I occasionally sent them letters to keep them informed about my activities and progress.

Interview complications

By interviewing in the homes, I met some of the parents' other children. Although the children sometimes talked to me about their memories of their brother or sister, their presence in the house during the interviews was often disruptive. Children interrupted six interviews with mothers by asking questions and demanding attention. One little boy just insisted on listening. He knew what the interview was about, and he wanted to hear his mother talk about what had happened to the baby. He even tried to console his mother when she began to cry while describing her experience. Children were present during only two interviews with fathers. Although these children interrupted occasionally, the fathers tolerated fewer interruptions than the mothers. I tried to let the parents decide how to handle their children's presence and their interruptions. Two couples did not have children at home anymore.

The interviews were disrupted by telephone calls and people coming to the door. After the first couple of interviews, I thought I should make sure that in the future there were no such disruptions. During my analysis of these interviews, however, I realized that these interruptions actually provided me with examples of how parents had to keep setting aside their pain to respond to the needs of others. One man took a call in the middle of a teary description of his experience. On the telephone, his voice and conversation gave no hint of his underlying pain; he seemed to welcome the break. While the men did not reveal to callers that they were in the middle of an interview, the women usually did, and they usually explained the reason for the interview. The women showed their tears to their children when they interrupted the interview; the men usually hid their tears from their children.

Interview issues

Most women seemed comfortable enough with either themselves or me or perhaps both to cry when they felt the need. I tried to acknowledge their pain without stopping its expression. A few women seemed surprised by the intensity of their reactions since their baby had died many years ago, but they did not seem self-conscious about their tears. Most talked while they cried. With the men, this was not the case. One man began to sob during his interview and seemed upset with himself for losing control. He asked me to stop recording until he could regain his composure. Other men seemed equally uncomfortable with their reactions to the interview. They took deep breaths, looked away, found excuses to leave the room, changed the subject, and welcomed interruptions. Although I tried to react to the men's tears the same way I did with the women, there was a part of me that was uncomfortable. I reacted to their embarrassment, whether I wanted to or not, by reassuring them it was all right to cry. By focusing attention on it, I may have inadvertently increased their discomfort.

One other issue should be mentioned. I typically respond to another's tears and pain with my own tears. They just quietly roll down my cheeks, and I have had to learn to accept that as a part of me. After this happened during the first interview, I remembered in subsequent interviews to warn the informants that I might cry with them. I did not want my tears to upset them or inhibit the free expression of their own pain. My tears seemed to signal the degree to which I felt the parents' pain, and the parents did not seem bothered by them.

Managing and analyzing the data

Managing the data

This study is based predominantly on the words and actions of parents whose babies died of SIDS. I used a diary format to record my struggle to understand the interviews and to "conceptualiz[e]...[my] ideas" (Hutchinson, 1986, p. 123). This activity is called memoing, and it provided my second source of data. The third source of data came from a selective sampling of related literature. I used it to contrast and compare my findings with people who had similar experiences. To manage all this data, I needed a sophisticated but flexible system.

As soon as possible after I completed each interview, I transcribed it into my computer. I also wrote memos to myself about the thoughts and questions that the interview stimulated. Then I put the interview into QUALPRO, a software package designed only to store and sort textual data, not to analyze it (Blackman, 1987a, 1987b; Tesch, 1989). Once the interview is loaded into the program, QUALPRO numbers the lines in the interview. Then, it merely stores and sorts the data in whatever way the researcher dictates (see Swanson-Kauffman [1986] for a detailed description of this process). Once I finished coding each line and entering the location and code name into QUALPRO, I could command the program to sort the interview into the categories and produce a print out of all data assigned to each specific code. I also catalogued and labeled my memos as they accumulated.

Coding and analyzing the data

According to Charmaz (1995), "Coding is the process of defining what the data are all about" (p. 37). It forges a link between the data that have been collected and the way the researcher uses that data to develop a theory to explain it. Any description of the coding process will, of necessity, appear linear. The analysis, however, is actually circular or, as Creswell (1998) describes it,"a zigzag process" (p. 57). I began with the words of my informants, and then, no matter how abstract the theory became, I always had to come back to their words. What I learned from one interview, I used to generate questions for the next. At first, this circular or zigzag process confused me; nothing seemed fixed or predictable. I could not see where I had been and where I was going. Eventually, through continuous data analysis and the constant comparative method, I began to see a structure underlying the parental grief experience. I used three levels of coding to uncover this structure.

Level I coding

After transcribing the initial two interviews and entering them into QUALPRO, I began Level I (Hutchinson, 1986) or open coding (Strauss & Corbin, 1990) by examining each interview line by line and asking the question, "What is going on here?" For this level of coding, I used "in vivo codes" (Charmaz, 1995, p. 41), that is, I borrowed the informant's words to succinctly answer that question and to label the elements of the experience. Originally, I found 80 labels, but this was far too cumbersome, so I reorganized the codes into 13 major categories. Then I recoded the first two interviews and entered their locations into QUALPRO. After reviewing the results and feeling satisfied that these 13 codes could capture all elements of the experience, I began to use them to analyze the other interviews.

As I coded, I asked questions of the data continually. For example, when examining the category *communication*, I wondered:

- What did parents want or not want to talk about?
- When could they talk, and when could they not talk?

- What kind of environment could they talk or not talk in?
- Who wanted to talk, and who did not?
- When parents said they wanted to "talk about it," what was "it?"

By returning to the interviews with these questions, I slowly discovered the properties and dimensions of actions related to the parents' ability to communicate.

Level II coding

Level II coding (Hutchinson, 1986) is also called axial coding (Strauss & Corbin, 1990). This level of coding involves examining the data to find connections within and between the categories. The researcher looks for "conditions, context, action/interactional strategies, and consequences" (Strauss & Corbin, 1990, p. 96). Using the steps outlined by Strauss and Corbin (1990), I made connections between the categories and uncovered patterned relationships. To illustrate this step, I will use one aspect of communication.

As I discovered by constant comparisons between and within the interviews, the "it" in "talking about it" could mean the parent's grief, the baby's life or the baby's death. I wanted to see what the connection was between the parent's ability or lack of ability to "talk about it" and the health of their marital relationship. By studying the interviews and all the data coded *communication*, I found the following connections: When their baby dies of SIDS (causal condition), parents grieve (phenomena). Grieving occurs within a marital relationship, a certain time frame, and community setting (context). When one partner is silent about his or her grief, perhaps because of ethnic or gender socialization (intervening condition), the communicative partner may react by trying to force the silent one to talk (interaction strategies). This behavior sometimes triggered resistance and an increase in marital tension (consequence 1). Using another possible interaction strategy, some communicative parents accepted their spouse's silence. They decided it reflected their usual method of dealing with stress. This reaction usually led to an increase in marital satisfaction or, at the very least, to the maintenance of the previous level of marital tension (consequence 2). By varying conditions in the model, I discovered factors that could make significant differences to marital health after a baby dies of SIDS. Then I continually compared and contrasted these developing hypotheses with the experiences of my informants until I felt I had uncovered all the factors. I did this with each set of patterned relationships. Then it was time to move to a higher level of abstraction.

Level III coding

Also known as selective coding (Strauss & Corbin, 1990), Level III coding produces "theoretical constructs" (p. 120). At this level, relationships between the categories of experience become more abstract; they begin to resemble a theory. Gradually, through constant comparison of each of the interviews and with the models I developed, I uncovered phases of parental grief that occurred over the years. This level of analysis, called "the story" (Strauss & Corbin, 1990, p. 116), incorporates the significant elements uncovered during the earlier analysis but raises them to a level beyond that of the individual parent's experience. At this point, diagramming the process became more meaningful and useful. Then I took the next step: searching for the core category or variable.

The core category or variable "is the central phenomenon around which all the other categories are integrated" (Strauss & Corbin, 1990, p. 116). It holds "the story" together, occurs throughout the data, ties the various elements together, and explains any differences found among the informants (Hutchinson, 1986). Because my core category, ***searching for reason***, describes a process that occurs over time and in varying conditions, it is called a Basic Social Psychological Process or BSPP (Glaser, 1978). As evidenced by my use of this core category to explore how people deal with other traumatic situations, ***searching for reason*** is a "transsituational" process (Prus, 1996, p. 142).

Validating, saturating, and searching for the negative case

As I developed hypotheses about the relationships between concepts, I tested each one by going back to relevant parts of the interviews to see if they proved to be right. When a relationship was not supported by data from an interview, I looked for reasons why. Sometimes the hypothesis had to be modified, and sometimes through this process, I realized I had uncovered a new set of conditions that I had not seen before. This discovery would take me back to the data again. I continued this circular process until all the relationships in the theory were solid. By comparing my findings with those in related literature and by sharing and discussing my findings with a group of SIDS parents, I began to feel confident that my theory was valid.

According to Hutchinson (1986), "Saturation refers to the completeness of all levels of codes when no new conceptual information is available to indicate new codes or the expansion of existing ones" (p. 125). By carefully reviewing my data and the coding I used to categorize it, I kept track of the level of saturation. I made sure that each category of experience was complete and that it was fully described and explained.

I also made sure that any negative case could be explained. A negative case is one that does not fit with the developing theory. Often such cases help researchers broaden their understanding of the experience.

Making connections

Besides learning from my informants, I also connected with other people's life experiences in a variety of ways. I used the popular media: a radio interview with parents who had experienced a miscarriage; television interview programs about people coping with minor and major life problems; newspaper reports about families dealing with tragedy; and movies about families coping with loss. I also read autobiographical accounts of people trying to cope with the death of a child. This kind of connecting helped me understand some difficult concepts at first. Later, it provided me with a testing ground as I developed a theory about how people cope with devastating events.

I also talked informally with a variety of people who were experiencing some kind of life crisis, such as coping with depression, coping with breast cancer, and trying to decide whether to end their marriage. Besides asking questions about how these people were dealing with their problem, I also showed them my theoretical model and asked them to critique it. Their comments helped ensure that the model was clear, understandable, and useful.

As the theory developed, I turned to research-based literature. Related literature helped me to look at my data differently when I was stuck, to ask sharper questions, and to define some of my concepts more clearly. I also tested and compared my theory with the findings of others who studied how people coped with traumatic events.

Validity and Reliability of the Study

Field and Morse (1985) define validity as "the extent to which the research findings represent reality" (p. 139). Since reality is a subjective term when it comes to dealing with the human experience, I would add "the reality of those being studied" to their definition. To ensure the validity of this study, I interviewed parents who had lost a baby to SIDS and who were willing to share their "reality" with me. Then I used a consistent set of procedures to understand and analyze the parents' experiences. To be sure that the developing theory was grounded in the parents' reality, I did three things. I compared the theoretical categories and sets of relationships with and across all the interviews. I also shared my initial findings with the informants and then more theoretical findings with other SIDS parents I met during the study; they agreed with my findings. When I began to attend a support group as their advisor, I repeatedly heard parents echo my findings. Finally, my findings corresponded with those of other researchers.

Reliability is defined as "the measure of the extent to which random variation may have influenced the stability and consistency of results" (Field & Morse, 1985, p. 139). The issue here is whether the informants adequately and truthfully described the "reality" of their situation and whether the researcher adequately and consistently collected, analyzed, and presented the data. First, I speak to the reliability of my informants.

Twenty-one parents volunteered to tell me what it was like for them to lose a baby to SIDS. I have no doubt that to the best of their ability these parents told me their perception of their experience as they remember it. Some may have been concerned with giving me socially desirable answers, but this is difficult in a lengthy narrative-type interview. In fact, often parents told me things they had never told anyone else. Although these parents varied in their ability to be articulate and reflective about their experience, I was studying communication problems. Parents not only told me about their communication problems, they unknowingly showed them to me. Also, with this many informants, I could compare experiences from one person to another. In addition, by hearing the stories of both the husband and wife in nine couples, I could compare one spouse's story with the other spouse's story. I learned that some couples had very different perceptions of the experience and of each other's behavior and intentions. The incongruities often became part of the data that I analyzed. Finally, the real test of reliability occurs when those who have lived the experience agree with the study's findings. When I shared my findings both with my informants and with other bereaved parents, they said I had accurately captured their experience.

As to the researcher's reliability, I conducted all the interviews to ensure consistency of style and approach. I tape-recorded and transcribed all the interviews myself and checked one against the other for accuracy. Using the methods described by Strauss and Corbin (1990), I analyzed and re-analyzed the data until a solid theory emerged. I compared my findings from one interview to another and across all the interviews. I shared my findings with many of my informants and presented them to groups of parents whom I had not interviewed. They said it was like I had lived through their experience. The last thing I did was compare my findings to relevant literature to be sure that the findings were reliable.

Ethical Considerations

I explained the purpose of this study in the written invitation and when I talked to prospective informants. I explained the study's purpose again when I began each interview and when I showed the informants the consent form (see Appendix D). I asked the informants to read the form and ask any questions they might have but not to sign the form until they finished the interview. This gave them one more opportunity to decide if they wanted to have their story included in the study. I ensured the parents' confidentiality by developing an identification code for each person. I used the code on the tapes and the transcripts, but I made sure that I did not write the code on any document that included the person's name. Tapes were stored separately in a secure environment.

One ethical problem that I had to deal with was how to protect the anonymity of my informants while still providing enough relevant background about them. Confidentiality was an issue for two reasons: first, I interviewed husbands and wives separately, and I promised them complete confidence; and second, most of my informants came from the relatively small SIDS support community where most members know one another and their circumstances. With these two considerations in mind, I chose to include only personal information that was absolutely vital to the reader's comprehension of the issues. To prevent one member from recognizing another's story, I have left out or altered personal information that might help identify any particular parent. I did not use pseudonyms for the parents, and I did not reveal family characteristics. I revealed the gender of those quoted in the study only when it contributed to a better understanding of the situation. Sometimes I changed the baby's gender to hide the identity of the parents.

Appendix B
Invitation to participate

A SPECIAL INVITATION

This is an invitation to participate in a research project that will help future SIDS parents understand and cope with their loss. I hope that you will take the time to read this invitation and will consider participating.

First, let me introduce myself. My name is Karen Martin, and I am finishing my Master's degree in Sociology at the University of Alberta. I am also a volunteer consultant for the Bereavement Society of Alberta. In the past, I have worked as a nurse, family life educator, counselor, and program coordinator for a bereavement support program. I am married and have two teenagers.

I am interested in learning how your child's death to SIDS has affected you and how you have coped with it. Although survey research on SIDS parents has been done, I do not believe that your personal stories have been adequately heard. My goal is to listen to the stories of many SIDS parents so that I can develop a picture of the experience and its impact upon all areas of life. This information will be used to help future SIDS parents and those who try to provide support. To develop this picture, I need parents to volunteer to be interviewed.

Because I am interested in how this experience affects parents over time, I will be dividing parents into two groups: those whose children died seven or more years ago (there is no maximum time) and those whose children died less than seven years ago (there is no minimum time).

Parents whose children died seven or more years ago will be interviewed first. For this group only, I require the participation of both parents. Each parent will be interviewed alone and in complete confidence a maximum of three times. Although all interviews will be tape-recorded, your identity will be protected.

Parents whose children died less than seven years ago will then be interviewed. Individual parents can participate even if their spouses do not want to be involved. All interviews will be tape-recorded and conducted in complete confidence. Your identity will be protected. We will meet one or two times.

The results of this research will be published in my master's thesis. I am also willing to do a presentation for your support group. This project has been approved by the Ethical Review Committee of the Department of Sociology. My supervisor's name is Dr. Lyle Larson. He may be reached at 492-2977.

If you are interested in talking to me about this further, please call the Department of Sociology at 492-5234 and leave your name and home number. I will return calls in the evening. Since I want to begin this project as soon as possible, please call soon.

I know that losing a child to SIDS can be a devastating experience, but sharing your story now may help others in the future. I hope you will consider participating in this important project.

Appendix C
Letter to invite participation

My name is Karen Martin, and I am completing my Master's degree in Sociology at the University of Alberta. I am currently working on the research for my thesis: how parents cope with the loss of a child to SIDS. When I mentioned this to [a classmate], she said that she knew someone who might be interested in being interviewed. She did not give me your name, and I have asked her to deliver this letter to you. At the moment, I am particularly interested in interviewing parents who lost children at least seven years ago. There is no maximum time since the loss. In fact, I have been interviewing parents whose children died up to 27 years ago.

To help you decide whether to participate, let me tell you something about myself and then about the project. In addition to being a student, I am also a volunteer consultant with the Bereavement Society of Alberta, an educational organization devoted to teaching people about the grief process. I am frequently called upon to speak in schools when there is a sudden death of a student or staff member. Prior to my attendance at university, I worked as a nurse, family life educator, counselor, and program coordinator for the Family Service Association of Edmonton. I am married and have two teenagers.

I am interested in learning how your child's SIDS death affected you as a person, parent, and partner in marriage and also how it affected your other children. My plan is to listen to the stories of many SIDS parents—I have already interviewed three couples—and to develop a comprehensive picture of the experience. I am also trying to develop a long-term picture of the grief process. This information will be used to help future SIDS parents and those who try to provide them with support.

Because I am interested in how both parents view their experience, both husband and wife must agree to be interviewed. Each will be interviewed separately at least twice. Nothing one says will be shared with the other. Interviews will last from an hour and a half to two hours. They may be held in your home if you prefer and will be scheduled at your convenience. All interviews will be audio-taped, and I will be the one who types them. Anonymity will be insured.

The results of this research will be published in my Master's thesis. This project has been approved by the Ethical Review Committee of the Department of Sociology. My supervisor's name is Dr. Lyle Larson. He may be reached at 492-2977.

I do hope that you will consider participating in this important research. If you are interested in talking to me about the project, please call the Department of Sociology (492-5234) and leave your name. Since I do not know your name, it would be helpful if you would mention that you are [classmate's name] friend. I will return your call in the evening. Thank you.

I know that losing a child to SIDS can be a devastating experience, but sharing your story may help others new to the experience. I hope you will consider participating in this project. I look forward to hearing from you soon.

Karen Martin

Appendix D
Parents' Consent Form

PARTICIPATION CONSENT FORM

PROJECT TITLE: After SIDS - A Study of the Experience of Parents

RESEARCHER: Karen Martin, Department of Sociology

ADVISOR: Dr. Lyle Larson, Department of Sociology, 492-2977 (office)

The purpose of this masters thesis project is to explore how the loss of a child might affect all areas of the parents' lives. Those who are interviewed might benefit from telling their story, but the greatest benefit will be to those who will lose children to SIDS in the future. The results of the project can be used to help them understand what is happening to them.

Up to a maximum of three interviews, each lasting an average of ninety minutes, may be conducted at your convenience. During each interview, you will be asked to tell about your feelings and experiences as they relate to the death of your child. The interviews will be recorded on audio-tapes. Only an identification number will be used on the tapes and transcripts so that your identity will be protected. Any other names or places on the tapes that will identify you will be disguised and will not be transcribed. Nothing you say during the interviews will be shared with your spouse or any other participant in this project.

THIS IS TO CERTIFY THAT

I,

(please print)

HEREBY AGREE TO PARTICIPATE AS A VOLUNTEER IN THE ABOVE NAMED PROJECT.

I understand that the interviews may bring up painful memories and that I may stop the interview or my participation in the project if I feel unable to continue.

I give permission to be interviewed and for these interviews to be recorded on audio-tape. I understand that these tapes may be used for educational purposes, and if used, a voice translator will protect my identity. Transcripts of the tapes will not have my name on them nor anything that might identify me. All tapes and transcripts will be kept in a locked drawer and only the researcher will have the key. I understand that the results of the study will be published but that my name and specific information that might identify me will not be used.

I understand that I am free to deny any answer to specific questions. I also understand that I am free to withdraw my consent and terminate participation at any time without penalty merely by saying that I no longer wish to be a participant in the study.

I have been given the opportunity to ask whatever questions I desire, and all such questions have been answered to my satisfaction. I have also been given a copy of this consent form.

Participant　　　　Witness

Researcher　　　　Date

Bibliography

Albas, C., & Albas, D. (1988). Emotion work and emotion rules: The case of exams. *Qualitative Sociology, 11*(4), 259–274.

Antonovsky, A. (1979). *Health, stress, and coping*. San Francisco, CA: Jossey Bass.

Antonovsky, A. (1987). *Unraveling the mystery of health: How people manage stress and stay well.* San Francisco, CA: Jossey Bass.

Arnold, J. H., & Gemma, P. B. (1991). Grief on the death of an infant. In C. A. Corr, H. Fuller, C. A. Barnickol, & D. M. Corr (Eds.), *Sudden Infant Death Syndrome: Who can help and how* (pp. 45–56). New York: Springer Publishing.

Attig, T. (1996). *How we grieve: Relearning the world.* Oxford: Oxford University Press.

Baker, J. E., & Sedney, M. A. (1996). How bereaved children cope with loss: An overview. In C. A. Corr & D. M. Corr (Eds.), *Handbook of childhood death and bereavement* (pp. 109–129). New York: Springer.

Ballard, R. (1979). Face to face with the unthinkable. In G. Lonsdale, P. Elfer, & R. Ballard (Eds.), *Children, grief, and social work* (pp. 115–124). Oxford, England: Basil Blackwell.

Beattie, M., & Stesin, N. (1991, August). Balloons for Shane. *Ladies Home Journal*, pp. 22, 27, 28.

Bergman, A. B., Pomeroy, M. A., & Beckwith, J. B. (1969). The psychiatric toll of the Sudden Infant Death Syndrome. *GP*, *xl*(6), 99–105.

Bergum, V. (1986). *The phenomenology of woman to mother: The transformative experience of childbirth.* Unpublished doctoral dissertation, University of Alberta, Edmonton, Alberta.

Bergum, V. (1989). *Woman to mother.* Granby, MA: Bergin and Garvey.

Blackman, B. I. (1987a). *QUALPRO* [computer program]. Tallahassee, FL: Impulse Development Company.

Blackman, B. I. (1987b). *QUALPRO* [computer manual, version 3.2]. Tallahassee, FL: Impulse Development Company.

Bluglass, K. (1993). The psychosocial consequences of Sudden Infant Death Syndrome: The nature of grief. In A. M. Walker, C. McMillen, & National SIDS Council of Australia (Eds.), *Second SIDS international conference* (pp. 53–63). Ithaca, NY: Perinatology Press.

Blumer, H. (1969). *Symbolic interactionism: Perspective and method.* Englewood Cliffs, NJ: Prentice Hall.

Bohannon, J. R. (1990–1991). Grief responses of spouses following the death of a child: A longitudinal study. *Omega*, *22*(2), 109–121.

Bolton, I. (1986). Death of a child by suicide. In T. A. Rando (Ed.), *Parental loss of a child* (pp. 201–212). Champaign, IL: Research Press.

Boyle, F. M., Vance, J. C., & Najman, J. M. (1993). Childbearing patterns and psychological adjustment following Sudden Infant Death Syndrome, neonatal death, and stillbirth. In A. M. Walker, C. McMillen, & National SIDS Council of Australia (Eds.), *Second SIDS international conference* (pp. 284–287). Ithaca, NY: Perinatology Press.

Brabant, S., Forsyth, C., & McFarlain, G. (1995). Life after the death of a child: Initial and long-term support from others. *Omega*, *31*(1), 67–85.

Bradey, R. (1989). Loss in the backyard pool: The great Australian leveler. *Australian Social Work*, *42*(2), 35–41.

Braun, M. J., & Berg, D. H. (1994). Meaning reconstruction in the experience of parental bereavement. *Death Studies*, *18*, 105–129.

Brazelton, T. B., & Cramer, B. G. (1990). *The earliest relationship: Parents, infants, and the drama of early attachment.* Reading, MA: Addison Wesley.

Brice, C. W. (1991). Paradoxes of maternal mourning. *Psychiatry*, *54*, 1–12.

Bright, M. A. (1992). Making place: The first birth in an intergenerational family context. *Qualitative Health Research*, *2*(1), 75–98.

Brown, A. A. (1987). How fathers and mothers perceive prenatal support. *MCN, 12*, 414–418.

Bugen, L. A. (1977). Human grief: A model for prediction and intervention. *American Journal of Orthopsychiatry, 47*(2), 196–206.

Bugen, L. A. (1983). Childhood bereavement: Preventability and the coping process. In J. E. Schowalter, P. R. Patterson, M. Tallmer, A. H. Kutscher, S. V. Gullnor, & D. M. Corr (Eds.), *The child and death* (pp. 357–365). New York: Columbia University.

Bunting, M. (1992, May). Jury says Gulf war killings "unlawful." *Manchester Guardian Weekly*, p. 1.

Burns, E., House, J. D., & Ankenbauer, M. R. (1986). Sibling grief in reaction to Sudden Infant Death Syndrome. *Pediatrics, 78*(3), 485–487.

Canadian Foundation for the Study of Infant Deaths. (no date). *Goals and objectives*. Toronto, ONT: Author.

Carroll, R., & Shaefer, S. (1993–94). Similarities and differences in spouses coping with SIDS. *Omega, 28*(4), 273–284.

Cassel, E. J. (1982). The nature of suffering and the goals of medicine. *New England Journal of Medicine, 306*, 639–645.

Charmaz, K. (1995). Grounded theory. In A. Smith, R. Harre, & L. Van Langenhov (Eds.), *Rethinking methods in psychology* (pp. 27–49). Thousand Oaks, CA: Sage.

Charon, J. M. (1979). *Symbolic interactionism: An introduction, an interpretation, an integration*. Englewood Cliffs, NJ: Prentice Hall.

Chartier, B. M. (1987, June). *Male role expectations and the suppression of grief*. Paper presented at the Annual Convention of the Canadian Psychological Association, Vancouver, BC.

Chodoff, P., Friedman, S., & Hamburg, D. A. (1964). Stress, defences and coping behavior: Observations in parents of children with malignant disease. *American Journal of Psychiatry, 120*, 743–749.

Cook, J. A. (1988). Dad's double binds: Rethinking fathers' bereavement from a men's studies perspective. *Journal of Contemporary Ethnography, 17*(3), 285–308.

Cook, J. A., & Wimberley, D. W. (1983). If I should die before I wake: Religious commitment and adjustment to the death of a child. *Journal for the Scientific Study of Religion, 22*(3), 222–238.

Cornwell, J., Nurcombe, B., & Stevens, L. (1977). Family response to loss of a child by Sudden Infant Death Syndrome. *Medical Journal of Australia, 1*, 656–658.

Craig, Y. (1977). The bereavement of parents and their search for meaning. *British Journal of Social Work*, 7(1), 41–54.

Creswell, J. W. (1998). *Qualitative inquiry and research design: Choosing among five traditions*. Thousand Oaks, CA: Sage.

Daly, P. (1992, June). Article missed some of the facts [Letter to the editor]. *The Edmonton Journal*, p. A9.

Davies, B., & Segal, S. (1991). Siblings and other children. In C. A. Corr, H. Fuller, C. A. Barnickol, & D. M. Corr (Eds.), *Sudden Infant Death Syndrome: Who can help and how* (pp. 83–100). New York: Springer Publishing.

Davis, D. L. (1991). *Empty cradle, broken heart: Surviving the death of your baby*. Golden, CO: Fulcrum Publishing.

Davis, C. G., Lehman, D. R., Thompson, S. C., Silver, R. C., & Wortman, C. B. (1991, June). *"If only it could be different": The undoing of life events*. Paper presented at the Annual Convention of the Canadian Psychological Association, Calgary, AB.

Day, R. D., & Hooks, D. (1987). Miscarriage: A special type of family crisis. *Family Relations, 36*, 305–310.

DeFrain, J. (1991). Learning about grief from normal families: SIDS, stillbirth, and miscarriage. *Journal of Marital and Family Therapy, 17*(3), 215–232.

DeFrain, J., & Ernst, L. (1978). The psychological effects of Sudden Infant Death Syndrome on surviving family members. *Journal of Family Practice, 6*, 985–989.

DeFrain, J., Ernst, L., Jakub, D., & Taylor, J. (1991). *Sudden Infant Death: Enduring the loss*. Lexington, MA: Lexington Books.

DeFrain, J., Jakub, D. K., & Mendoza, B. L. (1992). The psychological effects of Sudden Infant Death Syndrome on grandmothers and grandfathers. *Omega, 24*(3), 165–182.

DeFrain, J., Martens, L., Stork, J., & Stork, W. (1990). The psychological effects of stillbirth on surviving family members. *Omega, 22*(2), 81–108.

DeFrain, J., Taylor, J., & Ernst, L. (1982). *Coping with Sudden Infant Death*. Lexington, MA: Lexington.

Dershimer, R. A. (1990). *Counseling the bereaved*. New York: Pergamon Press.

DeVries, D., Lana, R. D., & Falck, V. T. (1994). Parental bereavement over the life course: A theoretical intersection and empirical review. *Omega, 29*(1), 47–69.

Doka, K. J. (1988). Seeking significance. *Loss, Grief, and Care, 2*(3/4), 33–38.

Downey, G., Silver, R. C., & Wortman, C. B. (1990). Reconsidering the attribution-adjustment relation following a major negative event: Coping with the loss of a child. *Journal of Personality and Social Psychology, 59*(5), 925–940.

Dunn, D. S., Goldbach, K. R. C., Lasker, J. N., & Toedter, L. J. (1991). Explaining pregnancy loss: Parents' and physicians' attributions. *Omega, 23*(1), 13–23.

Dyregrov, A. (1990). Parental reactions to the loss of an infant child: A review. *Scandinavian Journal of Psychology, 31*, 266–280.

Dyregrov, A., & Matthiesen, S. B. (1987a). Similarities and differences in mothers' and fathers' grief following the death of an infant. *Scandinavian Journal of Psychology, 28*, 1–15.

Dyregrov, A., & Matthiesen, S. B. (1987b). Stillbirth, neonatal death and Sudden Infant Death (SIDS): Parental reactions. *Scandinavian Journal of Psychology, 28*, 104–114.

Dyregrov, A., & Matthiesen, S. B. (1987c). Anxiety and vulnerability in parents following the death of an infant. *Scandinavian Journal of Psychology, 28*, 16–25.

Dyregrov, A., & Matthiesen, S. B. (1991). Parental grief following the death of an infant—A follow-up over one year. *Scandinavian Journal of Psychology, 32*, 193–207.

Farnsworth, E. B., & Allen, K. R. (1996). Mothers' bereavement: Experiences of marginalization, stories of change. *Family Relations, 45*(4), 360–367.

Feeley, N., & Gottlieb, L. N. (1988). Parents' coping and communication following their infant's death. *Omega, 19*(1), 51–66.

Fetus and Newborn Committee, Canadian Pediatric Society. (1983). Support for parents experiencing perinatal loss. *Canadian Medical Association Journal, 129*, 335–339.

Field, P. A., & Morse, J. M. (1985). *Nursing research: The application of qualitative approaches*. Rockville, MD: Aspen Publishers.

Fincham, F. D., Beach, S., & Nelson, G. (1987). Attribution precesses in distressed and non-distressed couples: 3. Causal and responsibility attributions for spouse behavior. *Cognitive Therapy and Research, 11*(1), 71–86.

Fincham, F. D., & Grych, J. H. (1991). Explanations for family events in distressed and non-distressed couples: Is one type of explanation used consistently? *Journal of Family Psychology, 4*(3), 341–353.

Finkbeiner, A. K. (1996). *After the death of a child: Living with loss through the years*. New York: Free Press.

Fish, W. C. (1986). Differences of grief intensity in bereaved parents. In T. A. Rando (Ed.), *Parental loss of a child* (pp. 415–428). Champaign, IL: Research Press.

Fitzpatrick, M. A. (1988). A typological approach to marital interaction. In P. Noller & M. A. Fitzpatrick (Eds.), *Perspectives on marital interaction* (pp. 98–120). Clevedon, Avon, England: Multilingual Matters.

Florian, V. (1989). Meaning and purpose in life of bereaved parents whose son fell during active military service. *Omega, 20*(2), 91–102.

Ford, D. (1993). Some reflections on the integration of self-help and professional support services to SIDS families. In A. M. Walker, C. McMillen, & National SIDS Council of Australia (Eds.), *Second SIDS international conference* (pp. 331–335). Ithaca, NY: Perinatology Press.

Friedman, N., & Sherman, R. (1987). *Handbook of measurements for marriage and family therapy*. New York: Brunner/Mazel.

Friedman, T. L. (1989). *From Beirut to Jerusalem*. New York: Anchor Books.

Futterman, E. H., & Hoffman, I. (1983). Mourning the fatally ill child. In J. E. Schowalter, P. R. Patterson, M. Tallmer, A. H. Kutscher, S.V. Gullor, & D. Peretz (Eds.), *The child and death* (pp. 366–381). New York: Columbia University.

Gage, M. G., & Holcomb, R. (1991). Couples' perception of stressfulness of death of the family pet. *Family Relations, 40*, 103–105.

Gauthier, J., & Marshall, W. L. (1977). Grief: A cognitive behavioral approach. *Cognitive Therapy and Research, 1*(1), 39–44.

Gilbert, K. R. (1989). Interactive grief and coping in the marital dyad. *Death Studies, 13*, 605–626.

Giljohann, B. A. (1993). The importance of family and friends for family recovery following the death of a baby from Sudden Infant Death Syndrome. In A. M. Walker, C. McMillen, & National SIDS Council of

Australia (Eds.), *Second SIDS international conference* (pp. 288–292). Ithaca, NY: Perinatology Press.

Glaser, B. G. (1978). *Theoretical sensitivity*. Hill Valley, CA: Sociology Press.

Goffman, E. (1959). *The presentation of self in everyday life*. Garden City, NY: Doubleday Anchor.

Gottlieb, L. N., Lang, A., & Amsel, R. (1996). The long-term effects of grief on marital intimacy following an infant's death. *Omega*, *33*(1), 1–19.

Greenberg, M., & Morris, N. (1974). Engrossment: The newborn's impact on the father. *American Journal of Orthopsychiatry*, *44*(4), 520–531.

Gregory, S. (1976). *The deaf child and his family*. London, England: George Allen & Unwin.

Guest, J. (1976). *Ordinary people*. New York: Viking Press.

Guist, C., & Larsen, J. E. (1991). Guidelines for emergency responders. In C. A. Corr, H. Fuller, C. A. Barnickol, & D. M. Corr (Eds.), *Sudden Infant Death Syndrome: Who can help and how* (pp. 140–157). New York: Springer Publishing.

Guthrie, D. M., & Noller, P. (1988). Spouses' perceptions of one another in emotional situations. In P. Noller & M. A. Fitzpatrick (Eds.), *Perspectives on marital interaction* (pp. 153–181). Clevedon, Avon, England: Multilingual Matters.

Halpern, W. I. (1972). Some psychiatric sequelae to crib death. *American Journal of Psychiatry*, *129*(4), 58–61.

Hamilton, V. L. (1980). Intuitive psychologist or intuitive lawyer: Alternative models of the attribution process. *Journal of Personality and Social Psychology*, *39*(5), 767–772.

Hewitt, J. P. (1984). *Self and society* (3rd ed.). Boston, MA: Allyn and Bacon.

Hewstone, M. (1983). Attribution theory and common sense explanations: An introductory overview. In M. Hewstone (Ed.), *Attribution theory: Social and functional extensions* (pp. 1–26). Oxford, England: Basil Blackwell.

Hillman, L. S. (1991). Theories and research. In C. A. Corr, H. Fuller, C. A. Barnickol, & D. M. Corr (Eds.), *Sudden Infant Death Syndrome: Who can help and how* (pp. 14–41). New York: Springer Publishing.

Hochschild, A. R. (1983). *The managed heart: Commercialization of human feeling*. Berkeley, CA: University of California Press.

Hogan, N., Morse, J. M., & Tasón, M. C. (1996). Toward an experiential theory of bereavement. *Omega, 33*(1), 43–65.

Horowitz, M. J., Bonanno, G. A., & Holen, A. (1993). Pathological grief: Diagnosis and explanation. *Psychosomatic Medicine 55*, 260–273.

Hutchins, S. H. (1986). Stillbirth. In T. A. Rando (Ed.), *Parental loss of a child* (pp. 129–144). Champaign, IL: Research Press.

Hutchinson, S. (1986). Grounded theory: The method. In P. L. Munhall & C. J. Oiler (Eds.), *Nursing research: A qualitative perspective* (pp. 111–130). Norwalk, CT: Century Crofts.

Irizarry, C., & Willard, B. (1993). Parental grieving: Together or alone. The effects of a Sudden Infant Death Syndrome on the parent's relationship. In A. M. Walker, C. McMillen, & National SIDS Council of Australia (Eds.), *Second SIDS international conference* (pp. 275–278). Ithaca, NY: Perinatology Press.

Jackson. M. (1992). *The mother zone*. Toronto: Macfarlane Walter & Ross.

Janoff-Bulman, R. (1992). *Shattered assumptions: Towards a new psychology of trauma*. New York: Free Press.

Jaspars, J. (1983). The process of causal attribution in common sense. In M. Hewstone (Ed.), *Attribution theory: Social and functional extensions* (pp. 28–44). Oxford, England: Basil Blackwell.

Johansen, B. B. (1988). Parental grief over the death of a child. *Loss, Grief and Care, 2*(3/4), 143–153.

Johnson-Soderberg, S. (1983). Parents who lost a child by death. In J. V. Sasserath (Ed.), *Minimizing high risk parenting* (pp. 55–61). No city: Johnson & Johnson.

Kaplan, L. J. (1995). *No voice is ever wholly lost*. New York: Touchstone.

Klass, D. (1988). *Parental grief: Solace and resolution*. New York: Springer.

Klass, D. (1992–1993). The inner representation of the dead child and the worldviews of the bereaved parents. *Omega, 26*(4), 255–272.

Klass, D. (1996). The deceased child in the psychic and social worlds of bereaved parents during the resolution of grief. In D. Klass, P. R. Silverman, & S. L. Nickman (Eds.), *Continuing bonds: New understandings of grief* (pp. 199–215). Washington, DC: Taylor & Francis.

Klass, D., & Marwit, S. J. (1988). Towards a model of parental grief. *Omega, 19*(1), 31–50.

Klass, D., Silverman, P. R., & Nickman, S. L. (Eds.). (1996). *Continuing bonds: New understandings of grief.* Washington, DC: Taylor & Francis.

Knapp, R. J. (1986). *Beyond endurance: When a child dies.* New York: Schocken Books.

Kruglanski, A. W., Baldwin, M. W., & Towson, S. M. J. (1983). The lay epistemic process in attribution making. In M. Hewstone (Ed.), *Attribution theory: Social and functional extensions* (pp. 81–95). Oxford, England: Basil Blackwell.

Kupst, M. J. (1986). Death of a child from a serious illness. In T. A. Rando (Ed.), *Parental loss of a child* (pp. 191–199). Champaign, IL: Research Press.

Kushner, H. S. (1983). *When bad things happen to good people.* New York: Avon.

Lalljee, M., & Abelson, R. P. (1983). The organization of explanations. In M. Hewstone (Ed.), *Attribution theory: Social and functional extensions* (pp. 65–80). Oxford, England: Basil Blackwell.

Lang, A., & Gottlieb, L. (1993). Parental grief reactions and marital intimacy following infant death. *Death Studies, 17,* 233–255.

Langer, E. J. (1975). The illusion of control. *Journal of Personality and Social Psychology, 32*(2), 311–328.

LaRossa, R. (1986). *Becoming a parent.* Beverly Hills, CA: Sage Publications.

LaRossa, R. (1988). Fatherhood and social change. *Family Relations, 37*(4), 451–457.

Lehman, D. R., Lang, E. L., Wortman, C. B., & Sorenson, S. B. (1989). Long-term effects of sudden bereavement: Marital and parent child relationships and children's reactions. *Journal of Family Psychology, 2*(3), 344–367.

Lehman, D. R., Wortman, C. B., & Williams, A. F. (1987). Long-term effects of losing a spouse or child in a motor vehicle crash. *Journal of Personality and Social Psychology, 52*(1), 218–231.

Lepore, S. J., Silver, R. C., Wortman, C. B., & Wayment, H. A. (1996). Social constraints, intrusive thoughts, and depressive symptoms among bereaved mothers. *Journal of Personality and Social Psychology, 70*(2), 271–282.

Lewis, C. (1982). "A feeling you can't scratch?": The effect of pregnancy on married men. In N. Beail & J. McGuire (Eds.), *Fathers: Psychological perspectives* (pp. 43–70). London, England: Junction Books.

l'Hoir, M. P., & Wolters, W. (1993). Psychological aspects of crib (cot) death: Assessment of posttraumatic stress disorders. In A. M. Walker, C. McMillen, & National SIDS Council of Australia (Eds.), *Second SIDS international conference* (pp. 293–297). Ithaca, NY: Perinatology Press.

Lietar, E. F. (1986). Miscarriage. In T. A. Rando (Ed.), *Parental loss of a child* (pp. 121–128). Champaign, IL: Research Press.

Lifton, R. J. (1982). Apathy and numbing: A modern temptation. In F. Dougherty (Ed.), *The meaning of human suffering* (pp. 196–231). New York: Human Sciences Press.

Lofland, L. H. (1982). Loss and human connection: An exploration into the nature of the social bond. In W. Ickes & S. Knowles (Eds.), *Personality, roles, and social behavior* (pp. 219–242). New York: Springer-Verlag.

Lord, C. (1992, June). Inquiry into pool drowning fails to satisfy victim's dad. *The Edmonton Journal*, p. D15.

Lovell, A. (1983). Some questions of identity: Late miscarriage, stillbirth and perinatal loss. *Social Sciences and Medicine*, *17*(11), 755–761.

Lowman, J. (1979). Grief intervention and Sudden Infant Death Syndrome. *American Journal of Community Psychology*, *7*(6), 665–677.

Mandell, F., Dirks-Smith, T., & Smith, M. F. (1988). The surviving child in the SIDS family. *Pediatrician*, *15*, 217–221.

Mandell, F., McAnulty, E. H., & Carlson, A. (1983). Unexpected death of an infant sibling. *Pediatrics*, *72*(5), 652–657.

Mandell, F., McAnulty, E. H., & Reece, R. M. (1980). Observations of paternal response to sudden unanticipated infant death. *Pediatrics*, *65*(2), 221–225.

Mandell, F., & Wolfe, L. C. (1975). Sudden Infant Death Syndrome and subsequent pregnancy. *Pediatrics*, *56*(5), 774–776.

Markusen, E., Owen, G., Fulton, R., & Bendiksen, R. (1978). SIDS: The survivor as victim. *Omega*, *8*(4), 277–284.

Martin, K., & Elder, S. (1993). Pathways through grief: A model of the process. In J. D. Morgan (Ed.), *Personal care in an impersonal world: A multidimensional look at bereavement* (pp. 73–86). Amityville, NY: Baywood Publishing.

May, H. J., & Breme, F. J. (1982). SIDS family adjustment scale: A method of assessing family adjustment to Sudden Infant Death Syndrome. *Omega*, *13*(1), 59–74.

May, K. A. (1979). *Management of detachment and involvement in pregnancy by first-time expectant fathers.* Unpublished doctoral dissertation, University of California, San Francisco, California.

May, K. A. (1980). A typology of detachment/involvement styles adopted during pregnancy by first-time expectant fathers. *Western Journal of Nursing Research, 2*(2), 445–453.

May, K. A. (1982). Three phases of father involvement in pregnancy. *Nursing Research, 31*(6), 337–342.

McClowry, S. G., Davies, E. B., May, K. A., Kulenkamp, E. J., & Martinson, I. M. (1987). The empty space phenomenon: The process of grief in the bereaved family. *Death Studies, 11*, 361–374.

McIntosh, D., Silver, R. C., & Wortman, C. B. (1993). Religion's role in adjustment to a negative life event: Coping with the loss of a child. *Journal of Personality and Social Psychology, 65*(4), 812–821.

Miles, M. S., & Crandall, E. K. (1983). The search for meaning and its potential for affecting growth in bereaved parents. *Health Values: Achieving High Level Wellness*, 7(1), 19–23.

Miles, M. S., & Demi, A. S. (1986). Guilt in bereaved parents. In T. A. Rando (Ed.), *Parental loss of a child* (pp. 97–118). Champaign, IL: Research Press.

Miles, M. S., & Demi, A. S. (1992). A comparison of guilt in bereaved parents whose children died by suicide, accident, or chronic disease. *Omega, 24*(3), 203–215.

Moos, R. H., & Schaefer, J. A. (1986). Life transitions and crises: A conceptual overview. In R. H. Moos (Ed.), *Coping with life crises: An integrated approach* (pp. 3–28). New York: Plenum Press.

Morrell, D. (1988). *Fireflies*. Markham, ON: Penguin Books.

Morse, J. M. (1989). Strategies for sampling. In J. M. Morse (Ed.), *Qualitative nursing research: A contemporary dialogue* (pp. 117–131). Rockville, MD: Aspen.

Morse, J. M., & Johnson, J. L. (1991). Understanding the illness experience. In J. M. Morse & J. L. Johnson (Eds.), *The illness experience: Dimensions of suffering* (pp. 1–12). Newbury Park, CA: Sage.

Nichols, J. A. (1986). Newborn death. In T. A. Rando (Ed.), *Parental loss of a child* (pp. 145–158). Champaign, IL: Research Press.

Nikolaisen, S. M., & Williams, R. A. (1980). Parent's view of support following the loss of their infant to Sudden Infant Death Syndrome. *Western Journal of Nursing Research, 2*(3), 593–601.

Oosterveen, G. (1988). *Too early frost.* Grand Rapids, MI: Zondervan Books.

Parkes, C. M. (1988). Bereavement as a psychosocial transition: Processes of adaptation to change. *Journal of Social Issues, 44*(3), 53–65.

Parkes, C. M., & Weiss, R. S. (1983). *Recovery from bereavement.* New York: Basic Books.

Peppers, L. G. (1987). Grief and elective abortion: Breaking the emotional bond? *Omega, 18*(1), 1–12.

Peppers, L. G., & Knapp, R. J. (1980). *Motherhood & mourning: Perinatal death.* New York: Praeger.

Price, M., Carter, B. D., Shelton, T. L., & Bendell, R. D. (1985). Maternal perceptions of Sudden Infant Death Syndrome. *Children's Health Care, 14*(1), 22–31.

Proudfoot, W., & Shaver, P. (1975). Attribution theory and the psychology of religion. *Journal for the Scientific Study of Religion, 14*(4), 317–330.

Prus, R. (1996). *Symbolic interaction and ethnographic research.* Albany, NY: State University of New York Press.

Rando, T. A. (1985). Bereaved parents: Particular difficulties, unique factors, and treatment issues. *Social Work, 30*(1), 19–23.

Rando, T. A. (1986a). The unique issues and impact of the death of a child. In T. A. Rando (Ed.), *Parental loss of a child* (pp. 5–43). Champaign, IL: Research Press.

Rando, T. A. (1986b). Parental bereavement: An exception to the general conceptualizations of mourning. In T. A. Rando (Ed.), *Parental loss of a child* (pp. 45–58). Champaign, IL: Research Press.

Rando, T. A. (1986c). Death of the adult child. In T. A. Rando (Ed.), *Parental loss of a child* (pp. 221–238). Champaign, IL: Research Press.

Ranney, M. D. (1991). SIDS and parents. In C. A. Corr, H. Fuller, C. A. Barnickol, & D. M. Corr (Eds.), *Sudden Infant Death Syndrome: Who can help and how* (pp. 57–82). New York: Springer Publishing.

Raphael, B. (1983). *The anatomy of bereavement.* New York: Basic Books.

Raphael, B., & Misso, V. (1993). Traumatic stress and Sudden Infant Death. In A. M. Walker, C. McMillen, & National SIDS Council of Australia (Eds.), *Second SIDS international conference* (pp. 298–303). Ithaca, NY: Perinatology Press.

Reinhartz, S. (1987). The social psychology of a miscarriage: An application of symbolic interaction theory and method. In M. J. Deegan & M. Hill

(Eds.), *Women and symbolic interactionism* (pp. 229–249). Boston, MA: Allen and Unwin.

Riches, G., & Dawson, P. (1996). "An intimate loneliness": Evaluating the impact of a child's death on parental self-identity and marital relationships. *Journal of Family Therapy, 18*, 1–22.

Rosenblatt, P. C. (1988). Grief: The social context of private feelings. *Journal of Social Issues, 44*(3), 67–78.

Rosenblatt, P. C., & Burns, L. H. (1986). Long-term effects of perinatal loss. *Journal of Family Issues, 7*(3), 237–253.

Rosenblatt, P. C., Spoentgen, P., Karis, T. A., Dahl, C., Kaiser, T., & Elde, C. (1991). Difficulties in supporting the bereaved. *Omega, 23*(2), 119–128.

Rosof, B. D. (1994). *The worst loss: How families heal from the death of a child.* New York: Henry Holt and Company.

Rubin, S. S. (1981). A two track model of bereavement: Theory and application in research. *American Journal of Orthopsychiatry, 51*(1), 101–109.

Rubin, S. S. (1985). Maternal attachment and child death: On adjustment, relationship, and resolution. *Omega, 15*(4), 347–352.

Rubin, S. S. (1993). The death of a child is forever: The life course impact of child loss. In M. S. Stroebe, W. Stroebe, & R. O. Hansson (Eds.), *Handbook of bereavement* (pp. 285–299). Cambridge: Cambridge University Press.

Rubin, S. S. (1996). The wounded family: Bereaved parents and the impact of adult child loss. In D. Klass, P. R. Silverman, & N. L Nickman (Eds.), *Continuing bonds: New understandings of grief* (pp. 217–232). Washington, DC: Taylor & Francis.

Sanders, C. M. (1980). A comparison of adult bereavement in the death of a spouse, child, and parent. *Omega, 10*(4), 303–322.

Sanders, C. M. (1986). Accidental death of a child. In T. A. Rando (Ed.), *Parental loss of a child* (pp. 181–190). Champaign, IL: Research Press.

Sanders, C. M. (1988). Risk factors in bereavement outcome. *Journal of Social Issues, 44*(3), 97–111.

Sanders, C. M. (1995). Grief of children and parents. In K. J. Doka (Ed.), *Children mourning, mourning children* (pp. 69–83). Bristol, PA: Taylor & Francis.

Scheff, T. J. (1985). Universal expressive needs: A critique and a theory. *Symbolic Interaction, 8*(2), 241–262.

Schmidt, J. D. (1986). Murder of a child. In T. A. Rando (Ed.), *Parental loss of a child* (pp. 213–221). Champaign, IL: Research Press.

Schwab, R. (1990). Paternal and maternal coping with the death of a child. *Death Studies, 14*, 407–422.

Scott, J., & Alwin, D. F. (1989). Gender differences in parental strain. *Journal of Family Issues, 10*(4), 482–503.

Silver, R. L., Boon, C., & Stones, M. H. (1983). Searching for meaning in misfortune: Making sense of incest. *Journal of Social Issues, 39*(2), 81–102.

Simos, B. G. (1979). *A time to grieve: Loss as a universal human experience.* New York: Family Service Association.

Smart, L. S. (1992). The marital helping relationship following pregnancy loss and infant death. *Journal of Family Issues, 13*(1), 81–98.

Smart, L. S. (1993–1994). Parental bereavement in Anglo-American history. *Omega, 28*(1), 49–61.

Smialek, Z. (1978). Observations on immediate reactions of families to Sudden Infant Death. *Pediatrics, 62*(2), 160–165.

Smith, A. C., & Borgers, S. B. (1988). Parental grief response to perinatal death. *Omega, 19*(3), 203–214.

Smith, J. E. (1983). *Preparation for fatherhood.* Unpublished master's thesis, University of Alberta, Edmonton, Alberta.

Soule, B., Standley, K., & Copans, S. A. (1979). Father identity. *Psychiatry, 42*, 255–263.

Spilka, B., Shaver, P., & Kirkpatrick, L. A. (1985). A general attribution theory for the psychology of religion. *Journal for the Scientific Study of Religion, 24*(1), 1–20.

Sprang, G., & McNeil, J. (1995). *The many faces of bereavement: The nature and treatment of natural, traumatic, and stigmatized grief.* New York: Bruner/Mazel.

Stahlman, S. D. (1996). Children and the death of a sibling. In C. A. Corr & D. M. Corr (Eds.), *Handbook of childhood death and bereavement* (pp. 149–164). New York: Springer.

Stainton, C. M. (1985). The fetus: A growing member of the family. *Family Relations, 34*(3), 321–326.

Staples, D. (1991, January). Victim's kin hope inquiry eases pain. *The Edmonton Journal*, p. C6.

Statistics Canada. (1994). *Causes of death.* Ottawa, ON: Minister of Industry.

Stephenson, J. (1986). Grief of siblings. In T. A. Rando (Ed.), *Parental loss of a child* (pp. 322–338). Champaign, IL: Research Press.

Stern, P. (1985). Using grounded theory method in nursing research. In M. M. Leninger (Ed.), *Qualitative research methods in nursing* (pp. 149–160). Orlando, FL: Grune & Stratton.

Stevens, M. J., Pfost, K. S., & Wessels, A. B. (1987). The relationship of purpose in life to coping strategies and time since the death of a significant other. *Journal of Counseling and Development*, *65*(8), 424–426.

Stinson, K. M., Lasker, J. N., Lohmann, J., & Toedter, L. J. (1992). Parents' grief following pregnancy loss: A comparison of mothers and fathers. *Family Relations*, *41*(2), 218–223.

Stinson, R., & Stinson, P. (1979). *The long dying of baby Andrew.* Boston/Toronto: Little, Brown and Company.

Storr, A. (1988). *Solitude: A return to the self.* New York: The Free Press.

Strauss, A., & Corbin, J. (1990). *Basics of qualitative research: Grounded theory procedures and techniques.* Newbury Park, CA: Sage.

Strauss, A., & Corbin, J. (1994). Grounded theory methodology: An overview. In N. K. Denzin & Y. S. Lincoln (Eds.), *Handbook of qualitative research* (pp. 273–285). Thousand Oaks, CA: Sage.

Stroebe, W., Stroebe, M. S., & Domittner, G. (1988). Individual and situational differences in recovery from bereavement: A risk group identified. *Journal of Social Issues*, *44*(3), 143–158.

Swanson-Kauffman, K. M. (1986). A combined qualitative methodology for nursing research. *Advances in Nursing Science*, *8*(3), 58–69.

Talbot, K. (1996–1997). Mothers now childless: Survival after the death of an only child. *Omega*, *34*(3), 177–189.

Taylor, J., DeFrain, J., & Ernst, L. (1986). Sudden Infant Death Syndrome. In T. A. Rando (Ed.), *Parental loss of a child* (pp. 159–180). Champaign, IL: Research Press.

Taylor, S. E. (1983). Adjustment to threatening events: A theory of cognitive adaptation. *American Psychologist*, *38*(11), 1161–1173.

Tesch, R. (1989). *Introductory guide to QUALPRO.* Desert Hot Springs, CA: Qualitative Research Management.

Thearle, M. J., Vance, J. C., Najman, J. M., Embelton, G., & Foster, W. J. (1995). Church attendance, religious affiliation, and parental responses to Sudden Infant Death Syndrome, neonatal death, and stillbirth. *Omega*, *31*(1), 51–58.

Thomas, V., Striegel, P., Dudley, D., Gibson, D., & Wilkins, J. (1992, November). *Parental grief of a perinatal loss: A qualitative and quantitative integration of individual and couple variables.* Paper presented at the Annual Conference of the National Council on Family Relations, Orlando, FL.

Ulmer, A., Range, L. M., & Smith, P. C. (1991). Purpose in life: A moderator of recovery from bereavement. *Omega, 23*(4), 279–289.

Vaillant, G. E. (1985). Loss as a metaphor for attachment. *The American Journal of Psychoanalysis, 45*(1), 59–67.

Valdes-Dapena, M. A. (1991). The phenomenon of Sudden Infant Death Syndrome and its challenges. In C. A. Corr, H. Fuller, C. A. Barnickol, & D. M. Corr (Eds.), *Sudden Infant Death Syndrome: Who can help and how* (pp. 2–13). New York: Springer Publishing.

Valeriote, S., & Fine, M. (1987). Bereavement following the death of a child: Implications for family therapy. *Contemporary Family Therapy, 9*(3), 202–217.

Vance, J. C., Foster, W. J., Najman, J. M., Embelton, G., Thearle, M. J., & Hodgen, F. M. (1991). Early parental responses to sudden infant death, stillbirth, or neonatal death. *The Medical Journal of Australia, 155*, 292–297.

Vance, J. C., Thearle, M. J., Najman, J. M., Embelton, G., & Foster, W. J. (1993). Alcohol and drug ingestion following Sudden Infant Death Syndrome, stillbirth, and neonatal death. In A. M. Walker, C. McMillen, & National SIDS Council of Australia (Eds.), *Second SIDS international conference* (pp. 279–283). Ithaca, NY: Perinatology Press.

Vance, J. C., Najman, J. M., Thearle, M. J., Embelton, G., Boyle, F. M., & Lutvey, C. (1995). Long-term outcome of SIDS families: A longitudinal study including comparisons with other forms of infant loss. In T. O. Rognum (Ed.), *Sudden Infant Death Syndrome: New trends in the nineties* (pp. 273–276). Oslo: Scandinavian University Press.

Videka-Sherman, L. (1982). Coping with the death of a child: A study over time. *American Journal of Orthopsychiatry, 52*(4), 688–698.

Wallis, C. L. (Ed.). (1965). *The treasure chest.* New York: Harper & Row.

Walsh, F., & McGoldrick, M. (1991). Loss and the family: A systemic perspective. In F. Walsh & M. McGoldrick (Eds.), *Living beyond loss: Death in the family* (pp. 1–29). New York: W. W. Norton & Company.

Weinstein, S. E. (1978). Sudden Infant Death Syndrome: Impact on families and a direction for change. *American Journal of Psychiatry, 135*(7), 831–834.

Weiss, R. S. (1988). Loss and recovery. *Journal of Social Issues, 44*(3), 37–52.

Wheeler, I. (1993–1994). The role of meaning and purpose in life in bereaved parents associated with a self-help group: Compassionate Friends. *Omega, 28*(4), 261–271.

Williams, R. A., & Nikolaisen, S. M. (1982). Sudden Infant Death Syndrome: Parents' perceptions and responses to the loss of their infant. *Research in Nursing and Health, 5*, 55–61.

Winnicott, D. W. (1987a). The beginning of the individual. In C. Winnicott, R. Shepherd, & M. Davis (Eds.), *Babies and their mothers* (pp. 51–58). Reading, MA: Addison Wesley. (Original work published 1966)

Winnicott, D. W. (1987b). Dependence in child care. In. C. Winnicott, R. Shepherd, & M. Davis (Eds.), *Babies and their mothers* (pp. 83–88). Reading, MA: Addison Wesley. (Original work published 1966)

Wolfelt, A. D. (1993, January/February). Identification of "grief avoidance" response patterns: A growing phenomenon. *The Forum* (*Newsletter of Association for Death Education and Counselling*), *18*(1), 1, 16–18.

Wong, P. T. P., & Weiner, B. (1981). When people ask "why" questions, and the heuristics of attributional search. *Journal of Personality and Social Psychology, 40*(4), 650–663.

Worden, J. W. (1982). *Grief counseling and grief therapy.* New York: Springer Publishing.

Worden, J. W. (1991). *Grief counseling and grief therapy* (2nd ed.). New York: Springer Publishing.

Wortman, C. B., & Silver, R. C. (1986). Coping with irrevocable loss. In G. R. Vandenbos & B. K. Bryant (Eds.), *Cataclysms, crises, and catastrophes: Psychology in action* (pp. 189–235). Washington, DC: American Psychological Association.

Wortman, C. B., & Silver, R. C. (1989). The myths of coping with loss. *Journal of Consulting and Clinical Psychology, 57*(3), 349–357.

Wuthnow, R., Christiano, K., & Kuzlowski, J. (1980). Religion and bereavement: A conceptual framework. *Journal for the Scientific Study of Religion, 19*(4), 408–422.

Zagdanski, D. (1995). The pain of losing a child: A personal account. In T. O. Rognum (Ed.), *Sudden Infant Death Syndrome: New trends in the nineties* (pp. 300–303). Oslo: Scandinavian University Press.

Zielke, H. R., Meny, R. G., O'Brien, M. J., Smialek, J. E., Kutlar, R., Huisman, T. H. J., & Dover, G. J. (1989). Normal fetal hemoglobin levels in the Sudden Infant Death Syndrome. *The New England Journal of Medicine, 321*(21), 1359–1363.

Index